KU-777-687

Introduction to
Image Processing

#122663896

Introduction to Image Processing

André Marion

Translated by
Charles Polley
Services for Export and Language,
University of Salford

ANDERSONIAN LIBRARY
*
WITHDRAWN
FROM
LIBRARY
STOCK
*
UNIVERSITY OF STRATHCLYDE

2 0. MAY

UNIVERSITY OF STRATHCLYDE

CHAPMAN AND HALL
London • New York • Tokyo • Melbourne • Madras

UK	Chapman and Hall, 2–6 Boundary Row, London SE1 8HN
USA	Van Nostrand Reinhold, 115 5th Avenue, New York NY10003
JAPAN	Chapman and Hall Japan, Thomson Publishing Japan, Hirakawacho Nemoto Building, 7F, 1-7-11 Hirakawa-cho, Chiyoda-ku, Tokyo 102
AUSTRALIA	Chapman and Hall Australia, Thomas Nelson Australia, 480 La Trobe Street, PO Box 4725, Melbourne 3000
INDIA	Chapman and Hall India, R. Seshadri, 32 Second Main Road, CIT East, Madras 600 035

Original French language edition *Introduction aux Techniques de Traitement d'Images* published by Editions Eyrolles, Paris.
© Editions Eyrolles, 1987
English edition 1991

© 1991 Chapman and Hall

Printed in Great Britain by
T.J. Press (Padstow) Ltd, Padstow, Cornwall

ISBN 0-412-37890-6 (HB)
ISBN 0-442-31202-4 (USA)

All rights reserved. No part of this publication may be reproduced or transmitted, in any form or by any means, electronic, mechanical, photocopying, recording or otherwise, or stored in any retrieval system of any nature, without the written permission of the copyright holder and the publisher, application for which shall be made to the publisher.

British Library Cataloguing in Publication Data

Marion, André
  An introduction to image processing.
  1. Image processing
  I. Title   II. De traitement d'images. *English*
  621.367

  ISBN 0-412-37890-6

Library of Congress Cataloging-in-Publication Data is available

ANDERSONIAN LIBRARY

2 0. MAY 91

UNIVERSITY OF STRATHCLYDE

621.367
MAR

Contents

ANDERSONIAN LIBRARY
★
WITHDRAWN
FROM
LIBRARY
STOCK
★
UNIVERSITY OF STRATHCLYDE

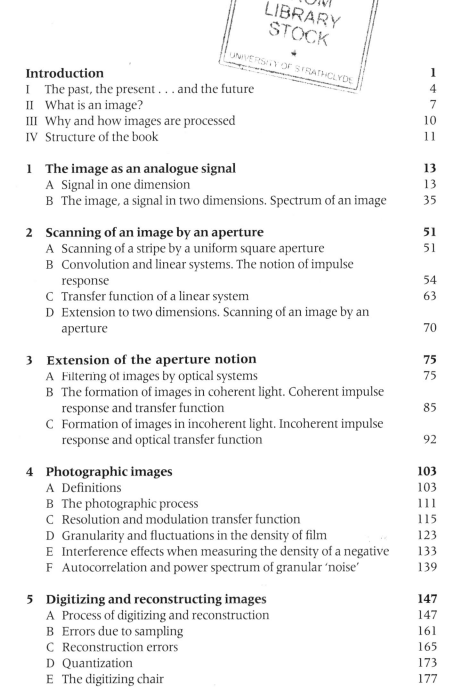

Introduction

I. The past, the present ... and the future

It is possible to take the view that ever since it began, the "ancient" branch of physics known as Optics has been concerned with processing images. But since the Nineteen-Thirties increasingly close ties have been forming between Optics, which until then had been largely based on instruments, and the sciences of communication and information arising out of mathematics and electronics. Such developments follow naturally, since communication systems and image-forming systems are all designed to receive or transmit information. Furthermore the same mathematical forms are used for describing the behaviour of electrical and optical systems. It is a question of systems theory, particularly linear systems, and of Fourier's analysis methods, which together constitute an important part of *Signal Theory*.

In the case of communication systems carrying signals of an electrical nature, information is time-related or temporal. Transmitted signals are one-dimensional and functions of a single variable, time t. In the case of optical systems information is spatial in nature. Signals are distributions of light intensity in space. In general they are treated as two-dimensional signals, being functions of two spatial variables written as x and y.

In the early Fifties the way forward became clearer still when some scientists at the Institut d'Optique in Paris began using *optical filtering* techniques in coherent light in order to enhance the quality of photographs. The possibilities of coherent filtering were exploited subsequently in the field of radar signal processing and later in the analysis of seismic waves. More recently, adapted filtering techniques using optical channels have been successfully applied to problems of *character identification*, which is just one aspect of the vast subject known as pattern recognition. The main attractions of optical processing are its simplicity, its moderate cost, its speed and the large amount of information which can be processed at one time.

The signals of images processed by these methods have one important characteristic: they are essentially continuous in nature. They are described as *analogue signals*, and since they are also two-dimensional it is possible to represent them mathematically as continuous functions of two variables: $f(x, y)$.

While all this research was taking place, developments in the computer field were opening up the concept of signals which were digital or *numerical* in nature. The information in such signals is represented and transmitted in the form of numbers in accordance with a selected coding convention (generally using binary code). Ever since 1920 it has been possible to transmit images digitally between New York and London by submarine cable for reconstitution on arrival. To use such techniques the continuous type of image mentioned above must first be digitized, that is transformed into an array or matrix of numbers, then processed as necessary by computer and (or) transmitted. For the purpose of retrieval and display, the digital image is then converted back to a continuous image. This process is the reverse of *digitization*, and is known as *reconstruction*.

Digital *image processing* is only a relatively recent development, starting in the Sixties when third generation computers made their appearance. In fact, as we shall see, an image of even modest size carries a large quantity of information. Due to progress in storage capacity and speed of calculation, these computers could be used to develop algorithms for processing a multitude of applications.

One of the first fields to use digital processing for the enhancement of images was space research. It was in 1964 that the Jet Propulsion Laboratory in Pasadena, California, used a computer to correct camera distortion in pictures of the lunar surface transmitted back to Earth from the Ranger 7 probe. Since that time many techniques for image enhancement and restoration have been developed in connection with the Surveyor, Mariner and Apollo missions.

At the same time the field of application for digital image processing has been gradually but decidedly growing. It now finds applications in medicine (radiography, tomography, scintigraphy), biology, geography, cartography, meteorology, astronomy, geology, archaeology, physics (spectroscopy, plasma physics, microscopy), military applications and industrial uses (materials radiography, non-destructive testing etc). The nature of the images processed is as highly varied as the subjects involved. There are aerial photographs, X-ray photographs, physical spectra, radar images, optical or electronic photomicrographs etc. Some typical applications will be mentioned in the course of this book.

Today the list is no longer limited to scientific or technical disciplines. It is true to say that no field of activity escapes or will escape the need to make use of image processing. Examples abound in live entertainment, video, fashion and every sector of artistic creation.

There are further practical applications in prospect, ranging from medical diagnostics to visual recognition by computer in the field of robotics and artificial intelligence, including automatic recognition of text, handwriting and shapes of objects by a machine for replacing inspection by the human eye.

The abundance of uses for image processing has had two important consequences:

1. There has been a growth in the number of specialised application packages as well as "standard" processing packages with virtually universal application, generally written in high-level language and easily portable to any type of large or medium-size computer.

2. Small processing workstations are now being marketed on a "turnkey" basis. These are usually organised around an expandable image memory and include a colour display console, a keyboard and visual display unit, mass storage devices such as hard disk, floppy disk, cassette and magnetic tape, as well as optional output devices such as screen dump printers, colour printers etc. Many of these systems have the double advantage of being programmable by the user for special applications and equipped with a number of standard programs which can be accessed easily by "menu" so that they can be used with ease by a non-specialist in computing.

These two differing philosophies, which may be summed up as the large computer centre and the small stand alone system, are complementary rather than competing. The choice depends above all on the type of application in question:

- For applications handling heavy and repetitious calculations, large amounts of data and algorithms which are fully-defined or needing only minor adjustment, a large computer seems most suitable.

- On the other hand, for research into new methodologies, or for the development of new algorithms, if the amount of data being processed is not prohibitive then it is very helpful to have the flexibility and *interaction* of a stand alone system, even if it is less powerful. In fact, interaction is often a selection criterion of prime importance for assessing the true effectiveness of an image processing system.

It should also be mentioned that there seems to be much promise for the future in hybrid systems which combine the advantages of computerized digital techniques with analogue optical filtering methods.

II. What is an image?

There are many definitions of the word "IMAGE". If we look in the dictionary we find that one of the definitions, relating to an image in the abstract sense, is along these lines: "An exact or analogous representation of a being or thing". An image can therefore be thought of as anything which represents something else. If we use "object" to mean anything which has a material or immaterial existence, that is any being, thing or concept, then images are obviously a form of object and we can divide objects in general into two categories: objects and the images of objects. The latter can be subdivided into three groups:

1. *Visible physical* images which are entirely real and either transitory or permanent in nature. Transitory images are either optical, composed of photons in the visible range (such as images produced by optical instruments, holograms and so on), or electro-optical (the screen of a cathode ray tube, light-emitting diode displays and things of that sort). Permanent images are reproductions of every kind, summed up in the more restrictive word "picture", including photographic negatives, drawings, paintings, engravings, sculptures, printed documents, hard-copy screen dumps and the like.

2. *Non-visible physical* images: these are optical images outside the visible range or images of an "unreal" nature. They include physical spectra, maps showing population, temperature or pressure and representations of any physical parameter in general which cannot be viewed by direct means. Thus a view in infra-red is a non-visible image, but after printing a film which is sensitive to this form of radiation it becomes a visible

physical image. The three-dimensional images produced by tomography are also in this class.

3. *Mathematical images*. These are concepts, and therefore invisible by their very nature. They may be continuous, for instance a function $f(x, y)$ or they may be discrete, in which case they are arrays or matrices of numbers. Such is the situation with purely synthetic images created by computer, at least before they are restored and displayed on a suitable system. Apart from discrete mathematical images, all other images are generally continuous, at least as far as our macroscopic scale of observation is concerned.

Any form of processing which converts a continuous image (the input image) into another continuous image (the output image) is known as *analogue processing*. This includes calculations carried out on analogue computers (which nowadays are used only rarely) as well as optical processing techniques. Similarly *digital processing*, which is usually carried out by computer, converts a discrete input image into a discrete output image. To make this possible, therefore, the image which requires processing has to be converted from the continuous to the discrete form. To do this requires a *digitization* system.

The table below summarizes these definitions:

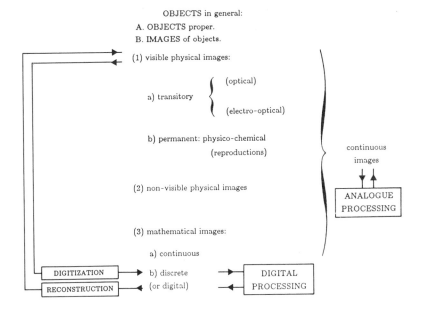

Once digital processing has been carried out, a visible physical image has to be retrieved from it. This may be done by producing for instance a display on a television screen, another photograph, or a printed representation. This job is performed by *display* or *playback* systems.

An example of the classic procedure for processing, starting with the object under investigation all the way through to the production of a processed photograph, consists of the following steps:

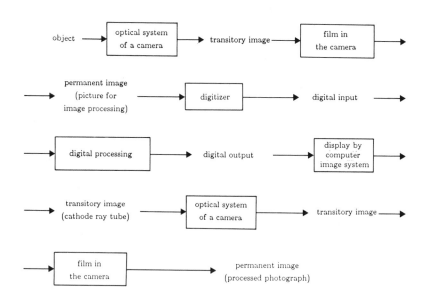

This book examines these various stages.

Thus we shall consider in succession how optical systems form images, the process by which an image is created on a photographic medium, digitization systems, reconstruction systems and digital processing methods using computers. We shall see that each of these stages introduces defects and restrictions of various kinds, such as noise, distortion and calculation artefacts, all of which degrade perception of the object being studied. There is therefore a need for caution when interpreting a processed image.

The visible physical images which we need to digitize are often of the two-dimensional monochrome or single-colour variety such as a so-called "black-and-white" photograph. Figure 0.1 shows just such an image. This is represented by a function $f(x, y)$ expressing the light intensity of a point with coordinates x and y. Similarly it is possible to represent a three-colour image such as the classic "colour" photograph by three functions $f_R(x, y)$, $f_G(x, y)$ and $f_B(x, y)$ expressing the intensity of each of the three primary component colours red, green and blue at point (x, y) on the image.

More generally we shall make reference to a multispectral image, being an image represented by a set of n components $f_1(x, y)$, $f_2(x, y)$ ... $f_n(x, y)$. We have an instance of this when a satellite records n views of the same region of the earth in n wavelength bands.

III. Why and how images are processed

It can be said that an image is being processed as soon as information begins to be extracted from it.

This viewpoint has nothing whatever to do with using a computer to produce purely synthetic images. Artificial image creation, or image synthesis, is not a part of the field commonly described by the term "image processing", and this book will not be dealing with it.

Having made this clear, we can say that there are many ways in which images can be processed. One way of classifying the types of processing which exist is by objective, in other words the reason for wanting to process the image in the first place.

1) There may be a need to improve its quality. This may be subjective, such as making it more attractive to look at. It may be a quality which can be measured objectively, such as increasing contrast, improving the ability to make out certain details or contours,

Fig.0.1 - A monochrome "analogue" image is a continuous distribution of light intensity represented as a function of the two spatial variables x and y: $f(x, y)$.

enhancing the clarity of certain zones or shapes, or reducing the noise or interference which can have a variety of causes and make the information less useful.

It is therefore a matter of *enhancement* techniques which make use of such varied procedures as histogram modification, convolution, linear filtering, non-linear filtering etc., in order to produce smoothing, contour accentuation, enhancement and so on. Most of these processes will be examined in this book.

2) Enhancing the quality of an image may also mean the search for an "ideal" image of the object if it has become degraded in a number of ways. There is a need to correct geometrical or photometric distortions introduced by a sensor, to reduce fluctuations caused by atmospheric turbulence, or to correct haze arising from camera shake etc. These are therefore *restoration* techniques. Here again, various types of linear or non-linear filters are used, including inverse

filters and Wiener's filtering. Some of these will be dealt with in the final chapter.

3) There may be a need to look for certain shapes, contours or textures of a particular kind, but no need to keep the other information in the image. We are referring here to *detection*, one of the classic problems of signal theory, concerning the need to extract a signal of a known shape when everything other than the useful signal is behaving like a sea of noise.

4) An important aspect of image processing is the enormous amount of information which has to be handled when transmitting one or more images. It is helpful to find a way of reducing the quantity of information involved. "Compressing" it to improve the transmission rate also reduces the size of the equipment and storage space required. All this needs to be achieved whilst sacrificing as little of the image quality as possible. This field concerns coding, data compression and image approximation. It is one of the more difficult aspects of information theory, and will not be given detailed treatment in this book. Readers interested in knowing more about this topic may refer to the works numbered 1, 3, 5, 8 and 12 in the bibliography.

5) Image processing also involves the analysis and comprehension of images. One of the aims of this activity is to equip machines with the ability to see. Machine vision leads us straight into the realms of robotics. *Image analysis*, also known as scene analysis, seeks to extract the information contained in the various objects in a scene without placing any interpretation on them. The basic techniques are **attribute extraction**, including the analysis of shapes, contours and textures; and **segmentation** of the image into zones exhibiting specific characteristics, by thresholding, by extracting and following contours, by erosion and enlargement, and by other methods. *Pattern recognition* techniques rely on the classification of shapes into preset categories on the basis of mathematical morphology. At a higher level, various models based on knowledge of the chosen goal are used for making the decisions and estimates needed to interpret the image. Image comprehension is the starting point of machine vision and other techniques based on artificial intelligence.

Another classification of processing operations involves dividing them according to the nature of the mathematical operations carried out. Thus within enhancement and restoration as well as detection we find both *linear* and *non-linear processing*. An operation or system is said to be linear when any linear combination of input signals gives the same linear combination of output signals. A large part of this work is devoted to examining linear systems.

A distinction is also made between operations which are *shift invariant* (or *stationary*) and those which are not. In a shift invariant operation a large-scale displacement of the input image is matched by identical displacement of the output image.

In section IV, "STRUCTURE OF THE BOOK", we shall see the meaning of the terms: *point operations, local operations* and *global operations*. We should also bear in mind the distinction between *analogue processing, digital processing* and *hybrid processing*.

IV. Structure of the book

This general introduction is followed by chapter I. Its aim is to familiarize the reader with the basic mathematical ideas behind the theory of *analogue signals*. We begin with a one-dimensional signal, such as the electrical signal representing a sound in a high-fidelity channel, which is a function of time. We use it to explain the concepts of the frequency *spectrum* and the *Fourier transform*. The same ideas are then extended to include images, considering them as continuous signals in two dimensions.

Chapter II is devoted to the fundamental concept of a linear system, regarded as both a *convolution* system and a *frequency filter*. To explain the principle of convolution we consider the scanning of a simple luminous object, in this case by a square aperture being moved across a stripe. We then define the *impulse response* and *transfer function* of a linear system, and give examples of simple square, circular and Gaussian apertures.

Chapter III discusses how *optical systems* form images. In appropriate circumstances these systems can be treated as linear. This is the case with systems which are said to be "diffraction limited". Their impulse response and transfer function, as determined by the system exit pupil, are examined first in coherent lighting and then in incoherent.

One kind of image which is commonly being processed is the photographic image. Chapter IV is devoted to how images are formed on photographic media. It studies the process from exposure to development as well as examining the properties of photographic emulsions. Having defined such concepts as density, transmittance and the basic characteristics of an emulsion, we consider resolution and the *modulation transfer function* (MTF).

The grain of the emulsion limits the perception of fine details and creates fluctuations in the observed density. This fluctuation may be thought of as a "noise" analogous to electronic hum. This means we can refer to an emulsion's signal-to-noise ratio and define the notion of equivalent quantum efficiency (EQE). We then go on to define both the autocorrelation and the power spectrum, or *Wiener's spectrum*, of this noise.

In order to be processed by computer the image in question, such as the photograph in chapter IV, must first be digitized. Once processing has been carried out the digital image so obtained is generally displayed, or restored in a form which is visible to the eye of the observer. This may be done by producing for instance a display on a television screen, a printed image or another photograph. Chapter V examines the processes of *digitization* and *reconstruction*. Particular attention is paid to the errors and limitations which these processes introduce. The distinction is drawn between the errors inherent in the operations themselves (especially errors arising during sampling and quantization of the analogue image) and the technological limitations caused by the less than perfect characteristics of the equipment, digitizers and restorers used.

In chapter VI we see the *basic techniques* used in image processing. We begin with important definitions of the *histogram* and cumulative histogram of an image. We then consider a number of procedures known as *point operations*, in which each point on the output image is simply a function of the same point on the input image, without taking account of neighbouring points. In this context we meet classic techniques such as histogram equalisation, obtaining a histogram of a given form and correcting the non-linear characteristics of sensors and restorers.

Chapter VII is devoted to the simple *algebraic operations* which can be carried out between two or more images, such as addition, subtraction or multiplication. These, too, are point operations, in which each point on the derived output image depends only on the point with the same coordinates on each of the other images involved. The chapter then examines the effect which such operations have on the histogram, and illustrates their usefulness by introducing some typical applications. So for example by averaging a series of images of the same scene it is possible to improve the signal-to-noise ratio considerably.

Coloured image displays can often be useful. If the image is naturally in colour, the primary components are used to reconstitute the original colours by an additive or subtractive process. On this basis the screen of a colour display monitor produces a coloured image by an additive process, whereas a photograph or printout from a colour printer uses a subtractive process. This mode of representation, called *"true colour"* mode, preserves the colour information in the image and analyses it as necessary into its different components.

There may also be a need for symbolic representation of a series of images of the same scene, for example photographs taken in different bands of the spectrum, such as red, infra-red and so on. The scene, or rather the multispectral image of the scene, is then said to be represented in *"false colour"* mode. The colours chosen can be purely arbitrary. Thirdly a coloured display of a black-and-white image may be produced by conventionally assigning a colour to each grey level. This is *"pseudo-colour"* mode, the main aim of which is to improve the ease with which certain details, contours or zones can be perceived without adding any spurious information. These techniques are explained in chapter VIII.

Chapter IX is the last chapter in the book and certainly the most important. It deals with *linear processing* of images, in both the analogue domain (principally by optical filtering) and the digital domain. The convolution concept is extended to the digital domain in the form of discrete convolution, first in one dimension and then in two. A certain number of applications are considered in which the image is convoluted with a window of finite size. This means that a *local operation* is carried out. This is one where each point on the processed image is a function not only of the corresponding point on the input image but also of all the neighbouring points contained in the window. In this way various types of filtering may be performed, including smoothing, directional filtering and contour accentuation. It is also possible to carry out filtering by operating in the frequency domain. This extends the concept of the Fourier transform to digital signals, and is known as the *discrete Fourier transform* (DFT) in one or two dimensions. In this case filtering is a *global operation*, since every point on the processed image is calculated by taking account of every point on the source image. Various classic applications are considered in the field of *restoration* of a degraded image. In particular these include such techniques as inverse filtering, Wiener's filtering and interactive restoration.

1

The image as an analogue signal

We can consider that a continuous monochrome image is a distribution of light intensities within a plane of x and y coordinates, and that it may be represented by a function $f(x, y)$ of the two spatial variables x and y (fig.0.1). We shall call this a two-dimensional signal and write it as $s(x, y)$. In introducing the concept of an image frequency spectrum (also known as a Fourier spectrum), we shall first consider the simpler case of a signal in one dimension, that is a function of a single variable.

A. Signal in one dimension

Taking time as a variable t: a signal in one dimension is then a function $s(t)$. It may be the sound of a musical instrument, the voltage at a given point in a circuit, or something similar.

1. Sinusoidal signal and the notion of spectrum

Let us consider a sinusoidal signal with a frequency f_0, such as the "pure" sound of a tuning-fork. It may be represented by the function:

$$s(t) = c \cos 2\pi f_0 t = c \cos 2\pi \frac{t}{T} \qquad (1)$$

where c is the signal amplitude and $T = f_0$ is its period.
The structure of this signal is shown in figure I.1.a. If time-shifted by quantity τ, it becomes:

$$s(t) = c \cos (2\pi f_0 t - \Phi)$$

where $\Phi = 2\pi f_0 \tau$. Ignoring for the moment phase shift Φ a sinusoidal signal is fully described by its frequency f_0 and its amplitude c.

This signal consists of a single frequency f_0. Its *frequency spectrum* will therefore be represented by a line of amplitude c located at frequency f_0 (fig.I.1.b).

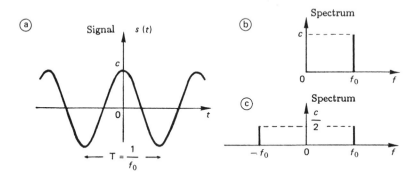

Fig.I.1 - Sinusoidal signal of frequency f_0: $s(t) = c \cos 2\pi f_0 t$; a) time structure, b) spectral representation of physical (positive) frequencies only, c) spectral representation including negative frequencies.

It should be noted that c can be calculated by the equation:

$$c = 2f_0 \int_{t_0}^{t_0+T} s(t) \cos 2\pi f_0 t \, dt \qquad (2)$$

where t_0 is any time.

By introducing complex exponentials

$$e^{jx} = \cos x + j \sin x \quad (j^2 = -1)$$

and using equation $\cos x = \frac{1}{2} (e^{jx} + e^{-jx})$ it is possible to write signal $s(t)$ in the form:

$$s(t) = \frac{c}{2} (e^{2\pi j f_0 t} + e^{-2\pi j f_0 t}) = \frac{c}{2} e^{2\pi j f_0 t} + \frac{c}{2} e^{2\pi j(-f_0)t}$$

It may therefore be thought of as the sum of two complex exponential signals with an "amplitude" of $\frac{c}{2}$ and symmetrical frequencies of f_0 and $-f_0$. Naturally only the positive frequency f_0 has any physical reality. The usefulness of this form of notation will soon become apparent, even if at the moment it seems more complicated than necessary.

In the frequency domain it is possible to represent the spectrum of $s(t)$ by including the negative frequencies. The spectrum will then consist of two symmetrical lines with an amplitude of $\frac{c}{2}$, located at frequencies f_0 and $-f_0$ (fig.I.1.c).

If period T becomes infinitely long, that is if frequency f_0 approaches zero, the signal becomes constant. Its amplitude, a, has a continuous level in the time domain shown in figure I.2.a. At the same time, in the frequency domain the spectra of figures I.1.b or I.1.c take on the appearance of figure I.2.b. There is a single line with amplitude a and frequency zero. The following expression now corresponds to equation (2):

$$a = f_0 \int_{t_0}^{t_0+T} s(t) \, dt \tag{3}$$

Let us suppose that we now add continuous level a to the sinusoidal signal $c \cos 2\pi f_0 t$ by imposing a vertical shift of a (fig.I.3.a):

$$s(t) = a + c \cos 2\pi f_0 t = a + \frac{c}{2} e^{2\pi j f_0 t} + \frac{c}{2} e^{-2\pi j f_0 t} \tag{4}$$

The spectrum of this signal is shown in figure I.3.b (including negative frequencies) and consists of three lines. It should be noted that the zero frequency line has an amplitude which is described by equation (3) representing the mean signal value (also known as its continuous component).

2. Periodic signal. Fourier series

We shall now consider a signal $s(t)$ with a period of $T = \frac{1}{f_0}$ (for instance fig.I.4.a). It can be shown that such a signal may be thought

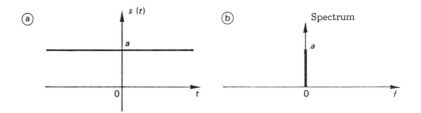

Fig.I.2 - Constant signal: $s(t) = a$; a) time structure, b) frequency spectrum.

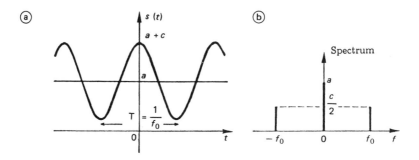

Fig.I.3   -   Sinusoidal   signal   superimposed   on   a   continuous   level: $s(t) = a + c \cos 2\pi f_0 t$; a) time structure, b) frequency spectrum.

of in general terms as the sum of the following:

- a constant signal c_0 (mean level of $s(t)$)
- a sine wave at a frequency of f_0 called the *fundamental*
- an infinite number of sine waves at frequencies of nf_0, being multiples of f_0, known as the *harmonics*.

Since these various sine waves are not necessarily in phase, it is possible to write:

$$s(t) = c_0 + c_1 \cos (2\pi f_0 t - \Phi_1) + c_2 \cos (4\pi f_0 t - \Phi_2) + \text{etc.}$$

This analysis of the signal into a *Fourier series* may be condensed into the following form:

$$s(t) = \sum_{n=0}^{\infty} c_n \cos (2\pi n f_0 t - \Phi_n) \text{ with } \Phi_0 = 0 \tag{5}$$

The corresponding spectrum (fig.I.4.b) is again a *line spectrum* (or discrete spectrum), and this is characteristic of periodic signals. Only amplitudes c_n are shown but it is also necessary to include phases Φ_n. In practice many of these lines may not exist, especially beyond a certain range. As a general rule they decrease towards the higher frequencies.

To calculate amplitudes c_n and phase shifts Φ_n, it is convenient to use a different form of notation for the Fourier series.

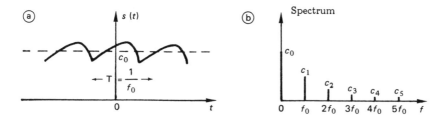

Fig.I.4 - Periodic signal with a period of $T = \dfrac{1}{f_0}$; a) time structure, b) spectrum

(positive frequencies only).

Since:

$$\cos (2\pi n f_0 t - \Phi_n) = \cos 2\pi n f_0 t \cos \Phi_n + \sin 2\pi n f_0 t \sin \Phi_n$$

it is possible to analyse $s(t)$ as a sum of cosines and sines:

$$s(t) = \sum_{n=0}^{\infty} (c_n \cos \Phi_n \cos 2\pi n f_0 t + c_n \sin \Phi_n \sin 2\pi n f_0 t)$$

Let: $a_n = c_n \cos \Phi_n$ and $b_n = c_n \sin \Phi_n$. Then:

$$s(t) = \sum_{n=0}^{\infty} (a_n \cos 2\pi n f_o t + b_n \sin 2\pi n f_o t) \qquad (6)$$

Then for $n \neq 0$ it is easy to find:

$$a_n = 2f_0 \int_{t_0}^{t_0+T} s(t) \cos 2\pi n f_o t \; dt$$

$$(7)$$

$$b_n = 2f_0 \int_{t_0}^{t_0+T} s(t) \sin 2\pi n f_o t \; dt$$

(where t_0 is any instant in time).

These equations are generalised expressions of equation (2).

For $n = 0$ we have: $a_0 = f_0 \int_{t_0}^{t_0+T} s(t) \; dt = c_0$ and $b_0 = 0$ as gener-

alised t_0 expressions of equation (3).

Since we know the values of a_n and b_n it is easy to calculate c_n and Φ_n. In particular $c_n = \sqrt{a_n{}^2 + b_n{}^2}$. The spectrum is represented by the a_n and b_n lines.

In fact, it is easier to handle complex exponentials than trigonometric functions. This is why it is useful to represent a signal as a *complex Fourier series*, including negative frequency lines as above.

Let:
$$A_n = \frac{1}{2} (a_n - jb_n) = \frac{1}{2} c_n e^{-j\Phi_n}$$

$$s(t) = \sum_{n=0}^{\infty} c_n \cos (2\pi n f_o t - \Phi_n)$$

$$= \sum_{n=0}^{\infty} \left[\frac{c_n}{2} \left(e^{2\pi j n f_0 t} e^{-j\Phi_n} + e^{-2\pi j n f_0 t} e^{j\Phi_n} \right) \right]$$

$$= \sum_{n=0}^{\infty} [A_n e^{2\pi j n f_0 t} + A_n^* e^{-2\pi j n f_0 t}]$$

where A_n^* is the conjugate complex of A_n. It can be shown that for real signals, which are the only ones we are considering here, $A_n^* = A_{-n}$.

This gives the complex Fourier series

$$s(t) = \sum_{n=-\infty}^{+\infty} A_n e^{2\pi j n f_0 t} \qquad (8)$$

Coefficients A_n, called Fourier coefficients, are in general complex. In order to calculate them, equations (7) give us:

$$A_n = \frac{1}{2} (a_n - jb_n)$$

$$= f_0 \int_{t_0}^{t_0+T} s(t) \cos 2\pi n f_0 t \, dt - f_0 \int_{t_0}^{t_0+T} s(t) j \sin 2\pi n f_0 t \, dt$$

$$= f_0 \int_{t_0}^{t_0+T} s(t) (\cos 2\pi n f_0 t - j \sin 2\pi n f_0 t) \, dt$$

being

$$A_n = f_0 \int_{t_0}^{t_0+T} s(t) e^{-2\pi j n f_0 t} \, dt \qquad (9)$$

Since coefficients A_n are complex, the spectral representation is once more a double set of lines. If we choose to represent the real parts and the imaginary parts we obtain a_n, b_n. Or we can represent the moduli and the arguments, in which case we obtain c_n, Φ_n.

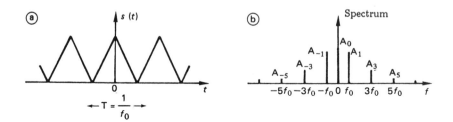

Fig.I.5 - Example of a periodic signal: repeated sawtooth signal with a period of $T = \dfrac{1}{f_0}$; a) time structure, b) frequency spectrum.

It can be shown that for an even signal $b_n = \Phi_n = 0$, so that a single representation is enough. In addition, coefficients A_n are also even ($A_{-n} = A_n$). For the sake of simplicity we shall always use this form. An example of a periodic and even sawtooth signal is given in figure I.5.a. Its spectrum is shown in figure I.5.b.

3. Any form of signal. Fourier transformation

Any form of signal, in general a non-periodic one, may be considered the limit of a periodic signal for which the period becomes infinitely long. The components move further and further apart until only one is left, consisting of the non-periodic signal concerned. Meanwhile in the frequency domain, the frequency of the fundamental tends towards zero and the frequencies of the harmonics bunch together. The spectral lines eventually touch and the discrete spectrum becomes continuous.

The Fourier series itself begins to take on the form of a "continuous summation", that is a definite integral. On the basis of expression (5), for example, the following integral is obtained:

$$s(t) = \int_0^\infty c(f) \cos [2\pi ft - \Phi(f)] \, df \qquad (10)$$

This equation expresses the analysis of $s(t)$ into an infinite number of sinusoidal components with infinitely close frequencies and infinitesimal amplitudes $c(f) \, df$, each sine wave being affected by a phase shift $\Phi(f)$ which is a function of its frequency.

As with a periodic signal, it is possible to rewrite the equation using complex exponentials:

$$s(t) = \int_0^\infty \frac{1}{2} c(f) \, e^{2\pi jft} \, e^{-j\Phi(f)} \, df + \int_0^\infty \frac{1}{2} c(f) \, e^{-2\pi jft} \, e^{j\Phi(f)} \, df$$

Let

$$S(f) = \frac{1}{2} c(f) e^{-j\Phi(f)}$$

$$s(t) = \int_0^\infty S(f) \, e^{2\pi jft} \, df + \int_0^\infty S^*(f) \, e^{-2\pi jft} \, df.$$

Here too it can be shown that for a real signal $S^*(f) = S(-f)$ which gives:

$$s(t) = \int_{-\infty}^\infty S(f) \, e^{2\pi jft} \, df \qquad (11)$$

(this equation is the analogue of (8)).

$S(f)$ is called the *Fourier transform* of $s(t)$. The spectrum of signal $s(t)$ is a representation of functions $c(f)$ and $\Phi(f)$. The first of these is twice the modulus of $S(f)$ and the second is its argument. It is also possible to represent $S(f)$ by its real part and its imaginary part. If we let $S(f) = A(f) - jB(f)$ then the following equations, which are the analogues of (7), can be shown:

$$A(f) = \int_{-\infty}^{\infty} s(t) \cos 2 \pi ft \, dt$$

(12)

$$B(f) = \int_{-\infty}^{\infty} s(t) \sin 2 \pi ft \, dt$$

giving

$$S(f) = \int_{-\infty}^{\infty} s(t) \, e^{-2\pi jft} \, dt$$

(13)

(this equation is the analogue of (9)).

This integral is perfectly symmetrical with integral (11) and can be used to calculate the Fourier transform $S(f)$ for signal $s(t)$. Functions $s(t)$ and $S(f)$ are also said to be Fourier transform pairs (abbreviated to F.T).

- *Examples*:

1) Figure I.6.a: A signal known as a "Lorentz" signal

$$s(t) = \frac{1}{1 + \dfrac{t^2}{a^2}}.$$

Its mid-height width is $2a$. It can be shown that its Fourier transform is a symmetrical exponential $S(f) = \pi \, a \, e^{-2\pi a|f|}$ (fig.I.6.b).

2) Figure I.7.a: A signal known as a "Gaussian" signal

$$s(t) = e^{-\frac{t^2}{2\sigma^2}}$$

Its width at $\dfrac{1}{\sqrt{e}} \simeq$ at 60% of height is 2σ. It can be shown that its Fourier transform is also Gaussian (fig.I.7.b):

$$S(f) = \sigma\sqrt{2\pi} \, e^{-\frac{f^2}{2\sigma^2}} \qquad \alpha = \frac{1}{2\pi\sigma}$$

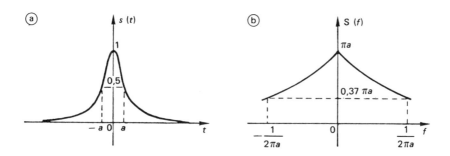

Fig.I.6. - "Lorentz" signal: $s(t) = \dfrac{1}{1 + \dfrac{t^2}{a^2}}$; a) time structure, b) Fourier trans-

form $S(f) = \pi\, a\, e^{-2\pi a|f|}$.

Width at 60% of height is 2α.

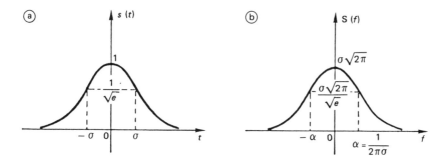

Fig.I.7 - "Gaussian" signal: $s(t) = e^{-\dfrac{t^2}{2\sigma^2}}$; a) time structure, b) Fourier trans-

form $S(f) = \sigma\sqrt{2\pi}\, e^{-\dfrac{f^2}{2\alpha^2}}$

Exercise: Let us calculate the Fourier transform for a symmetrical square-wave signal with a height of unity and a width of a (fig.I.8.a), also known as a symmetrical "gate" function.

$$S(f) = \int_{-\infty}^{+\infty} s(t)\, e^{-2\pi jft}\, dt = \int_{-a/2}^{a/2} e^{-2\pi jft}\, dt$$

$$= \left[\frac{e^{-2\pi jft}}{-2\pi jf} \right]_{-a/2}^{a/2} = \frac{e^{\pi jaf} - e^{-\pi jaf}}{2\pi jf}$$

$$= \frac{\sin \pi af}{\pi f} = \frac{a \sin \pi af}{\pi af} = a \; \text{sinc} \; \pi af$$

At the same time let $\dfrac{\sin x}{x} = \text{sinc}\; x$, a function called "cardinal sine". $S(f)$ passes through zero for the first time in respect of frequency $f = \dfrac{1}{a}$ (fig.I.8.b).

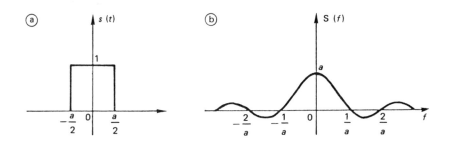

Fig.I.8 - Square-wave signal or "gate function" having width a; a) time structure, b) Fourier transform S(f) = a sinc π af.

4. Properties of the Fourier transform

We shall now examine the important properties of the Fourier transform, and some of their implications.

    a) **Linearity**: This arises from the linear property of the integral. If two signals $s_1(t)$ and $s_2(t)$ have a F.T. of $S_1(f)$ and $S_2(f)$ respectively, the signal for the summation $s_1(t) + s_2(t)$ has an F.T. consisting of the summation $S_1(f) + S_2(f)$.

In more general terms if n signals $s_1(t)$, $s_2(t)$, ... $S_n(t)$, have as their F.T. $S_1(f)$, $S_2(f)$, ... $S_n(f)$ respectively, any form of linear combination of these signals $\sum_{i=1}^{n} a_i s_i(t)$ has as its F.T. the same linear combination of F.T., that is to say: $\sum_{i=1}^{n} a_i S_i(f)$

$$\sum_{i=1}^{n} a_i s_i(t) \rightarrow \sum_{i=1}^{n} a_i S_i(f)$$

b) **Correlation between signal width and spectrum width:** The wider the signal, the narrower will be its spectrum, and vice versa. This means that the F.T. of a short signal is widely spaced in the higher frequencies.

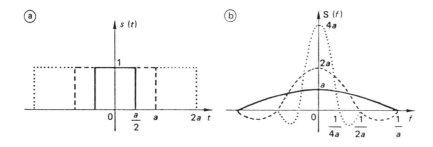

Fig.I.9 - a) Square-wave signals with a height of unity and increasing widths a, 2a, 4a, b) the corresponding Fourier transforms, each of unit area.

We can show this in the case of a "gate" signal. First (fig.I.9.a) let us assume that the gate width increases from a to $2a$, then to $4a$, in general terms to $2ka$. The corresponding spectrum (fig.I.9.b) becomes narrower and higher. In other respects, the surface area of this spectrum remains constant because it is equal to:

$$\int_{-\infty}^{+\infty} S(f)\ df$$

This represents the value assumed by the integral (11), when we choose $t = 0$, or in other words $s(0) = 1$.

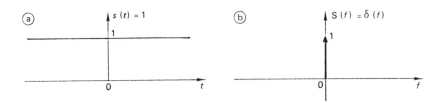

Fig.I.10 - a) Constant signal s(t) = 1, b) its Fourier transform is a Dirac signal located at frequency zero: δ(f); this infinitely narrow signal with a surface area of unity is shown conventionally as a vertical arrow with a height of 1.

In the limiting case ($k = \infty$) we obtain a signal which is constant and equal to 1 (fig.I.10.a). It can be shown that the Fourier transform at the limit of the cardinal sine, a sinc π af, tends towards an infinitely narrow and infinitely high "function" with a surface area of unity, which is a *Dirac signal* (or impulse) $\delta(f)$. Strictly speaking, in mathematical terms this is no longer a function but a distribution. Pulse $\delta(f)$ is represented conventionally as a vertical arrow located at frequency 0 with a height of 1 (to represent its surface area) (fig.I.10.b), thus bringing us back to the situation in figure I.2.

Let us now consider gates which decrease in width $\left[a, \frac{a}{2}, \frac{a}{4}, \frac{a}{2k}\right]$ and increase in height $\left[\frac{1}{a}, \frac{2}{a}, \frac{4}{a}, \frac{2k}{a}\right]$ in such a way that their surface area remains constant and equal to 1 (fig.I.11.a).

Their Fourier transforms are cardinal sines, each wider than the last (sinc πaf, sinc $2\pi af$, sinc $4\pi af$, sinc $2k\pi af$) (fig.I.11.b). If k becomes very large, signal $s(t)$ tends towards a Dirac signal at time $t = 0$ (fig.I.12.a) whereas the F.T. $S(f)$ becomes a constant of unity (fig.I.12.b).

To sum up:

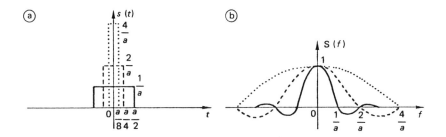

Fig.I.11 - a) Square-wave signals with a surface area of unity and decreasing
widths, a, $\frac{a}{2}$, $\frac{a}{4}$, b) the corresponding Fourier transforms.

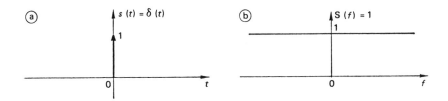

Fig.I.12 - a) Dirac signal at instant in time = origin: $\delta(t)$, b) its Fourier transform
$S(f) = 1$.

$$\boxed{\begin{array}{l} \delta(t) \xrightarrow{\text{F.T.}} 1 \\[2ex] 1 \xrightarrow{\text{F.T.}} \delta(f) \end{array}} \qquad (14)$$

c) **Interchanging the function $\longleftrightarrow$ F.T. roles:** The symmetrical property shown in figures I.6 to I.12 is valid for all even signals.
If it is true that $s(t)$ has a F.T. of $S(f)$ it is possible to write:

$$s(t) = \int_{-\infty}^{+\infty} S(f)\ e^{2\pi jft}\ df$$

Exchanging the roles of time variable t and frequency variable f gives:

$$s(f) = \int_{-\infty}^{+\infty} S(t)\ e^{2\pi jft}\ dt$$

So if we write the F.T. of $S(t)$ as $\overline{S(f)}$ we have:

$$\overline{S(f)} = \int_{-\infty}^{+\infty} S(t)\ e^{-2\pi jft}\ dt = s(-f)$$

Thus in the special case where $s(t)$ is even we find:

$$\overline{S(f)} = s(f),$$

which means: if an even signal $s(t)$ has an F.T. of $S(f)$ (also even), then conversely signal $S(t)$ has an F.T. of $s(f)$.

d) **Change of scale:**

$$\boxed{s(at) \xrightarrow{\text{F.T.}} \frac{1}{|a|} S\left(\frac{f}{a}\right)} \tag{15}$$

The reader may wish to check this property as an exercise.

e) **Shift in the time domain:**

$$\boxed{s(t - \tau) \xrightarrow{\text{F.T.}} S(f)\ e^{-2\pi jf\tau}} \tag{16}$$

A shift of τ in the time domain has the effect of multiplying the

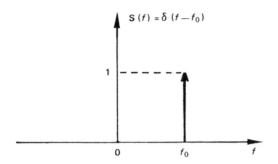

Fig.I.13 - The Fourier transform of complex signal $s(t) = e^{2\pi j f_0 t}$ is a Dirac signal located at frequency f_0: $S(f) = \delta(f-f_0)$.

F.T. $S(f)$ by the phase factor $e^{-2\pi j f\tau}$.
In fact assume:

$$\int_{-\infty}^{+\infty} s(t - \tau) \, e^{-2\pi j f t} \, dt.$$

Letting $t - \tau = t'$, then by substitution:

$$\int_{-\infty}^{+\infty} s(t') \, e^{-2\pi j f(t'+\tau)} \, dt' = e^{-2\pi j f\tau} \int_{-\infty}^{+\infty} s(t') \, e^{-2\pi j f t'} \, dt' = e^{-2\pi j f\tau} \, S(f)$$

f) **Shift in the frequency domain:**

$$s(t) \, e^{2\pi j f_0 t} \quad \xrightarrow{\text{F.T.}} \quad S(f-f_0) \qquad (17)$$

This property is a corollary of the preceding one, and can be demonstrated immediately.

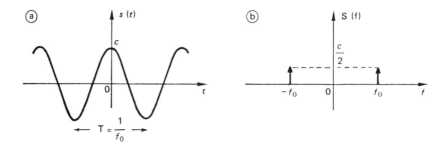

Fig.I.14 - a) Sinusoidal signal $s(t) = c \cos 2\pi f_0 t$ b) Fourier transform $S(f) = \frac{c}{2}$

$[\delta(f-f_0) + \delta(f+f_0)]$; this spectral representation is comparable with figure I.1.c.

$$\int_{-\infty}^{+\infty} s(t)\, e^{2\pi j f_0 t}\, e^{-2\pi j f t}\, dt = \int_{-\infty}^{+\infty} s(t)\, e^{-2\pi j (f-f_0) t}\, dt = S(f-f_0)$$

This makes it possible to find the F.T. of complex exponential signal $e^{2\pi j f_0 t}$. In fact $e^{2\pi j f_0 t} = 1 \times e^{2\pi j f_0 t}$.

But 1 has a F.T. of $\delta(f)$. Thus the F.T. of $e^{2\pi j f_0 t}$ is $\delta(f-f_0)$, in other words a straight line located at frequency f_0 (fig.I.13).

This gives the transformation of a sinusoidal signal as:

$$\cos 2\pi f_0 t = \frac{1}{2} (e^{2\pi j f_0 t} + e^{-2\pi j f_0 t}) \qquad \text{(fig.I.14.a)}.$$

In accordance with property a) (linearity) we find the F.T. to be:

$$\frac{1}{2} (\delta(f-f_0) + \delta(f+f_0))$$

which is represented by two lines located symmetrically at frequencies f_0 and $-f_0$.

The corresponding spectral representation, using Dirac functions (fig.I.14.b), is comparable to figure I.1.c.

So it can be seen that by using Dirac functions it is possible to consider the F.T. of a periodic signal, whereas we began by defining this concept for non-periodic signals only. From this it is apparent that the form of the F.T. is more general than of the Fourier series.

A periodic signal $s(t)$ can be developed into a complex Fourier series:

$$s(t) = \sum_{n=-\infty}^{+\infty} A_n \, e^{2\pi j n f_0 t}$$

Its F.T. will be:

$$S(f) = \sum_{n=-\infty}^{+\infty} A_n \, \delta(f-nf_0) \tag{18}$$

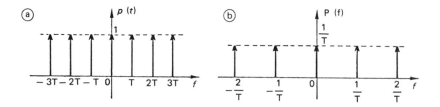

Fig.I.15 - a) Dirac comb signal with a period of T: $p(t) = \sum_{n=-\infty}^{+\infty} \delta(t-nT)$,

b) its Fourier transform is still a comb with a period $\frac{1}{T}$:

$$P(f) = \frac{1}{T} \sum_{n=-\infty}^{+\infty} \delta(f-\frac{n}{T}).$$

Example: The periodic function with a period of T is called the *sampling function*, or *Dirac comb function:*

$$p(t) = \sum_{k=-\infty}^{+\infty} \delta(t-kT) \tag{fig.I.15.a}$$

We can represent this as a Fourier series and write:

$$p(t) = \sum_{n=-\infty}^{+\infty} A_n \, e^{2\pi jn \frac{t}{T}}$$

Equation (9) can be used to calculate the A_n coefficients as follows:

$$A_n = \frac{1}{T} \int_{t_0}^{t_0+T} \sum_{K=-\infty}^{+\infty} \delta(t-KT) \, e^{-2\pi jn \frac{t}{T}} \, dt$$

$$= \frac{1}{T} \sum_{K=-\infty}^{+\infty} \int_{t_0}^{t_0+T} \delta(t-KT) \, e^{-2\pi jn \frac{t}{T}} \, dt$$

Using the equation $f(x)\delta(x-a) = f(a)\delta(x-a)$ we easily find that A_n

$= \frac{1}{T}$ and thus $p(t) = \frac{1}{T} \displaystyle\sum_{n=-\infty}^{+\infty} e^{2\pi jn \frac{t}{T}}$ and the Fourier transform

$$\boxed{P(f) = \frac{1}{T} \sum_{n=-\infty}^{+\infty} \delta\left(f - \frac{n}{T}\right)} \qquad (19)$$

In other words the F.T. of a comb with teeth spaced T apart is still a comb with teeth spaced $\frac{1}{T}$ apart and multiplied by $\frac{1}{T}$ (fig.I.15.b).

Exercise

Calculate the F.T. of a symmetrical periodic square wave with a period of T.

The height of each rectangle is equal to 1 and the width is half the period (fig.I.16.a).

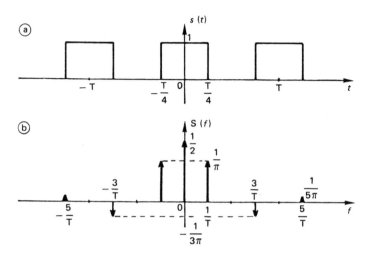

Fig.I.16 - Periodic square-wave signal; a) time structure, b) Fourier transform: apart from the zero frequency line representing mean signal level $\frac{1}{2}$, the spectrum consists of the fundamental and odd harmonics only.

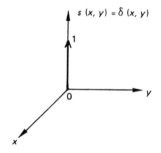

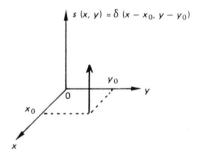

Fig.I.17 - Two-dimensional Dirac signal $\delta(x,y)$ representing a point of light at the origin.

Fig.I.18 - A point of light at a location having the coordinates (x_0,y_0) represented by a Dirac signal $\delta(x-x_0,y-y_0)$.

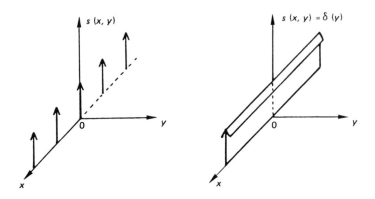

Fig.I.19 - "Comb" signal on Ox axis.   Fig.I.20. - "Blade" signal on
Ox axis: $\delta(y)$ representing a
line of light.

According to (17) $\delta(f) = \displaystyle\sum_{n=-\infty}^{+\infty} A_n \, \delta\left(f - \frac{n}{T}\right)$ and, according to (9):

$$A_n = \frac{1}{T} \int_{t_0}^{t_0+T} s(t) \, e^{-2\pi jn \frac{t}{T}} \, dt$$

As an example we shall choose $t_0 = -\dfrac{T}{2}$:

$$A_n = \frac{1}{T} \int_{-T/2}^{T/2} s(t) e^{-2\pi jn \frac{t}{T}} \, dt = \frac{1}{T} \int_{-T/4}^{T/4} e^{-2\pi jn \frac{t}{T}} \, dt$$

$$= -\frac{1}{2\pi jn}\left[e^{-2\pi jn\frac{t}{T}}\right]_{-T/4}^{T/4} = \frac{e^{\pi j\frac{n}{2}} - e^{-\pi j\frac{n}{2}}}{2\pi jn} = \frac{\sin \pi \frac{n}{2}}{\pi n}$$

with $A_0 = \frac{1}{2}$.

This gives the spectrum in figure I.16.b, where we have represented:

$$A_1 = A_{-1} = \frac{1}{\pi}$$

$$A_3 = A_{-3} = -\frac{1}{3\pi}$$

$$A_5 = A_{-5} = \frac{1}{5\pi}$$

(even-numbered harmonics do not exist).

B. The image, a signal in two dimensions. Spectrum of an image

1. Image signals

A continuous image is a distribution of light intensities within a plane xOy, that is to say it is a two-dimensional signal $s(x, y)$. This bi-variate function can be represented spatially.

By this means a single point of light located at the origin of the coordinates will be represented by a two-dimensional *Dirac signal* $\delta(x, y)$ (fig.I.17).

In the same way, a point of light at a location having the coordinates (x_0, y_0) will be written $\delta(x-x_0, y-y_0)$ (fig.I.18).

A set of regularly spaced points on the Ox axis, all having the same intensity, forms a *comb* (fig.I.19). There is a similar comb on the Oy axis.

A line of light of uniform intensity along the Ox axis is a signal known as a *"blade"* function $\delta(y)$ (fig.I.20). In the same way it would be possible to have a blade $\delta(x)$ located on the Oy axis.

A cluster of parallel and equidistant lines of light is a set of blades (fig.I.21). If T equals the distance between the blades we can

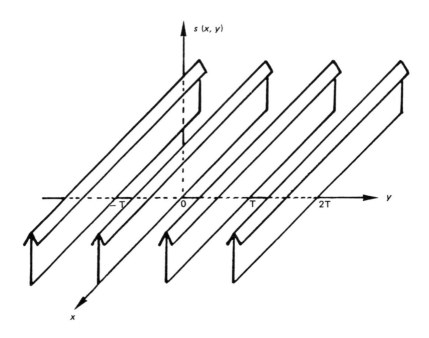

Fig.I.21 - Set of blades parallel to Ox and equidistant by amount T:

$$s(x, y) = \sum_{n=-\infty}^{+\infty} \delta(y-nT).$$

write:

$$s(x, y) = \sum_{n=-\infty}^{+\infty} \delta(y-nT)$$

A set of light points located at the nodes of an orthogonal grid is called a two-dimensional sampling signal, or *"brush"* function (fig.I.22). It should be noted that the grid spacing is not necessarily the same for axis Ox and axis Oy.

An object which varies sinusoidally in intensity with respect to Ox between 0 and 2a and is constant with respect to Oy is a signal,

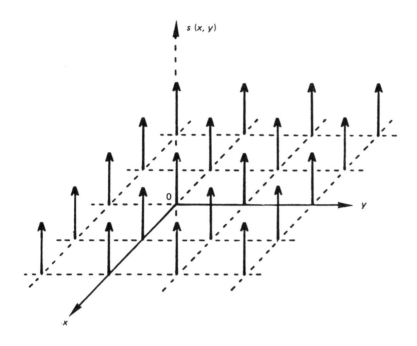

Fig.I.22 - "Brush" signal.

such that: $s(x, y) = a(1 + \cos 2\pi f_0 x)$, where $\dfrac{1}{f_0}$ is the period of the sine wave (fig.I.23.a and fig.I.24).

2. Spectra of two-dimensional signals

By generalising the concept of the Fourier transformation $S(f)$ for a one-dimensional signal $s(x)$, we shall see that the F.T. of an image $s(x, y)$ is a function $S(u, v)$. The two variables u and v represent the spatial frequencies of the image with respect to directions Ox and Oy respectively. Let us begin our reasoning with periodic-type images.

a) Periodic-type images

Let us return to signal $s(x, y) = a(1 + \cos 2\pi f_0 x)$, which is not dependent on variable y (fig.I.23.a). Through applying the results for signals which are a function of a single variable (in this case x) and

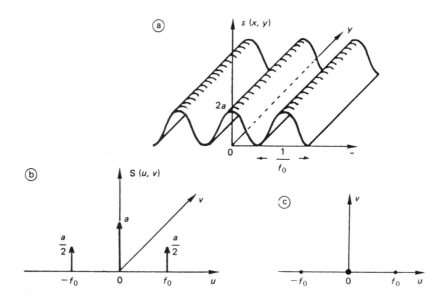

Fig.I.23 - Signal representing a luminous object varying sinusoidally in intensity with respect to Ox and constant with respect to Oy: $s(x, y) = a(1 + \cos 2\pi f_0 x)$; a) spatial aspect, b) spectral representation as a function of spatial frequencies u and v by the Fourier transform: $S(u,v) = a\delta(u,v) + \frac{a}{2}[\delta(u-f_0) + \delta(u+f_0)]$, c) spectrum represented as luminous points in the plane (u,v).

writing the frequency as u, we know that such a signal has a F.T. which consists of a Dirac signal with a frequency of $u = 0$ and a sur-face area of a, representing continuous component a, and two Dirac signals with a surface area of $\frac{a}{2}$ located at frequencies $u = f_0$ and $u = -f_0$. We say that u is the spatial frequency with respect to Ox. If we write v for the spatial frequency with respect to Oy, which is not shown in this instance, we can write this F.T. as follows:

$$S(u, v) = a\,\delta(u, v) + \frac{a}{2}\,(\delta(u - f_0) + \delta(u + f_0))$$

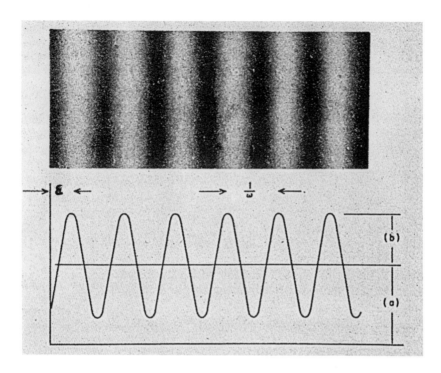

Fig.I.24 - Luminous object varying sinusoidally in intensity with respect to Ox
and constant with respect to Oy: spatial frequency ω, phase ϵ, modulation a
(from J.C. Dainty and R. Shaw). [8]

It is possible to represent $S(u, v)$ spatially (fig.I.23.b). A plane representation is also possible, and this is analogous to an image, as if we were viewing $S(u, v)$ from above (fig.I.23.c). The Dirac signals are then light points with an intensity proportional to their surface area, meaning the height of the arrow. By convention they may be drawn as points, with the intensity of each represented by its surface area. The larger the point, the greater the light intensity.

In the same way, an image varying sinusoidally with respect to Oy is a signal $s(x, y) = a(1 + \cos 2\pi f_0 y)$.

Its F.T. is $S(u, v) = a\, \delta(u, v) + \frac{a}{2}\, (\delta(v - f_0) = \delta(v + f_0))$ which

consists of three luminous points on the Ov axis representing the spatial frequencies with respect to direction Oy.

A signal which is periodic with respect to Ox and constant with respect to Oy (fig.I.25.a), with a period of T, has a spectrum composed of an infinite number of equidistant lines on the Ou axis with frequencies of $0, \pm\frac{1}{T}, \pm\frac{2}{T}, \dots \pm\frac{n}{T}$, etc., (fig.I.25.b and I.25.c). The line at the origin represents the mean image level, the lines at a frequency of $u = \pm\frac{1}{T}$ are the fundamental and the lines at a frequency of $u = \pm\frac{k}{T}$ are the k'th harmonic.

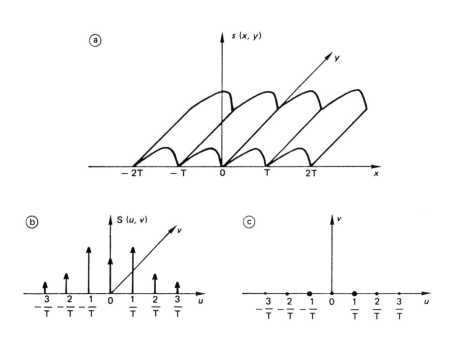

Fig.I.25 - Luminous object which is periodic with respect to Ox and constant with respect to Oy; a) spatial aspect, b) spectrum: Fourier transform S(u,v) c) spectrum "viewed from above".

For example figure I.26.a represents a periodic test pattern made up of black stripes on a white background, with a Fourier spectrum consisting of luminous points decreasing in intensity and aligned on the Ou axis (see fig.I.16). Figure I.26.b shows a copy of the test pattern on large grain film (see chapter IV) together with its corresponding Fourier spectrum. The edges of the stripes in the pattern have been softened by the film response (modulation transfer function), showing up in the spectrum as a decrease in the intensity of the high frequencies. Roughness of the background is due to the film grain size, and shows in the spectrum as a widening of the zero frequency spot.

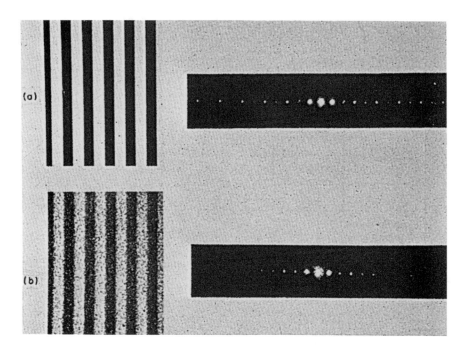

Fig.I.26 - a) Periodic test pattern of black stripes on a white background (luminous object varying in intensity as a square wave in the x direction and constant in the y direction), and its Fourier spectrum consisting of luminous points decreasing in intensity and aligned on the Ou axis, b) copy of the test pattern on large grain film and its corresponding Fourier spectrum. The edges of the stripes in the pattern have been softened by the film response, showing up in the spectrum as a decrease in the intensity of the high frequencies. Roughness of the background is due to the film grain size, and shows up in the spectrum as a widening of the zero frequency spot (from J.C. Dainty and R. Shaw). [8]

An image which is periodic in the direction O*y* and constant with respect to O*x* has a F.T. consisting of equidistant lines arranged in the direction O*v*, which is the axis of the spatial frequencies in the direction O*y* (fig.I.27).

An image which is periodic with respect both to O*x* and O*y* will have a spectrum of the type shown in figure I.28, where it is assumed that the period in *x* is half the period in *y*. If both periodic intervals occur in any two directions OA and OB on the plane, with periods T_1 and T_2 respectively (fig.I.29.a), the spectrum consists of points aligned in the same directions OA and OB of plane *u*O*v*, separated by $\dfrac{1}{T_1}$ and $\dfrac{1}{T_2}$ respectively (fig.I.29.b).

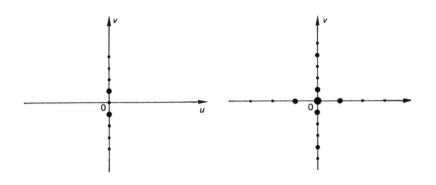

Fig.I.27 - Spectrum (top view) of a luminous object with constant intensity with respect to O*x* but periodic in type with respect to O*y*.

Fig.I.28 - Spectrum (top view) of a luminous object with periodic intensity in both the O*x* and O*y* directions. The period in *x* is half the period in *y*.

Other examples

The reader can easily check the following results:

• a set of blades parallel to O*x* (equidistant infinitely narrow lines with a separation of T) has a spectrum consisting of points of uniform intensity $\dfrac{1}{T}$ apart aligned in the direction O*v*, that is to say a comb aligned on O*v* (fig.I.30).

• the F.T. of a blade located on the O*x* axis is a blade situated on the O*v* axis (simply let T tend towards infinity in the preceding example). Similarly, the spectrum of a blade aligned with O*y* is a

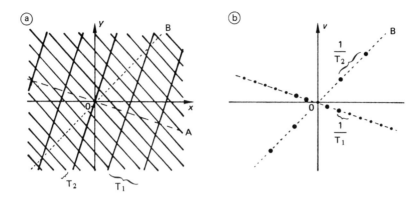

Fig.I.29 - a) Schematic representation of a luminous object which is periodic in any two directions OA and OB on the plane xOy, b) the spectrum of this object, viewed from above, consists of points aligned in the same directions OA and OB of the plane of spatial frequencies uOv.

blade aligned with O*u* (see fig.I.35.b).

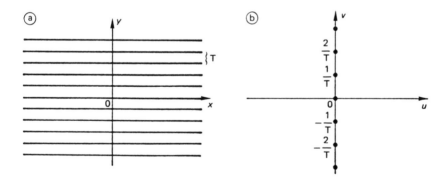

Fig.I.30 - a) A set of equidistant blades parallel to Ox with a separation of T, b) the spectrum consists of points of uniform intensity $\frac{1}{T}$ apart, aligned on the Ov axis.

- a brush function with period T_1 in the x direction and period T_2 in the y direction (fig.I.31.a) has a F.T. consisting of a brush with period $\dfrac{1}{T_1}$ in the u direction and period $\dfrac{1}{T_2}$ in the v direction (fig.I.31.b).

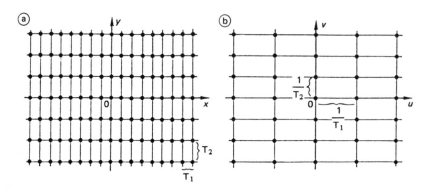

Fig.I.31 - a) "Brush" signal with period T_1 in the x direction and T_2 the y direction. b) the spectrum is also a brush with period $\dfrac{1}{T_1}$ in the direction Ou and $\dfrac{1}{T_2}$ in the direction Ov.

b) Any images

Any non-periodic image may be considered as the sum of an infinite number of sinusoidal components w ith infinitesimal amplitudes, having all possible spatial frequencies in both the Ou and the Ov directions. It is written as follows in complex notation:

$$s(x, y) = \int_{-\infty}^{+\infty}\int_{-\infty}^{+\infty} S(u, v)\ e^{2\pi j(ux+vy)}\ du\ dv \qquad (20)$$

It is the analogue of $s(x) = \displaystyle\int_{-\infty}^{+\infty} S(f)\ e^{2\pi jft}\ df$ for one dimensional signals.

$S(u, v)$ is the two-dimensional F.T. of $s(x, y)$. It is expressed as a function of the image by the following double integral:

$$S(u, v) = \int_{-\infty}^{+\infty}\int_{-\infty}^{+\infty} s(x, y)\ e^{-2\pi j(ux+vy)}\ dx\ dy \qquad (21)$$

This is the analogue of $S(f) = \int_{-\infty}^{+\infty} s(x)\ e^{-2\pi jfx}\ dx$

Each of the functions $S(u, v)$ and $s(x, y)$ is therefore the F.T. of the other.

Calculation is much easier in cases where the variables can be separated, that is $s(x, y)$ can be written as the product of two functions, one of which contains only variable x and the other only variable y:

$$s(x, y) = s_1(x)\ s_2(y)$$

Double integral (20) can then be reduced to a product of two simple integrals:

$$S(u, v) = \int_{-\infty}^{+\infty} s_1(x)\ e^{-2\pi jux}\ dx\ .\ \int_{-\infty}^{+\infty} s_2(y)\ e^{-2\pi jvy}\ dy = S_1(u).S_2(v)$$

$S(u, v)$ is the product of the one-dimensional F.T. for $s_1(x)$ and $s_2(y)$.

Example 1: $s(x, y) = P_1(x)\ P_2(y)$

This product of two "gate" functions (width a in x, b in y) represents a luminous rectangle with an intensity of unity and sides a and b (fig.I.32.a). We find straight away that: $S(u, v) = ab$ sinc $\pi\ ua$ sinc π vb (fig.I.32.b and I.32.c).

Example 2:

A luminous disc with a diameter of D and an intensity of unity (fig.I.33.a). This image has circular symmetry, and is not a separable signal. The calculation is rather more complex, and yields a F.T.

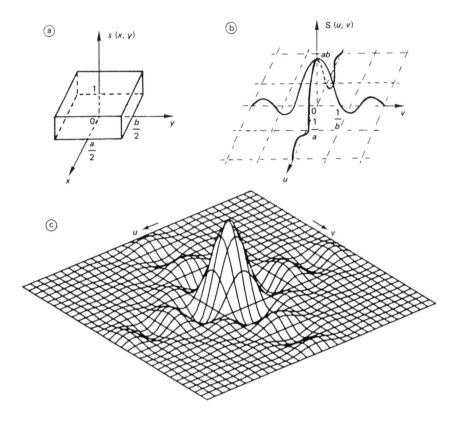

Fig.I.32 - a) Luminous rectangle with an intensity of unity and sides a and b in
directions Ox and Oy respectively, b) and c): the Fourier transform is the pro-
duct of two functions in $\frac{\sin u}{u}$ and $\frac{\sin v}{v}$: $S(u, v) = ab$ sinc π ua sinc π vb.

which also has circular symmetry, with a cross-section defined by the
function

$$\frac{\pi D^2}{2} \frac{J_1(\pi D\rho)}{\pi D\rho}$$

where ρ is the radius ($\rho = \sqrt{u^2 + v^2}$) and where J_1 is the Bessel function of the first order: it passes through zero for the first time when

$\rho = \dfrac{1.22}{D}$ (fig.I.33.b and c).

Example 3:

A circular Gaussian image, with cross-section $e^{-\frac{r^2}{2\sigma^2}}$ where r is the radius ($r = \sqrt{x^2 + y^2}$) (fig.I.34.a). As in the one-dimensional case, (see fig.I.7) we show that the F.T. is also Gaussian. It is in fact a circular Gaussian model with cross-section $2\pi\sigma^2 e^{-\frac{\rho^2}{2\alpha^2}}$ where ρ is the radius ($\rho = \sqrt{u^2 + v^2}$ and where $\alpha = \dfrac{1}{2\pi\sigma}$ (fig.I.34.b and c).

Figure I.35 shows various images and their spectra:

a) a small luminous disc: (see fig.I.33)

b) a line in the direction Oy (neither infinitely narrow nor infinitely long) with a spectrum tending towards a line in the direction Ou.

c) two small discs which are symmetrical with respect to the origin. They may be thought of as the result of convolution (see chapter II) between a disc centred on the origin as in a), and two Dirac signals (luminous points) located at the centre of the discs. The F.T. is the product of the F.T. of the disc and the F.T. of the two points. But the transform of a sine wave consists of two points. Conversely the F.T. of two points is a sine wave (see fig.I.23). This explains the appearance of the spectrum obtained.

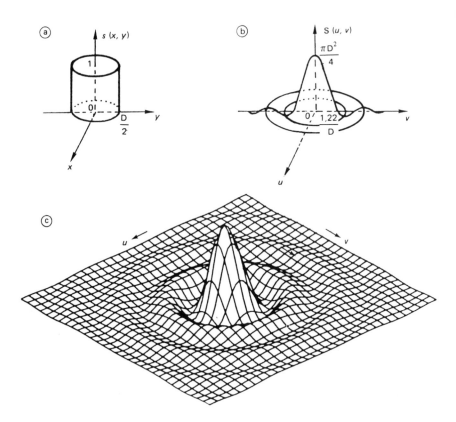

Fig.I.33 - a) Luminous disc with a diameter of D and intensity unity (object with circular symmetry). b) and c) The Fourier transform also has circular symme-

try and cross-section described by the function $\dfrac{\pi D^2}{2} \dfrac{J_1(\pi D\rho)}{\pi D\rho}$ where ρ is the

radius ($\rho = \sqrt{u^2 + v^2}$) and where J_1 is the Bessel function of the first order.

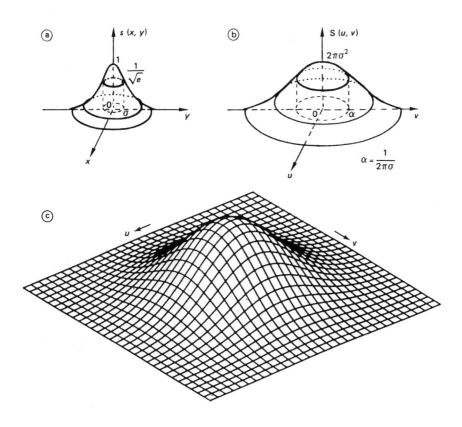

Fig.I.34 - a) Two-dimensional Gaussian signal, with cross-section $e^{-\left(\frac{r^2}{2\sigma^2}\right)}$ where r is the radius $(r = \sqrt{x^2 + y^2})$, b) and c): the Fourier transform is also a circular Gaussian model with cross-section $2\pi\sigma^2 e^{\left(-\frac{\rho^2}{2\alpha^2}\right)}$ where ρ is the radius $(\rho = \sqrt{u^2 + v^2})$ and where $\alpha = \frac{1}{2\pi\sigma}$.

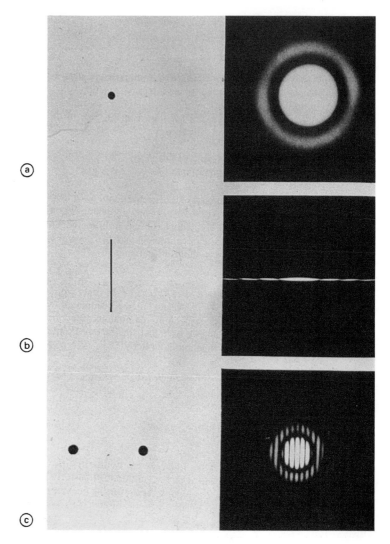

Fig.I.35 - Two-dimensional objects and their Fourier spectra: a) small disc (see fig.I.33), b) a line in the direction Oy, with a spectrum aligned on Ou, c) two small discs which are symmetrical with respect to the origin. They may be thought of as the result of convolution (see chapter II) between a disc centred on the origin as in a), and two Dirac signals (luminous points) located at the centre of the discs. This explains the appearance of the spectrum obtained. It is the product of a type a) spectrum and a cosine function (from R.C. Gonzalez and P. Wintz). [1]

2

Scanning of an image by an aperture

There are many physical systems for forming images. These include such things as optical equipment, image creation by photographic processes and so on. In suitable conditions they can be modelled to a first approximation using linear systems. The same applies to many processing methods, both digital and analogue. It is therefore essential to study linear systems closely. We shall see that in the spatial domain these systems carry out an operation called *convolution*, and in the spectral domain they perform *frequency filtering*. To introduce the concept of convolution, it is convenient to consider how an image is scanned by an aperture moving across it. We shall start by reducing the problem to a single dimension.

A. Scanning of a stripe by a uniform square aperture

Let us look at figure II.1.a. A uniformly transparent square aperture, in other words a hole, moves from left to right across a white stripe on a black background. The sides of the aperture are a in length and the stripe is ℓ wide. We shall assume that $a < \ell$. If we capture the luminous flux passing through the aperture, we see that it varies according to where the aperture is positioned, and we obtain the trapezoidal variation shown in the figure. Five particular positions of the aperture are considered.

The stripe can be shown as a gate function $e(x)$ with a width of ℓ (fig.II.1.b), and the aperture can be shown as a gate function $o(x)$ with a width of a (fig.II.1.c). Signal $e(x)$ can be thought of as the input signal to the system.

The captured flux is output signal $s(x)$: in figure II.1.d the maximum amplitude has been arbitrarily chosen as equal to 1. The relationship between $s(x)$ and $e(x)$ can be precisely defined. For each aperture position x', identified by reference to the centre of the stripe, the

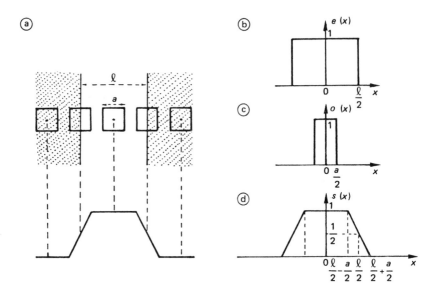

Fig.II.1 - a) Scanning a stripe ℓ wide with a uniform square aperture of side a, and the signal shape obtained, b) stripe shown as an input signal e(x): gate width ℓ, c) aperture shown as a signal o(x): gate width a, d) derived output signal s(x).

quantity of light passing through is proportional to the illuminated surface, in other words to the integral:

$$\int_{-\infty}^{+\infty} e(x)\, o(x-x')\, \mathrm{d}x \qquad \text{giving:} \qquad \int_{-\infty}^{+\infty} s(x') = e(x)\, o(x-x')\, \mathrm{d}x \,(1)$$

Figures II.2.a.b.c.d. illustrate this relationship in the particular a case of $x' = \frac{\ell}{2}$. We then have $s(x') = \frac{a}{2}$.

To obtain the expression for $s(x)$ we simply reverse the roles of the variables x and x' in equation (1). This gives

$$s(x) = \int_{-\infty}^{+\infty} s(x) = e(x')\ o(x'-x)\ dx' \tag{2}$$

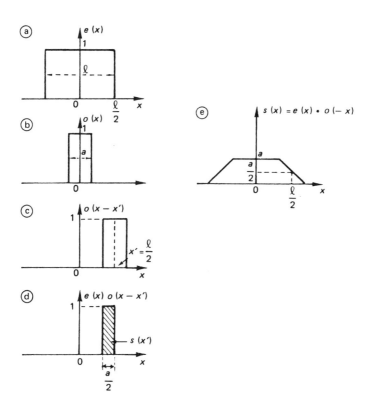

Fig.II.2 - Convolution e(x) * o(-x); a) signal e(x), b) signal o(x), c) shifted signal

o(x-x′) for $x' = \frac{\ell}{2}$, d) product e(x) o(x-x′): the surface area of this product

represents $s(x') = \int_{-\infty}^{+\infty} e(x)o(x-x')dx$ which is the value of the output signal

for $x = x' (= \frac{\ell}{2})$, e) output signal s(x) = e(x) * o(-x).

We are dealing here with a *convolution integral*. Let us recall what we mean by the convolution of two functions $f(x)$ and $g(x)$, writing the operation as * :

$$f(x) * g(x) = \int_{-\infty}^{+\infty} f(x') \, g(x-x') \, dx'$$

By this definition integral (2) represents the convolution of $e(x)$ with $o(-x)$, being the reversed aperture function:

$$\boxed{s(x) = e(x) * o(-x)} \qquad (3) \text{ (fig.II.2.e)}$$

B. Convolution and linear systems.
The notion of impulse response

Any system in which the relationship between input and output is a convolution is an invariant linear system also called a linear filter.

Before considering what these terms mean we shall return to the example in section A. The system is characterised by aperture function $o(x)$, or equally by $o(-x)$ operating directly in convolution equation (3). This function is called its *impulse response*, and is written $R(x)$ so that $o(-x) = R(x)$. It takes its name from the fact that $R(x)$ effectively represents the system's response to a Dirac pulse $\delta(x)$, meaning in this case the output signal obtained when the stripe becomes infinitely narrow. By actually moving the aperture $o(x)$ across the stripe a signal is captured representing the aperture itself, but reversed. If the reader needs to be convinced of this, simply imagine a non-uniform aperture, for instance with greater transparency on the right than on the left. Moving this aperture from left to right will capture a decreasing amount of light. In this way $s(x) = o(-x) = R(x)$ (fig.II.3).

It is possible to write equation (3) in the form

$$\boxed{s(x) = e(x) * R(x)} \qquad (4)$$

and say that a linear system uses the impulse response $R(x)$ to perform convolution of the input signal.

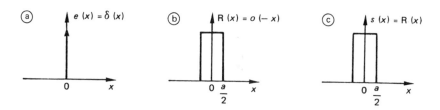

Fig.II.3 - a) Signal $e(x) = \delta(x)$ representing an infinitely narrow stripe, b) the impulse response of a uniform square aperture with a width of a, c) the output signal is equal to the impulse response of the aperture: $s(x) = \delta(x) * R(x) = R(x)$.

In its explicit form: $\quad s(x) = \displaystyle\int_{-\infty}^{+\infty} e(x')\ R(x-x')\ dx'$ \hfill (5)

Note

Convolution is a commutative operation. If variable substitution is carried out for $x - x' = X$ in integral (5), we find in fact:

$$s(x) = \int_{+\infty}^{-\infty} e(x-X)\ R(X)\ (-dX) = \int_{-\infty}^{+\infty} R(X)\ e(x-X)\ dX = R(x)*e(x)$$

Properties of linear systems

In general the following two properties define invariant linear systems, often known as "linear filters".

1. Linearity

a) If the input signal is multiplied by k, the output is also multiplied by k.

$$k\ e(x) \rightarrow k\ s(x) \hfill (5)$$

b) If $s_1(x)$ and $s_2(x)$ are the outputs corresponding to input signals $e_1(x)$ and $e_2(x)$ respectively, the response to the summed signal $e_1(x) + e_2(x)$ is the sum of the responses $s_1(x) + e_2(x)$:

$$e_1(x) + e_2(x) \rightarrow s_1(x) + s_2(x) \tag{6}$$

It is therefore possible to say that any linear combination of input signals has the same corresponding linear combination of output signals (known as the superposition principle).

$$\sum_i a_i\, e_i(x) \rightarrow \sum_i a_i\, s_i(x) \tag{7}$$

2. Shift invariance (also called stationarity)

If the input signal is shifted by any quantity, the output signal is shifted by the same amount.

$$e(x-x_0) \rightarrow s(x-x_0) \tag{8}$$

It is easy to check that the scanning system in section A has both of these properties.

We have also seen that a linear system is characterised by its impulse response $R(x)$, which is a response to input signal $\delta(x)$, and that the system uses $R(x)$ to convolute the input signal. We shall show that this is a consequence of properties 1) and 2), but first let us imagine the case of a system which does not modify the input signal. It therefore gives $s(x) = e(x)$. This means in particular that for $e(x) = \delta(x)$ the output is $R(x) = \delta(x)$ (fig.II.4). (This is the situation where we are scanning with an infinitely narrow aperture).

Consequently, convolution by $\delta(x)$ does not modify a signal. This can also be seen in figure II.4. It is then said that the Dirac signal is the *neutral element* of the convolution operator.

$$\left.\begin{array}{l} \delta(x) * R(x) = R(x) \\ e(x) * \delta(x) = e(x) \end{array}\right\} \tag{9}$$

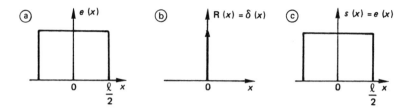

Fig.II.4 - a) Signal e(x) representing a stripe of width ℓ, b) impulse response of an infinitely narrow aperture: $R(x) = \delta(x)$, c) the output signal is equal to the input signal: $s(x) = e(x) * \delta(x) = e(x)$.

Symbolic representation of an invariant linear system

We shall use the diagram shown in figure II.5. This represents the linear system as a "black box" with an impulse response of $R(x)$ which transforms input signal $e(x)$ into an output signal $s(x) = e(x) * R(x)$.

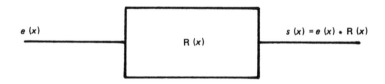

Fig.II.5 - Symbolic representation of an invariant linear system as a "black box" with an impulse response of R(x) which transforms input signal e(x) into an output signal: $s(x) = e(x) * R(x)$.

Demonstrating the convolution relationship

We shall begin with a "physical" interpretation of equation (9): $e(x) * \delta(x) = e(x)$.

Suppose that we construct an approximation of signal $e(x)$ from a series of small, adjacent rectangles each with a width of a, forming a step function (fig.II.6.a):

$$e(x) \simeq \sum_{n=-\infty}^{+\infty} e(na)\ o(x-na)$$

where $o(x)$ is the gate function with a width of a (fig.II.1.c). If we let a tend towards zero, rectangles $o(x-na)$ tend towards Dirac signals crowding ever more closely together. If we put $na = x'$ the previous discrete summation becomes the continuous summation

$$\int_{-\infty}^{+\infty} e(x')\ \delta(x-x')\ dx'$$

This gives the equation $e(x) = \displaystyle\int_{-\infty}^{+\infty} e(x')\ \delta(x-x')\ dx' = e(x) * \delta(x)$

It is therefore possible to interpret this as an integral, representing a signal as the sum of an infinite number of Dirac signals all with "infinitesimal" amplitudes $e(x')\ dx'$ and located at points x' which are infinitely close together (fig.II.6.b).

This integral enables the relationship for input-output convolution (4) to be found by using the properties of linearity and invariance in the system. In this way, if we examine the responses to successive input signals $\delta(x)$, $\delta(x-x')$, etc., we obtain:

$$\delta(x) \rightarrow R(x)$$

$$\delta(x-x') \rightarrow R(x-x') \qquad \text{property of invariance (8)}$$

$$e(x')\ \delta(x-x')\ dx' \rightarrow e(x')\ R(x-x')\ dx' \qquad \text{property of linearity (5)}$$

$$\int e(x')\ \delta(x-x')\ dx' \rightarrow \int e(x')\ R(x-x')\ dx' \qquad \text{property of linearity (7)}$$

so that $e(x) \rightarrow e(x) * R(x)$

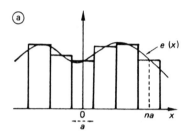 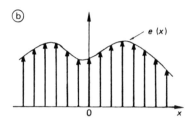

Fig.II.6 - a) Close approximation to a signal e(x) made from a series of small,

adjacent rectangles $e(x) \simeq \sum_{n=-\infty}^{+\infty} e(na) \, o(x-na)$ where o(x) is the gate func-

tion with a width of a (fig.II.1.c), b) when a tends towards zero, the small rectangles become Dirac signals, the discrete summation becomes an integral and
the approximation at a) becomes an equation. This is the convolution integral:

$$e(x) = \int_{-\infty}^{+\infty} e(x') \, \delta(x-x') \, dx' = e(x) * \delta(x).$$

Example

Convolution of a rectangle (fig.II.7.a) with a triangle (fig.II.7.b).
If we assume that $R(x)$ represents an aperture which we move across
$e(x)$, we can calculate the surface area of the shared part of the product $e(x) \, R(x-x')$ for all possible values of x'. Symmetry means that
our reasoning can be confined to cases where $x' > 0$. We obtain the
results shown below in Figure II.7.c.

$$0 < x' < 1 \qquad s(x') = 1$$

$$1 < x' < 2 \qquad s(x') = 1 - \frac{1}{2}(x - 1)^2$$

$$2 < x' < 3 \qquad s(x') = \frac{1}{2}(3 - x)^2$$

$$x' > 3 \qquad s(x') = 0$$

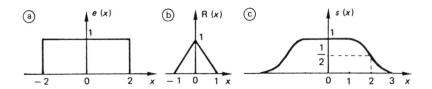

Fig.II.7 - Example: convolution of a rectangle and a triangle; a) square input signal, b) triangular impulse response, c) derived output signal.

Application

The foregoing example shows that convolution rounds or blurs the edges of the rectangle. In other words it attenuates the higher frequencies in the signal. This effect is often used to "clean up" a signal overlaid with a burst of much higher frequency interference which is causing "noise" (fig.II.8.a). By convoluting with an impulse response which is wide compared to the period of the noise, but narrow enough not to cause too much distortion to the useful signal itself (fig.II.8.b), most of the disturbance is eliminated (fig.II.8.c). This is known as smoothing.

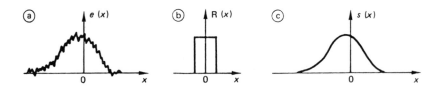

Fig.II.8 - Using convolution to smooth a signal affected by noise; a) input signal distorted by noise, b) square impulse response, c) smoothed signal obtained as output from the filter.

Exercise 1

A periodic test pattern is being scanned. Its period is ℓ and the width of each stripe is $\frac{\ell}{2}$. Uniform square apertures of increasing width a are being used where: $a = 0, \frac{\ell}{8}, \frac{\ell}{4}, \frac{\ell}{2}, \frac{3\ell}{4}, \ell, \frac{3\ell}{2}, 2\ell$. Draw the shape of the output signals derived.

The results are shown in figure II.9.

It will be noticed that as a increases the sides of each succeeding trapezium are less steep.

For $a = \frac{\ell}{2}$ they become adjacent triangles.

For $a = \frac{3\ell}{4}$ the contrast is reduced, and for $a = \ell$ it is zero, meaning that the derived signal is constant ($a = 2\ell$ gives the same result, as in general does $n\ell$). For $a = \frac{3\ell}{2}$ we find the contrast is inverted. This result may be interpreted with the aid of the transfer function.

Exercise 2

Demonstrate that convolution of a signal by means of a Dirac signal located at $x = a$ is the same as shifting this signal by the quantity a.

We wish to prove that $s(x) = e(x) * \delta(x-a) = \int_{-\infty}^{+\infty} e(x')\delta(x-a-x')dx'$

But $e(x) = e(x) * \delta(x) = \int_{-\infty}^{+\infty} e(x')\delta(x-x')\, dx'$. Comparing both integrals we find that:

$$e(x) * \delta(x-a) = e(x-a)$$

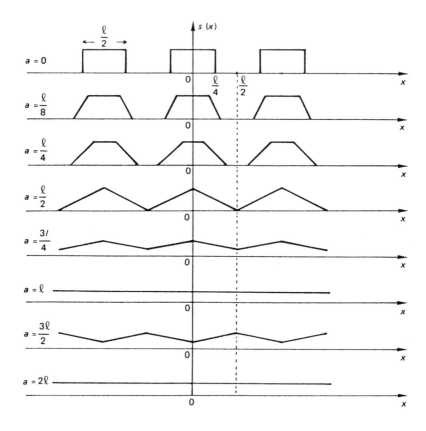

Fig.II.9 - Scanning a periodic test pattern with a period of ℓ using square apertures with a width of a: results obtained as a function of a. For a = ℓ, 2ℓ, ...
nℓ a constant signal is obtained. For a = $\dfrac{3\ell}{2}$ we find inversion of the test
pattern.

C. Transfer function of a linear system

1. Sinusoidal input of frequency f_0:

being
$$e(x) = \cos 2\pi f_0 x = \frac{1}{2} e^{2\pi j f_0 x} + \frac{1}{2} e^{-2\pi j f_0 x}$$

a) We shall begin our reasoning from the complex signal $e^{2\pi j f_0 x}$. The response to this signal, given by the linear system with an impulse response of $R(x)$, is as follows:

$$R(x) * e^{2\pi j f_0 x} = \int_{-\infty}^{+\infty} R(x') e^{2\pi j f_0 (x-x')} \, dx'$$

$$= e^{2\pi j f_0 x} \int_{-\infty}^{+\infty} R(x') e^{-2\pi j f_0 x'} \, dx'$$

The integral is familiar as the Fourier transform of $R(x)$ for the frequency $f = f_0$. If we write this F.T. as $G(f)$ we can write the derived signal as:

$$e^{2\pi j f_0 x} G(f_0)$$

b) Similarly, signal $e^{-2\pi j f_0 x}$ will give the response:

$$e^{2\pi j f_0 x} G(-f_0)$$

c) Now let us consider $e(x) = \cos 2\pi f_0 x$. The linearity of the system will ensure that the output signal will be the sum of the responses to signals $\frac{1}{2} e^{2\pi j f_0 x}$ and $\frac{1}{2} e^{-2\pi j f_0 x}$, being:

$$s(x) = \frac{1}{2} e^{2\pi j f_0 x} G(f_0) + \frac{1}{2} e^{-2\pi j f_0 x} G(-f_0)$$

By explicitly writing the modulus and argument of $G(f)$ we have:

$$G(f) = |G(f)| \, e^{-j\phi(f)}$$

Since $R(x)$ is moreover real, we know that:

$$G(-f) = G*(f) = |G(f)| \, e^{j\phi(f)}$$

Therefore

$$s(x) = \frac{1}{2} |G(f_0)| (e^{2\pi j f_0 x} e^{-j\phi(f_0)} + e^{-2\pi j f_0 x} e^{j\phi(f_0)})$$

being $s(x) = |G(f_0)| \cos [2\pi f_0 x - \Phi(f_0)]$ (10)

Therefore *the output is a sinusoidal signal of the same frequency* f_0 as the input signal. This signal is:

-          amplified or attenuated depending on the value $|G(f_0)|$ taken by the modulus of $G(f)$ for frequency f_0,

-          phase-shifted by $\Phi(f_0)$, being the argument of $G(f)$ for frequency f_0.

The F.T. $G(f)$ of impulse response $R(x)$ is called the *transfer function* (or "complex gain") of the system. This characteristic is equivalent to the impulse response which expresses the frequency response of the system.

Writing the F.T. with the notation $\mathcal{F}$ we have:

$$\boxed{G(f) = \mathcal{F} [R(x)]}$$ (11)

This property of sine wave conservation is summarised in figure II.10, and is fundamental to linear systems. It forms the basis of all methods for measuring frequency response using sinusoidal test signals, such as sine wave generators for electricity and sinusoidal test patterns for optics. These methods comprise the *harmonic analysis* of the system.

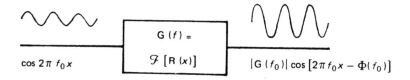

Fig.II.10 - A fundamental property of invariant linear systems: sine wave conservation. Definition of the gain or transfer function G(f), Fourier transform of the impulse response R(x).

2. Any type of input

As we saw in the previous chapter (chap.I. equation 10), any form of input signal $e(x)$ may be analysed into a summation of sinusoidal components in accordance with the Fourier integral

$$e(x) = \int_0^{+\infty} 2 \, |E(f)| \, \cos \, (2\pi f x - \Phi_e(f)) \, df$$

where $E(f) = |E(f)|e^{-j\phi e(f)}$ is the F.T. of signal $e(x)$. But we know from the first part of our study (equation 10) that the response to signal $\cos 2 \, \pi f x$ is the sinusoidal signal

$$|G(f)| \, \cos \, (2\pi f x - \Phi(f))$$

where $G(f) = |G(f)|e^{-j\phi(f)}$ is the system transfer function. As the system is linear, the output corresponding to signal $e(x)$ will be the same linear combination of sine waves, namely the same integral:

$$s(x) = \int_0^{+\infty} 2 \, |E(f)| \, |G(f)| \, \cos(2\pi f x - \Phi_e(f) - \Phi(f)) \, df$$

But $s(x)$ is written:

$$s(x) = \int_0^{+\infty} 2 \, |S(f)| \, \cos(2\pi f x - \Phi_s(f)) \, df$$

where $S(f) = |S(f)|e^{-j\phi_s(f)}$ represents its Fourier transform. We can use this information to deduce the following equivalences between moduli and arguments:

$$\left\{ \begin{array}{c} |S(f)| = |E(f)| \, |G(f)| \\ \Phi_s(f) = \Phi_e(f) + \Phi(f) \end{array} \right\}$$

These are expressions of the equation $\boxed{S(f) = E(f) \, G(f)}$ (12)

The F.T. of the output signal is obtained by multiplying the F.T. of the input signal by the system transfer function $G(f)$. A linear system thus performs *frequency filtering*.

We can say in mathematical terms that a *convolution* in the x domain (time or space) has a corresponding *multiplication* in the frequency domain f. We can show that the reverse is equally true. The F.T. of the product of two signals is given by convolution in the f domain between the F.T.'s of these signals. These properties are summarised below:

$$\begin{array}{cc} x \text{ domain} & f \text{ domain} \end{array}$$

$$\left\{ \begin{array}{rcl} e(x) & \longleftrightarrow & E(f) \\ R(x) & \longleftrightarrow & G(f) \\ e(x) * R(x) & \longleftrightarrow & E(f) \cdot G(f) \end{array} \right\}$$

$$\left\{ \begin{array}{rcl} e_1(x) & \longleftrightarrow & E_1(f) \\ e_2(x) & \longleftrightarrow & E_2(f) \\ e_1(x) \cdot e_2(x) & \longleftrightarrow & E_1(f) * E_2(f) \end{array} \right\}$$

Example

A stripe ℓ wide is being scanned by a uniform square aperture of the same width. Figure II.11.a shows $e(x)$ and $R(x)$, and their F.T. $E(f)$ and $G(f)$ are shown in figure II.11.b: $E(f) = G(f) = \ell$ sinc $\pi\ell f$.

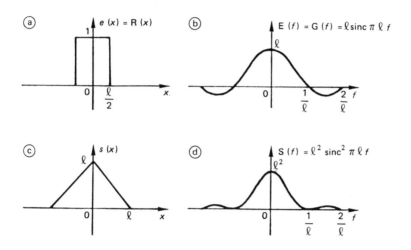

Fig.II.11 - A stripe ℓ wide being filtered by a square aperture of the same width; a) input signal $e(x)$ and impulse response $R(x)$, b) input signal Fourier transform $E(f)$ and system gain $G(f)$, c) sawtooth output signal obtained: $s(x) = e(x) * R(x)$, d) output signal Fourier transform: $S(f) = E(f) \cdot G(f)$.

We obtain a sawtooth output signal which is 2ℓ in width at the base (fig.II.11.c) with a F.T. of $S(f) = \ell^2 \operatorname{sinc}^2 \pi\ell f$. (fig.II.11.d).

Exercise 1

Spectrum of a periodic signal. Show that the spectrum of a periodic signal with period T is derived from that of the generator component by multiplying it by $\frac{1}{T}$ then taking (Dirac) lines from the spectrum with a separation of $\frac{1}{T}$.

It is always possible to consider a periodic signal $f(x)$ as if it had been derived by repeating a component $m(x)$ of duration T at a period of T. This is how it is possible to move from the gate in figure I.8 to the square wave in figure I.16 by choosing $a = \frac{T}{2}$:

$$f(x) = \sum_{n=-\infty}^{+\infty} m(x-nt)$$

But $m(x - nt) = m(x) * \delta(x-nT)$ and therefore:

$$f(x) = \sum_{n=-\infty}^{+\infty} m(x) * \delta(x-nT) = m(x) * \sum_{n=-\infty}^{+\infty} \delta(x-nT) = m(x) * p(x)$$

with $p(x)$ being the comb function of period T. To periodise a signal therefore is to convolute it with a comb function. Moving on to the frequency domain, we have the multiplication of each corresponding F.T. namely:

$$F(f) = M(f) \cdot P(f) = \tfrac{1}{T} M(f) \sum_{n=-\infty}^{+\infty} \delta\left(f - \tfrac{n}{T}\right)$$

For example this operation will lead from the spectrum of figure I.8.b, with $a = \dfrac{T}{2}$, to the line spectrum in figure I.16.b where the arrows lie within an envelope which is the function:

$$\tfrac{1}{T} \times \tfrac{T}{2} \text{ sinc } \pi \tfrac{T}{2} f = \tfrac{1}{2} \text{ sinc } \frac{\pi T f}{2}$$

The reader may wish to apply this principle by returning to exercise 1 in section B (fig.II.9) and reasoning within the frequency domain. The transfer function of the aperture is a cardinal sine of the type shown in figure II.11.b, where a replaces ℓ. In particular it allows us to explain the contrast inversion observed for $a = \dfrac{3\ell}{2}$. In fact we notice that except for the continuous component, all lines in the spectrum at figure I.16.b (where T becomes ℓ) become negative, and as such are shifted downwards once they have been multiplied by transfer function $\dfrac{3\ell}{2}\text{sinc } \dfrac{3\pi\ell}{2}f$.

Exercise 2

Convolution of a Gaussian with a Gaussian

$$e(x) = R(x) = e^{-x^2}$$

a) calculation in the spatial domain:

$$s(x) = e(x) * R(x) = \int_{-\infty}^{+\infty} e^{-x'^2} e^{-(x-x')^2} dx'$$

$$= e^{-x^2} \int_{-\infty}^{+\infty} e^{2xx'-2x'^2} dx' = e^{-x^2} \int_{-\infty}^{+\infty} e^{-2(x'-\frac{x}{2})^2} e^{\frac{x^2}{2}} dx'$$

$$= e^{-\frac{x^2}{2}} \int_{-\infty}^{+\infty} e^{-2(x'-\frac{x}{2})^2} dx'$$

If we put $x' - \frac{x}{2} = u$ and use the classic identity:

$$\int_{-\infty}^{+\infty} e^{-2u^2} du = \sqrt{\frac{\pi}{2}}$$

we find $s(x) = \sqrt{\frac{\pi}{2}} \; e^{-\frac{x^2}{2}}$ which is also Gaussian.

b) calculation in the frequency domain:

$$E(f) = G(f) = \sqrt{\pi} \; e^{-\pi^2 f^2} \qquad \text{(see figure I.7.a)}$$

therefore:

$$S(f) = \pi \; e^{-2\pi^2 f^2} \qquad \text{and} \qquad s(x) = \sqrt{\frac{\pi}{2}} \; e^{-\frac{x^2}{2}} \; .$$

D. Extension to two dimensions.
Scanning of an image by an aperture

1. Two-dimensional linear systems

The same definitions and properties apply.

Signals in the spatial domain become functions of the two variables x and y, and spectra become functions of the two spatial frequencies u and v. Convolution and Fourier integrals are now double integrals. In particular, the transfer function $G(u, v)$ is the two-dimensional F.T. of the impulse response $R(x, y)$, which represents the image of a luminous point $\delta(x, y)$ located at the origin, as it progresses through the system. $R(x, y)$ is called the point spread function in the literature, usually abbreviated to PSF.

We shall now summarise the main properties. If $e(x, y)$ is used for the input image, $E(u, v)$ for its Fourier transform, $s(x, y)$ for the output image and $S(u, v)$ for the F.T. of the latter, we obtain the following equations:

$$\boxed{s(x, y) = e(x, y) * R(x, y)} \qquad (13)$$

$$= \int_{-\infty}^{+\infty}\int_{-\infty}^{+\infty} e(x', y')\, R(x-x', y-y')\, dx'\, dy'$$

$$\boxed{S(u, v) = E(u, v)\, G(u, v)} \qquad (14)$$

$$E(u, v) = \mathscr{F}[e(x, y)] = \int_{-\infty}^{+\infty}\int_{-\infty}^{+\infty} e(x, y)\, e^{-2\pi j(ux+vy)}\, dx\, dy$$

$$S(u, v) = \mathscr{F}[s(x, y)] = \int_{-\infty}^{+\infty}\int_{-\infty}^{+\infty} s(x, y) \, e^{-2\pi j(ux+vy)} \, dx \, dy$$

$$G(u, v) = \mathscr{F}[R(x, y)] = \int_{-\infty}^{+\infty}\int_{-\infty}^{+\infty} R(x, y) \, e^{-2\pi j(ux+vy)} \, dx \, dy$$

2. Systems with an aperture

These are systems describing the scanning of an image $e(x, y)$ by a two-dimensional aperture $o(x, y)$. As with systems simplified to one dimension, it is easy to see that the impulse response is the aperture reversed in both x and y, so that $R(x, y) = o(-x, -y)$. For symmetrical apertures we have $R(x, y) = o(x, y)$. In this case the transfer function is the F.T. of the aperture itself. It is a convention that the continuous component of the signal (at a frequency of $u = v = 0$) is transmitted without attenuation, in other words that the mean intensity level of the image is conserved. This allows the normalisation of the transfer function so that $G(0,0) = 1$.

Figure II.12 represents three types of classic aperture and their normalised transfer functions.

a) **square aperture** transmitting uniformly (fig.II.12.a).

The impulse response $R(x, y)$ equals the product of two gate functions with a width of a, in both x and y. The normalised transfer function is:

$G(u,v) = $ sinc $\pi \, au$. sinc $\pi \, av$.   (See chap.I, section B.2.b, example 1).

b) **circular aperture** transmitting uniformly (fig.II.12.b).

This aperture has circular symmetry and a normalised transfer function which also has rotational symmetry. Its cross-section is given by:

$$G(u,0) = 2 \; \frac{J_1(\pi Du)}{\pi Du}$$

where D is the diameter of the aperture and J_1 the first order Bessel function which passes through zero for the first time when $u = \dfrac{1.22}{D}$ (see chapter I section B.2.b, example 2).

c) circular Gaussian aperture (fig.II.12.c)

This aperture is often used as a model to represent an electronic spot such as that obtained on the screen of a cathode ray tube.

The impulse response has cross-section $e^{-\frac{r^2}{2\sigma^2}}$ with $r = \sqrt{x^2 + y^2}$. The normalised transfer function is still a rotation Gaussian with cross-section $e^{\frac{\rho^2}{2\alpha^2}}$ where $\rho = \sqrt{u^2 + v^2}$ and where $\alpha = \dfrac{1}{2\pi\sigma}$ (see chapter I section B.2.b, example 3).

Figure II.13 compares the cross-sections $G(u,0)$ of the normalised transfer functions for the three aperture systems we have just examined. Curve {1} refers to the Gaussian aperture with parameter $\sigma = \dfrac{a}{2}$.

Curve {2} relates to the square aperture with a width of a and curve {3} is for the circular aperture with a diameter of a.

All these systems are low-pass filters which introduce no phase shift other than a possible change of sign (which is the same as a phase shift of π) for frequencies corresponding to the negative values of their transfer functions. This never occurs in the case of a Gaussian aperture.

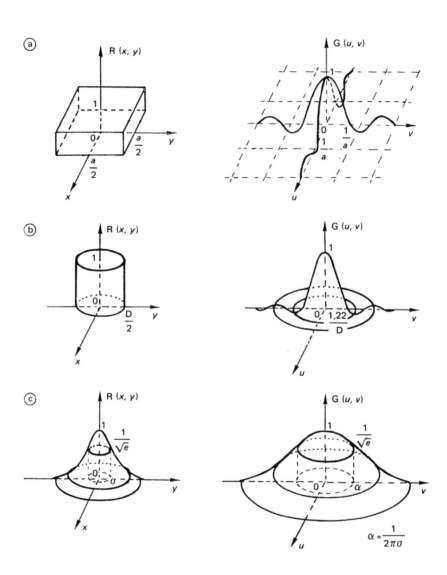

Fig.II.12 - Impulse responses and normalised transfer functions for aperture systems: a) square aperture with uniform transmission and a width of a, b) circular aperture with uniform transmission and a diameter of D, c) Gaussian aperture with parameter σ.

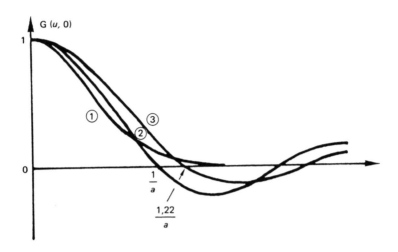

Fig.II.13 - Comparison between the normalised transfer functions in figure II.12 (along the cross-sections $G(u,0)$). {1} Gaussian aperture with parameter 2, {2} square aperture of side a, {3} circular aperture of diameter a.

3

Extension of the aperture notion

A. FILTERING OF IMAGES BY OPTICAL SYSTEMS

Elementary optics teaches us how to calculate the position and shape of an image after it has passed from an object through an optical instrument such as a magnifying glass or a microscope. To do this we use the laws of geometrical optics, and assume among other things that the image of a perfect point viewed through a centred optical lens system will itself be a perfect point. We lay down a set of conditions such as Gauss's approximation, whereby light beams have little slope relative to the axis and are very close to it, so that we can then ignore effects such as aberration.

In reality an optical system always shows the image of a point as a "blurred" luminous disc of greater or lesser diameter (fig.III.1). In this respect it resembles systems for scanning by an aperture. They show the image of a point through their impulse response. This is the aperture itself[1], and it is a "physical" aperture which therefore has finite dimensions (see chapter II).

There are many reasons why this is so:

- *focussing* defects
- geometrical and chromatic *aberrations*
- *diffraction* effects.

In this chapter we shall see that if we ignore aberration and consider only systems which are said to be "limited by diffraction", an optical system is both linear and invariant. Shift invariance assumes that if a point object is moved, its image moves by an equal amount with no distortion. This obviously presupposes magnification equal to

(1) except for reversal.

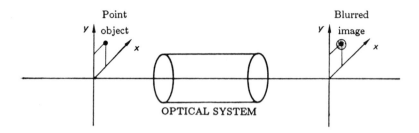

Fig.III.1 - A centred optical system shows the image of a point object as a
   "blurred disc".

+1, for otherwise we must postulate a scaling effect with a ratio
equal to the magnification. It also invokes the paraxial approximation
hypothesis (Gauss).

1. Focussing defects: an example

Let us imagine a circular thin lens which is perfectly free from diffraction or aberration (fig.III.2). Applying the laws of geometrical
optics, the image of a point object located on the axis is also a point
located on the axis. For example, if p is the distance between the
object and the lens and is equal to or twice the focal length, the
image will be a real image also situated at a distance of p from the
lens. Suppose that we now create a focussing defect by moving the
observation plane slightly away from the geometrical image plane by
a further distance d. The image becomes a small, blurred and uniformly illuminated disc with a radius of $r = R \dfrac{d}{p}$ (R = radius of the
lens).

If we move the object by a distance x perpendicular to the axis
but "not too far" from it, we shall see that the disc moves in the
opposite direction by the distance $y = x \dfrac{p + d}{p} \simeq x$ because d $<<$ p,
and that it does so without changing in size.

This system therefore behaves as if it were an invariant linear
system with the blurred disc as its impulse response. The response is
analogous to the cylindrical aperture with uniform transmission seen
in the previous chapter. The transfer function of this low-pass system
therefore includes some negative portions, and inverted contrast can
be observed for certain frequencies. This effect is made apparent in

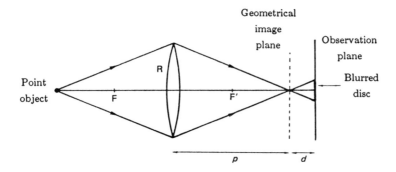

Geometrical
image
plane
Observation
plane
Blurred
disc

Fig.III.2 - Example of a focussing defect: the image of a point object is a blurred
and uniformly illuminated disc with a diameter of $r = R \dfrac{d}{p}$.

figure III.3, where the chosen object is a Foucault test pattern with
spatial frequencies increasing distance from centre, $\dfrac{1}{r}$. The lower
photograph shows the image obtained with a focussing defect.
Among other things we observe circles where frequencies are suppressed, corresponding to transfer function values close to zero. There
are other circles where the frequencies undergo contrast inversion
(phase opposition) and these correspond to negative transfer function
values (change of sign related to a phase shift of π).

2. Effects of light diffraction

a) Let us assume a strictly monochromatic point source S at a given
wavelength. It emits spherical light waves which are observed at a
remote plane (fig.III.4.a).

If the plane of observation is far enough from the source, spherical waves seem to behave as though moving on a front which has the
form of a boundless plane (fig.III.4.b). Vibrations received at any
point on the plane are in the form A cos (ωt - Φ), where ω is the
pulsation rate of the vibration and is linked with wavelength λ by the
relationship $\omega = 2\pi \dfrac{c}{\lambda}$ (c = velocity of light). Since the phase Φ is the
same for all points on the plane they vibrate in phase. They are said
to be illuminated by a *coherent light source*.

Vibration A cos $(\omega t - \Phi)$ may be thought of as the real part of the complex vibration A $e^{j(\omega t - \Phi)}$ = A $e^{j\omega t}$ $e^{-j\Phi}$.

Leaving aside the term $e^{j\omega t}$, the remaining quantity A $e^{-j\Phi}$ is called the *complex amplitude* of the wave. The real amplitude A is therefore the modulus of the complex amplitude.

b) The same result is obtained at finite distance by placing source S at the object focus of a convergent lens (fig.III.5) assumed to be:

- free of aberrations. Since aberrations have the effect of distorting wave surfaces, the wave front emerging from the lens would no longer be plane.

- geometrically semi-infinite. The reason for this will be seen later.

An object placed on any plane perpendicular to the optical axis is illuminated in coherent light. The complex amplitude of the light wave received from the object at any point is the same.

If we place an aperture of finite size on this plane (or amounting to the same thing, if we take a lens of finite dimensions) the aperture transmits a uniform complex amplitude which may be considered as equal to 1. This applies over the entire surface of the aperture (or lens) but not outside that area (fig.III.6).

c) **Diffraction of light**

According to the Huyghens-Fresnel principle [2, 7, 10] the wave transmitted by the above aperture may be considered as the envelope for "secondary" spherical waves emitted from every point on that aperture. They behave as if they were a multitude of small secondary sources. If the aperture is semi-infinite, it can easily be seen that the envelope returns a plane wave form. In these conditions, if we then position another lens L_2 which is also semi-infinite (fig.III.7), it transmits spherical waves converging towards the image focus, where we observe a perfect point image of the point source (called a geometrical image).

By contrast, if we position an aperture of finite size (fig.III.8), the envelope of secondary waves no longer returns a plane wave and the image obtained is no longer a point. To find what this image is we need to calculate the vibration impinging on each point of the image focal plane for lens L_2. This calculation is carried out by assuming that the various points on the aperture vibrating in phase emit plane waves in all directions (the waves are said to be diffracted

Fig.III.3 - Low-pass filtering with defective focussing. Upper picture: Foucault radial test pattern used as object. Spatial frequencies varying as $\frac{1}{r}$, where $r =$ distance from centre. Lower picture: image obtained with defective focussing. It is possible to observe among other things circles where frequencies are suppressed, corresponding to transfer function values close to zero, and circles where frequencies undergo contrast inversion corresponding to negative transfer function values (change of sign).

by the aperture). It is also assumed that there will be interference between these waves, the resultant of which is governed by their

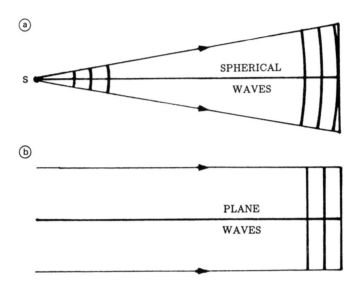

Fig.III.4 - a) Spherical waves emitted by a monochromatic point source which is
perfectly coherent, b) if the plane of observation is very remote from the
source, spherical waves seem to behave as though moving on a front which has
the form of a boundless plane.

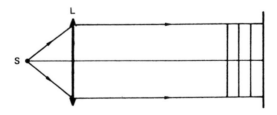

Fig.III.5 - Plane waves emitted by a monochromatic point source placed at the
object focus of a convergent semi-infinite lens L.

transmission angle.

If we return for the sake of simplicity to one dimension, let us
assume a point on the plane shown in figure III.8. Let us call x the
abscissa of a point on the aperture (origin O, diameter a) and x' the

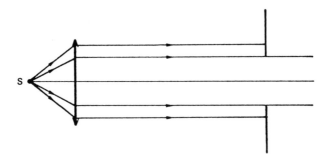

Fig.III.6 - Limiting the spread of plane waves by interposing
an aperture of finite size.

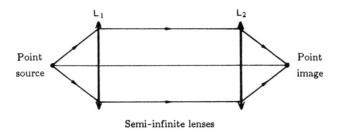

Semi-infinite lenses

Fig.III.7 - Since the lenses are assumed to be semi-infinite, there are no diffraction
phenomena. The point source located at the object focus of L_1 gives a point
image (geometrical image) at the image focus of L_2.

abscissa of the point on the image plane where all vibrations
transmitted at an angle of α will converge. The resultant of these
vibrations is given by the integral:

$$F(\alpha) = \int_{-a/2}^{a/2} \cos \omega \, [(t - \tau(x,\alpha))] \, dx$$

where $\tau(x,\alpha)$ represents the delay between the wave transmitted in
that direction by the point with abscissa x and the wave transmitted

at the same angle by the centre O of the aperture.

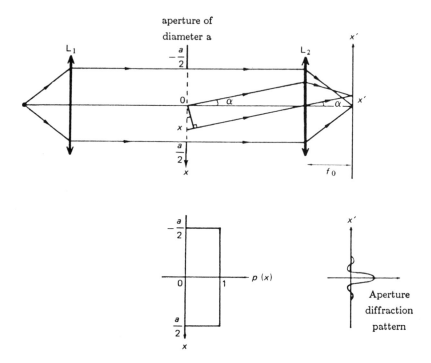

Fig.III.8 - The lenses are assumed to be semi-infinite in extent, but the aperture
limits the spread of the beam. The diffracted waves transmitted by the aperture have a resultant which is no longer a plane wave. The "image" observed
at the image plane of L_2 is no longer a point but a diffraction pattern characteristic of the aperture (the Fourier transform of that aperture). It is the coherent impulse response of the system.

According to the figure it is possible to write:

$$\tau(x, \alpha) = \frac{x \sin \alpha}{c} \qquad (c = \text{velocity of light})$$

or if α is small (paraxial approximation)

$$\tau(x, \alpha) \simeq x \frac{\alpha}{c}$$

which gives:

$$F(\alpha) = \int_{-a/2}^{a/2} \cos \omega \left[t - \frac{x\alpha}{c} \right] dx$$

Since lens L_2 is semi-infinite, all these waves duly converge at the point on the image plane with abscissa $x' = f_0 tg\ \alpha \simeq f_0 \alpha$ (f_0 = focal length). A characteristic diffraction pattern for the aperture is obtained on this plane. It can be shown that this pattern is in fact the F.T. of the aperture. To do so we put $u = \dfrac{x'}{\lambda f_0} = \dfrac{\alpha}{\lambda}$

$$\left[\lambda = 2\pi \frac{c}{\omega} \text{ wavelength of the light} \right].$$

$$\frac{x\alpha}{c} = x \frac{u\lambda}{c} = 2\pi x \frac{u}{\omega}$$

giving

$$F(\alpha) = F(u\lambda) = F_1(u) = \int_{-a/2}^{a/2} \cos(\omega t - 2\pi x u)\ dx$$

$$= \cos \omega t \int_{-a/2}^{a/2} \cos 2\pi x u\ dx + \sin \omega t \int_{-a/2}^{a/2} \sin 2\pi x u\ dx$$

$$= \cos \omega t\ A(u) + \sin \omega t\ B(u)$$

This expression represents a sinusoidal vibration with an amplitude of $\sqrt{A^2(u) + B^2(u)}$ and with:

$$A(u) = \int_{-a/2}^{a/2} \cos 2\pi xu \; dx = \int_{-\infty}^{+\infty} p(x) \cos 2\pi xu \; dx$$

$$B(u) = \int_{-a/2}^{a/2} \sin 2\pi xu \; dx = \int_{-\infty}^{+\infty} p(x) \sin 2\pi xu \; dx$$

(1)

while $p(x)$ is the aperture function (a gate function with a value of 1 within the aperture and 0 outside it).

The equations are the same as equation (12) in chapter 1. They show that $A(u)$ and $B(u)$ are the real part and the imaginary part of the Fourier transformation $P(u)$ for aperture $p(x)$:

$$P(u) = \int_{-\infty}^{+\infty} p(x) \; e^{-2\pi jux} \; dx$$

(2)

In other words the complex amplitudes observed in the image focal plane of L_2 represent the F.T. of the aperture.

The above calculation can easily be extended to two dimensions, giving the following result:

The image of the monochromatic point source is a diffraction pattern characteristic of the aperture. Its complex amplitude is the F.T. of that aperture. It is known as the *coherent impulse response* of the system.

We should note the important difference between an optical assembly and a system for scanning by an aperture. In the latter case the impulse response is the aperture itself (except for reversal), whereas for a coherent optical system the impulse response is the F.T. of the aperture which limits the beam.

If we wish to represent the coherent impulse response as a function of the spatial variable x' we use the relation $u = \dfrac{x'}{\lambda f_0}$.

For example, for a circular aperture with a diameter of a, we obtain a blurred disc with the complex amplitude shown in figure I.33.b, where the radius of the first zero ring is $u = \dfrac{1.22}{a}$ giving

$$x' = 1.22 \frac{\lambda f_0}{a} \tag{3}$$

Notes

1. These results may be generalised to situations where the aperture does not transmit uniformly. For example if an object with any degree of transparency is placed against the aperture, a diffraction pattern is observed with a complex amplitude which is the F.T. of the object.

2. The eye is not sensitive to the complex amplitude, but to the luminous intensity. This is the square of the true amplitude, being the square of the modulus of the complex amplitude (see a): $A^2(u) + B^2(u)$.

3. The same results are obtained with the system shown in figure III.9.a where the aperture is placed against a single lens. The F.T. of that aperture will be observed. Similarly in the case shown in figure III.9.b, where there is a lens of limited size, the F.T. of the lens aperture will be observed.

B. The formation of images in coherent light. Coherent impulse response and transfer function.

1. The example of a thin lens

Let the system be arranged as in figure III.10. A circular thin lens L with a diameter of a is situated at a distance of D from an object illuminated with coherent light and forms a real image of the object at the same distance (D $= 2f_0$ where f_0 is the focal length of the lens). In terms of geometrical optics the image is equal to the object in reverse (magnification $= -1$). A magnification of $+1$ can be assumed by reversing the x and y axes of the image plane with res-

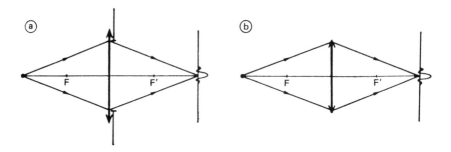

Fig.III.9 - These configurations give the same result as the arrangement in figure
III.7: a) aperture placed against a lens of unlimited extent, b) lens of limited
extent.

pect to those of the object plane.

Taking account of diffraction caused by the finite aperture of the
lens, a point O on the object gives an image with a complex amplitude which is the coherent impulse response $h_c(x, y)$. This is the
same as the F.T. of the aperture (or the diffraction pattern) centred
on the geometrical image I.

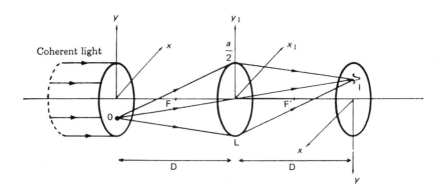

Fig.III.10 - Formation of the image I by a thin circular lens L of an object O illuminated by coherent light. The image is the convolution of the object with the
coherent impulse response of the lens.

Since the light is coherent, the light waves emitted from every point on the object are vibrating in phase. Since the system is linear and shift invariant, the complex amplitude at any point on the image can be found by adding together the individual impulse responses for all the points on the object, assigning each one its amplitude $o(x, y)$. This allows us to find the integral of the complex amplitudes:

$$s(x, y) = \iint_{\text{object}} o(x',y') \, h_c(x-x', \, y-y') \, dx' \, dy'$$

Since $o(x, y)$ is zero anywhere outside the object, it is possible to write:

$$s(x, y) = \int_{-\infty}^{+\infty} \int_{-\infty}^{+\infty} o(x',y') \, h_c(x-x', \, y-y') \, dx' \, dy'$$

This is the convolution product of the complex amplitude of the object and the coherent impulse response.

$$\boxed{s(x, y) = o(x, y) * h_c(x, y)} \qquad (3)$$

If we refer to the coordinates in the plane of the thin lens as x_1, y_1, we may recall the equation:

$$h_c(x, y) = \mathcal{F}(p(x_1, y_1)) \qquad (4)$$

where $p(x_1, y_1)$ represents the aperture of this lens and $h_c(x, y)$ is the *coherent impulse response*, also known as the "coherent point spread function".

If in fact we are taking account of the true geometrical dimensions, we must write [10]

$$\boxed{h_c(x, y) = \mathcal{F}(p(\lambda D x_1, \lambda D y_1))} = \frac{1}{\lambda^2 D^2} P\left(\frac{x}{\lambda D}, \frac{y}{\lambda D}\right) \qquad (5)$$

We must put $P(x, y) = \mathcal{F}(p(x_1, y_1))$. (D is the distance between the lens and the image plane).

Since the lens is circular with a diameter of a, we can find the radius of the first black ring in the diffraction pattern:

$$x = 1.22 \frac{\lambda D}{a} \qquad (6)$$

This is the analogue of equation (3) in the earlier example.

We should recall that the observed luminous intensity is $|s(x, y)|^2$ (the square of the modulus), and in particular that the intensity of the coherent point spread function is $|h_c(x, y)|^2$.

The *coherent transfer function* of the lens may be defined by the equation: $H_c(u, v) = \mathcal{F}[h_c(x, y)]$.

Equation (4) would give $H_c(u, v) = p(u, v)$.

In reality (5) gives: $\qquad H_c(u, v) = p(\lambda Du, \lambda Dv) \qquad (7)$

The coherent transfer function is therefore the aperture function itself but with a transfer of variable (fig.III.11).

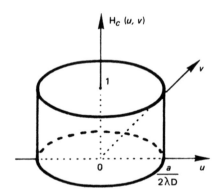

Fig.III.11 - The coherent transfer function of the system in figure III.10. To the nearest scale factor $\frac{1}{\lambda D}$, it is equal to the lens aperture function (or the "pupil" function of the system).

It is a perfect low-pass filter and completely blocks all spatial frequencies above the cut-off frequency:

$$u_c = \frac{a}{2\lambda D} \qquad (8)$$

The relationship between the F.T. of the object and that of the image is defined by the equation:

$$S(u, v) = O(u, v) \cdot H_c(u, v) \qquad (9)$$

Note

The convolution equation (3) can be found in another way by considering the "double diffraction" system in figure III.12. Lens L_1 creates a diffraction pattern in its image focal plane, which is actually the entrance surface of L_2. This pattern represents the F.T. of the object $o(x, y)$ which is just in front of it. If we ignore the scale factors mentioned above we can consider that the position of this plane is identified by the coordinates u and v and we can write this diffraction pattern $\mathcal{F}[o(x, y)] = O(u, v)$.

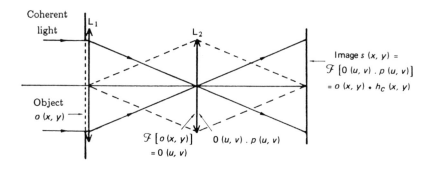

Fig.III.12 - "Double diffraction" system for finding directly the relationship: $s(x,y) = o(x, y) * h_c(x, y)$.

Beyond lens L_2 can be found the distribution of the complex amplitudes $O(u, v) \, p(u, v)$ where $p(u, v)$ is the aperture function of this lens.

The image recovered in the image focal plane of L_2 is given by another Fourier transformation:

$$s(x, y) = \mathscr{F}[O(u, v)\; p(u, v)] = \mathscr{F}[O(u, v)] * \mathscr{F}[p(u, v)]$$

so that $\qquad\qquad s(x, y) = o(x, y) * h_c(x, y)$

2. Centred optical system

a) Definition of entrance and exit pupils

A centred optical system consisting of a variety of lenses may be shown diagrammatically as a box crossed by a beam of light travelling from the object to the image. If we limit ourselves to the approximations of geometrical optics, we may give particular consideration to the beams leaving the object point located on the axis and converging on the image point which is also on the axis. The rays in these beams do not all reach the image point, because of the various obstacles to stop them on the way, including apertures, diaphragms and lens mounts. The useful beam, in this case the "fattest" beam which can possibly make the whole journey through the apparatus, is limited by a physical diaphragm or stop called the system pupil. This stop is the one whose image in the object space subtends the smallest angle (in comparison with the images of the other stops) when viewed from the object point. This image is known as the *entrance pupil* of the system.

In the same way the image of the pupil in the image space is viewed at the smallest angle from the image point. It is then called the *exit pupil*. Entrance pupil and exit pupil are therefore optical conjugates, or images, of one another.

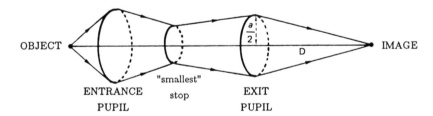

Fig.III.13 - The pupils of an optical system. "Smallest stop" means the one with an image which subtends the smallest angle when viewed from the object point. The images of this stop in the optical systems which precede and follow it are the entrance pupil and the exit pupil of the system respectively. They are therefore each other's optical conjugates.

Examples

a) An assembly as in figure III.10: the mounting for lens L is both entrance and exit pupil.

b) An assembly as in figure III.12: the mounting for lens L_2 is both entrance and exit pupil.

b) Coherent impulse response (point spread function) and coherent transfer function

It can be shown [10] that the equations obtained for a thin lens remain valid provided the lens aperture is replaced by the exit pupil for the system (still assuming magnification equal to 1).

$$s(x, y) = o(x, y) * h_c(x, y)$$
$$S(u, v) = O(u, v) \cdot H_c(u, v)$$

(3)
(9)

with

$$h_c(x, y) = \mathscr{F}[p(\lambda Dx_1, \lambda Dy_1)]$$
$$H_c(u, v) = p(\lambda Du, \lambda Dv)$$

(5)
(7)

$p(x_1, y_1)$ is the exit pupil function, D the distance between that pupil and the image plane.

Figure III.14 represents the coherent transfer functions of two optical systems limited by diffraction:

a. with a square exit pupil measuring *a* along each side.

b. with a circular exit pupil with a diameter of *a*.

It should be noted that a coherent transfer function is never negative, unlike $h_c(x, y)$.

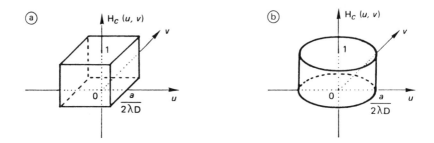

Fig.III.14 - Coherent transfer functions: a) square exit pupil of side a, b) circular exit pupil of diameter a.

C. Formation of images in incoherent light.
Incoherent impulse response and optical transfer function

1. Comparison with coherent light

So far we have assumed that the light is perfectly coherent and that it emanates from a monochromatic point source. We shall continue to assume that the light source is monochromatic or nearly so, but that it now has physical size. In these conditions the various atoms in the source will emit vibrations which are completely out of phase with one another and the phase difference between points on an illuminated object will not be constant. It is said that, spatially, the light is *incoherent*. For the same reasons, the impulse responses arriving at a given point on the image plane from points on the object are out of phase. It is no longer a matter of adding them all together to find the observed light intensity, since the phase variations are all statistically independent. But the observer, say a human eye or a photographic plate, takes an average for a moment of time which is very long when compared with the vibration period of the light. This means that in that moment phases can have taken every possible value at random, and their average is therefore zero.

Let us examine the situation for n object points:

- in the coherent example, we were retrieving at every given instant the sum of the complex amplitudes $\displaystyle\sum_{i=1}^{n} A_i e^{-j\Phi_i}$, where phases Φ_i were constant in time. Writing $\overline{}$ for the average-time operator, we we were therefore observing the intensity:

$$I_c = \overline{\left|\sum_{i=1}^{n} A_i\, e^{-j\Phi_i}\right|^2} = \left|\sum_{i=1}^{n} A_i\, e^{-j\Phi_i}\right|^2$$

- in the incoherent example, we have the same expression $\displaystyle\sum_{i=1}^{n} A_i\, e^{-j\Phi_i}$ but the phases Φ_i vary with time. In order to reveal the effect of these variations we should write the intensity at any moment as:

$$\sum_{i=1}^{n} A_i\, e^{-j\Phi_i(t)} \sum_{k=1}^{n} A_k^{*}\, e^{j\Phi_k(t)}$$

The following average intensity will be observed:

$$I_i = \overline{\sum_{i=1}^{n} A_i\, e^{-j\Phi_i(t)} \sum_{k=1}^{n} A_k^{*}\, e^{j\Phi_k(t)}} = \sum_{i=1}^{n}\sum_{k=1}^{n} A_i\, A_k^{*}\, \overline{e^{j(\Phi_k(t)-\Phi_i(t))}}$$

if $k = i$ $\qquad e^{j(\Phi_k-\Phi_i)} = e^{j0} = 1$ then $\overline{e^{j(\Phi_k-\Phi_i)}} = 1$

if $k \neq i$ $\overline{e^{j(\Phi_k-\Phi_i)}} = \overline{\cos(\Phi_k-\Phi_i) + j\,\sin(\Phi_k-\Phi_i)} = 0 + j0 = 0$

giving the result:

$$I_i = \sum_{i=1}^{n} |A_i|^2$$

In other words the system is still linear, not in relation to the complex amplitudes but with respect to the *intensities* (the squares of their moduli).

2. Incoherent impulse response and optical transfer function

The reasoning based on n object points remains valid for an infinite number of points. The foregoing discrete sum becomes a continuous integral. Since the intensity of an object point is $\left| h_c(x, y) \right|^2$, we obtain the intensity of the whole object by adding these individual responses together, weighting each with the intensity $o_i(x, y)$ of the corresponding object point.

So

$$s_i (x, y) = \int_{-\infty}^{+\infty} o_i (x', y') \left| h_c (x - x', y - y') \right|^2 dx' \, dy'$$

giving

$$\boxed{s_i(x, y) = o_i(x, y) * \left| h_c(x, y) \right|^2} \qquad (10)$$

To the nearest constant factor, $\left| h_c(x, y) \right|^2$ is called the *incoherent impulse response*, or incoherent point spread function.

By putting $\left| h_c(x, y) \right|^2 = h_i(x, y)$ it is possible to define the transfer function by reference to the F.T. of $h_i(x, y)$:

$$\mathscr{F}(h_i(x, y)) = \mathscr{F}\left(\left| h_c(x, y) \right|^2 \right) = \mathscr{F}(h_c(x, y) \cdot h_c^*(x, y))$$

$$= \mathscr{F}(h_c(x, y)) * \mathscr{F}(h_c^*(x, y)) = H_c(u, v) * H_c^*(-u, -v)$$

This function represents something known as the *autocorrelation function* of $H_c(u, v)$. It is easily calculated by offsetting function $H_c(u, v)$ within the plane uOv in relation to its original location and calculating the surface area of the overlap (coherent transfer functions are actually pupil functions, and are generally real and symmetrical). Figure III.15.a explains this calculation in the instance of a square exit pupil, and figure III.17.a does the same where the exit pupil is circular.

The incoherent transfer function actually used is a normalised function [7, 10] which takes a value of 1 for a frequency of zero. It is easy to check that this result is obtained by dividing the previous function by the surface area of coherent transfer function $H_c(u, v)$:

Surface area of overlap

total surface area

This function is written as $H_i(u, v)$ and called the optical transfer function (abbreviated to O.T.F.).

(By carrying out the same normalisation on $\left| h_c(x, y) \right|^2$ we obtain the incoherent impulse response).

Figures III.15.b and III.16 show the O.T.F. for a system with a square exit pupil.

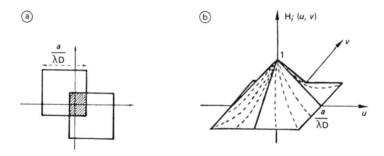

Fig.III.15 - Incoherent transfer function (or optical transfer function, abbreviated to OTF) of a diffraction-limited system having a square exit pupil of side a; a) calculating the surface area of the overlap, b) the corresponding OTF, being the pupil autocorrelation function.

Figure III.17.b shows a system with a circular exit pupil. This is a tent-shaped function with rotational symmetry.

The relationship between the F.T.'s of the intensity patterns for the object and the image may be expressed as follows:

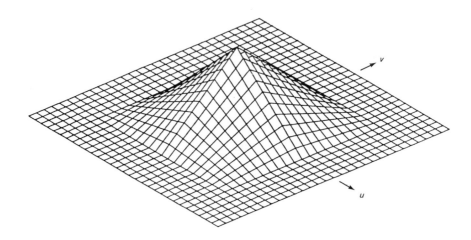

Fig.III.16 - Two-dimensional view of the OTF for figure III.15.b: diffraction-limited system having a square exit pupil.

$$\boxed{S_i(u, v) = O_i(u, v) \cdot H_i(u, v)}$$ (11)

with $\qquad\qquad\qquad S_i(u, v) = \mathscr{F}[s_i(x, y)]$

$$O_i(u, v) = \mathscr{F}[o_i(x, y)]$$

Aspects of the following functions are summarised in Figure III.18: coherent transfer function $H_c(u, v)$; optical transfer function $H_i(u, v)$; incoherent impulse response (incoherent point spread function) $h_i(x, y)$.

Two situations are shown:

a) a square exit pupil with sides measuring a.

b) a circular exit pupil with a diameter of a. In this second case the incoherent point spread function represents the Airy disc so familiar to opticians (the radius of the inner dark ring is 1.22 $\lambda D/a$)

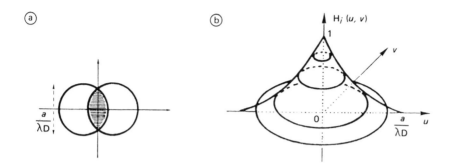

Fig.III.17 - OTF of a diffraction-limited system having a circular exit pupil with a diameter of a; a) calculating the surface area of the overlap, b) the corresponding OTF, or "tent" function.

It can be seen that the cut-off frequency of the O.T.F. is twice that of the coherent transfer function, and also that it is never negative for a diffraction-limited system (convolution of positive functions) (see sections 4.b and 4.d).

3. Rayleigh's criterion for resolution

Let us consider an optical instrument limited by diffraction, having a circular exit pupil with a diameter of a and an incoherent light source. The image of a point object is then an Airy disc which is the point spread function (impulse response) $h_i(x, y)$ in figure III.18.b.

Rayleigh's criterion for resolution lays down the principle that two point sources will be just resolved by the instrument if the centre of the Airy disc produced by one of them coincides with the inner dark ring of the Airy disc produced by the other, that is to say if the distance between the centres of the two diffraction patterns is:

$$\boxed{\delta_i = 1.22 \frac{\lambda D}{a}} \qquad (12)$$

This is the distance between the geometrical images of both points, and will also be the distance between the point sources if magnification is equal to 1. Since an optical instrument generally has a *magnification* of G ≠ 1 it is useful to have a way of expressing the

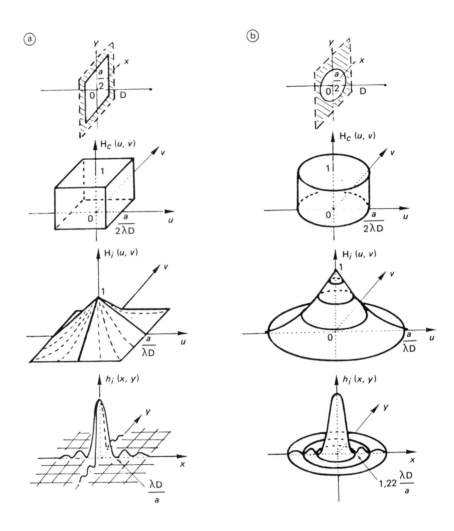

Fig.III.18 - Pupil function, coherent transfer function, incoherent transfer function (OTF) and incoherent impulse response (incoherent point spread function) of diffraction-limited systems: a) square exit pupil of side a, b) circular exit pupil of diameter a.

distance δ_0 between objects which can just be resolved.

We see from figure III.19 that the magnification is $G = \dfrac{D}{d}$ and distance δ_o equals:

$$\delta_O = \frac{\delta_i}{G} = 1.22 \, \frac{\lambda D}{a} \, \frac{d}{D} \qquad \boxed{\delta_o = 1.22 \, \frac{\lambda D}{a'}} \qquad (13)$$

In this instance $a' = a$, but this formula is general if d is the distance between the object and the entrance pupil, with a' as the diameter of this *entrance* pupil.

It is common to express δ_o as a function of a quantity called the *numerical aperture* (NA) of the instrument. NA is defined by a quantity $n \sin \alpha$, where n is the index of the object space and α is the half-angle at the apex of the effective beam, meaning the centred beam which passes through the entrance pupil of the system.

So in the case of figure III.19, if we assume $n = 1$ we have:

$$NA = \sin \alpha \simeq tg \, \alpha = \frac{a}{2d}$$

and

$$\boxed{\delta_o = \frac{0.6\lambda}{NA}} \qquad (14)$$

Worked example

$$NA = 0.15 \qquad \lambda = 0.5\mu \qquad G = 100$$

$$\delta_o = \frac{0.6 \times 0.5}{0.15} = 2\mu \qquad \delta_i = 2\mu \times 100 = 200\mu$$

4. Properties of the optical transfer function (O.T.F.)

a) All spatial frequencies above cut-off frequency f_c are completely eliminated. In this way a test pattern in the form of a periodic square wave (alternating black and white stripes) with a repetition frequency between 0.5 f_c and f_c has its fundamental as its image, in other words a perfectly sinusoidal pattern.

b) An O.T.F. is never negative for an aberration-free system. Contrast inversion is never observed.

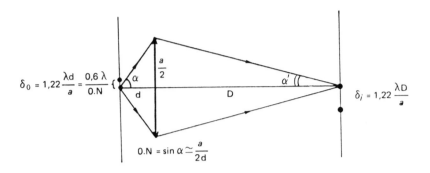

Fig.III.19 - Rayleigh's criterion for resolution. Two points on the object are resolved if the distance between them is greater than $\delta_o = 1.22 \dfrac{\lambda d}{a} = 0.6 \dfrac{\lambda}{NA}$.

c) If the system has a magnification $G \neq 1$, the O.T.F. is expressed as a function of the spatial frequencies in the image plane. Notice in particular that cut-off frequency $f_c = \dfrac{a}{\lambda D}$ is the cut-off frequency for the image plane (where a is the diameter of the exit pupil and D is the distance between the exit pupil and the image plane). Similarly the spatial variables x and y appearing in the impulse response $h_i(x, y)$ are those of the image plane.

As we saw with Rayleigh's criterion, if we wish to argue from the object plane, we must divide distances and multiply frequencies by G. Among other things the cut-off frequency becomes:

$$G f_c = G \frac{a}{\lambda D} = \frac{a'}{\lambda D}$$

where a' is the diameter of the entrance pupil and d is the distance between that entrance pupil and the object $\left[\text{or if } G f_c = \dfrac{2\,NA}{\lambda}\right]$.

Thus returning to the worked example in section 3 we have:

$$f_c = \frac{a}{\lambda D} = \frac{1.22}{\delta_i} = 6.10^{-3}\ \mu^{-1} = 6\ \text{mm}^{-1}$$

$$G\ f_c = 100\ f_c = 600\ \text{mm}^{-1}\ \left(= \frac{20N}{\lambda}\right)$$

d) The effect of aberrations

It can be shown [2, 10] that aberrations have the effect of reducing the amplitude of the O.T.F. so that it can even become negative
for certain frequency ranges. Contrast inversion may then be
observed at these frequencies. This phenomenon was first encountered in the case of a focussing defect, which may be thought of as a
special form of aberration.

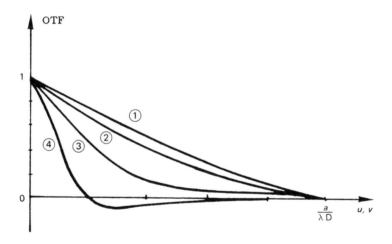

Fig.III.20 - The effect of a focussing defect on the OTF of a system with a circular exit pupil, shown as a function of the degree of defocussing. This is measured by the divergence d between the axial ray and the marginal rays.
(1) d = 0, (2) d = 0.2λ, (3) d = 0.5λ, (4) d = λ

Figure III.20 shows the effect of defocussing on the O.T.F. of a system with a circular exit pupil, as a function of the degree of defocussing. This is measured by the divergence d between the axial ray and the rays at the extremes.

curve (1) : d = 0   curve (2) : d = 0.2λ curve   (3) : d = 0.5λ

curve (4) : d = λ (where λ = wavelength of the light).

4

Photographic images

A. Definitions

1. Energy flow and light flow

- *Flux:* the *radiant flux* Φ emanating from a light source is the energy radiated by that source in a second. It is therefore a measure of power expressed in *watts* (W).

This quantity should not be confused with *luminous flux* F, which is a photometric (light flow) quantity. Every photometric measurement is linked to the visual impression on the human eye, which differs in sensitivity across the range of wavelengths. This sensitivity falls to nil for all forms of radiation outside the visible spectrum. There is therefore a curve of typical relative sensitivity $S(\lambda)$ (of the standard observer). If a source radiates with a spectral energy distribution of $E(\lambda)$, the luminous flux is defined [3] by:

$$F = K \int_0^\infty E(\lambda) \, S(\lambda) \, d\lambda$$

The unit of luminous flux is the *lumen* (lm) and K equals 685 lm/W. The relationship between a radiant energy quantity and its corresponding photometric quantity therefore depends on the spectrum of the light concerned, and there is no simple equivalence between units unless the light in question has a very narrow spectrum at around the $\lambda = 555$ nm level, where the $S(\lambda)$ curve equals 1. Then 1 W equals 685 lumens.

- The *intensity* of a *point source* in a given direction (fig.IV.1): this is the flux radiated per unit solid angle in a given direction. If $d\Phi$ is the elementary flux radiated into the lesser solid angle $d\Omega$, we have:

$$I = \frac{d\Phi}{d\Omega}$$ (1)

unit of radiant energy: watt/steradian
unit of photometric measurement: *candela* = lm/st
- *Illuminance* (or irradiance) received at a point, such as on a screen, is the flux received per unit of screen surface area around the point in question (fig.IV.1).

$$E = \frac{d\Phi}{dS'}$$ (2)

but $d\Phi = I\,d\Omega$ and $d\Omega = \dfrac{dS'\cos\alpha'}{r^2}$ giving $\boxed{E = \dfrac{I\cos\alpha'}{r^2}}$ (3)

unit of radiant energy: watt/m²
unit of photometric measurement: *lux* = lumen/m².

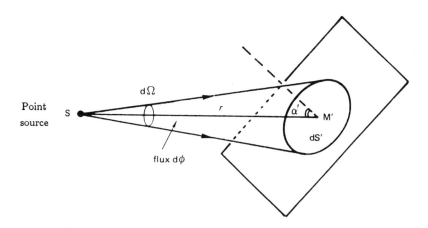

Fig.IV.1 - The intensity of point source S in the direction SM' is $I = \dfrac{d\Phi}{d\Omega}$. The illuminance received by the screen at point M' is $E = \dfrac{d\Phi}{dS'} = \dfrac{I\cos\alpha'}{r^2}$.

- The *intensity* of an extended source *element* in a given direction (fig.IV.2). If $d^2\Phi$ is the elementary flux emitted from dS into the lesser solid angle $d\Omega$ in the direction MM', we have:

$$dI = \frac{d^2\Phi}{d\Omega}$$

This creates the following illuminance at point M' on the screen:

$$dE = \frac{d^2\Phi}{dS'} = \frac{dI \cos \alpha'}{r^2}$$

- The *luminance* of a point on an extended source in a given direction. Element dS has an intensity of dI in direction MM' and emits a beam of light in that direction with a cross-section of dS cos α (fig.IV.2). The luminance of point M in that direction is:

$$\boxed{L = \frac{dI}{dS \cos \alpha}} \tag{4}$$

in other words the intensity per unit projected area in the specified direction.

unit of radiant energy: $\dfrac{\text{watt}}{\text{strd.m}^2}$

unit of photometric measurement: $\dfrac{\text{candela}}{\text{m}^2}$

- The *transported flux* in a beam limited by two elementary surfaces (fig.IV.2), or the flux from dS to dS', may be expressed as:

$$d^2\Phi = dI \, d\Omega = L \, dS \cos \alpha \, d\Omega \quad \text{but} \quad d\Omega = \frac{dS' \cos \alpha'}{r^2}$$

therefore

$$\boxed{d^2\Phi = L \, \frac{dS \, dS' \cos \alpha \cos \alpha'}{r^2} = L \, d^2U} \tag{5}$$

with $d^2U = \dfrac{dS \, dS' \cos \alpha \cos \alpha'}{r^2}$ the *geometrical spread* of the beam.

The elementary illuminance dE produced in M' by dS is:

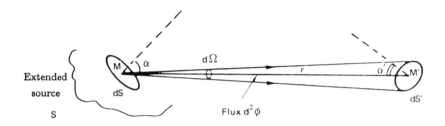

Fig.IV.2 - The intensity of source element dS from extended source S in the direc-

tion MM′ is $dI = \frac{d^2\Phi}{d\Omega}$. The illuminance received by the screen at point M′ is

$dE = \frac{d^2\Phi}{dS'} = \frac{dI \cos \alpha'}{r^2}$. The source luminance in the direction MM′ is

$L = \frac{dI}{dS \cos \alpha'}$. The transported elementary beam flux is

$d^2\Phi = L \frac{dS \, dS' \cos \alpha \cos \alpha'}{r^2} = L \, d^2U$ where d^2U is the spread of the beam.

$$dE = \frac{d^2\Phi}{dS'} = L \frac{dS \cos \alpha \cos \alpha'}{r^2} = L \, d\Omega' \cos \alpha'$$

with $d\Omega' = \frac{dS \cos \alpha}{r^2}$ the solid angle at which dS is viewed from point
M′.

- *Conservation of flux, spread and luminance* through an optical instrument.

Let us consider the arrangement in figure IV.3 where the object and image media are assumed to be identical. If there is neither absorption nor reflection by the glass in the lenses, the flux of the effective beam passing through the entrance pupil leaves again via the exit pupil.

The spread of the entrance beam is $d^2U_1 = dS \frac{S_1}{d_1^2} = dS \, d\Omega_1$.

The spread of the exit beam is $d^2U_2 = dS' \frac{S_2}{d_2^2} = dS' \, d\Omega_2$

where dS′ is the image of a small object element dS viewed through the system.

If we also assume that the Abbe sine relationship is satisfied we have $n_1 y_1 \sin u_1 = n_2 y_2 \sin u_2$ or in this case, because $n_1 = n_2$, $y_1 \sin u_1 = y_2 \sin u_2$. By deduction

$$\frac{\sin^2 u_1}{\sin^2 u_2} = \frac{y_2}{u_2}$$

But it is possible to express the solid angles $d\Omega_1$ and $d\Omega_2$ in the form $d\Omega_1 = \pi \sin^2 u_1$ and $d\Omega_2 = \pi \sin^2 u_2$.

Moreover the square of the magnification is equal to the ratio of the surface areas dS' and dS, being

$$\frac{y_1^2}{y_2^2} = \frac{dS'}{dS}$$

Therefore $\quad \dfrac{d\Omega_1}{d\Omega_2} = \dfrac{dS'}{dS} \quad$ or $\quad dS\, d\Omega_1 = dS'\, d\Omega_2$

This means that $d^2U_1 = d^2U_2$. Thus there is conservation of spread. Since the flux is $d^2\Phi = L\, d^2U_1 = L'd^2U_2$ it can be deduced that $L = L'$. Thus there is also conservation of luminance.

Consequently the illuminance received by dS' is

$$dE = \frac{d^2\Phi}{dS'} = L\,\frac{d^2U_2}{dS'} = L\, d\Omega_2$$

and is the same as that given by a source with a luminance of L located at the exit pupil.

Application: formation of images in incoherent light

To examine this problem let us return to the simple assembly with a magnification of 1 shown in figure III.10. In this example the entrance and exit pupils are the same as the aperture of lens L, which has a surface area of $S_p = \pi a^2$. We shall seek to clarify the relationship between input and output convolution (formula (10) in chapter III) by assigning a meaning to "intensities" of the object, the image and the point spread function. The object may be thought of as an extended source. This source includes a point which has coordinates of x and y and luminance of $o_i(x, y)$. The image can be seen as a distribution of illuminances $s_i(x, y)$. The point spread function (impulse response) will be normalised on the assumption that

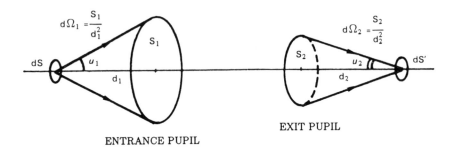

Fig.IV.3 - Conservation of flux, spread and luminance through an optical instrument. Conservation of flux $d^2\Phi$: flux entering the entrance pupil = flux leaving the exit pupil. Conservation of spread $d^2U_1 = d^2U_2$ with $d^2U_1 = dS\, d\Omega_1$
and $d^2U_2 = dS'd\Omega_2$. Conservation of luminance: $d^2\Phi = L\, d^2U_1 = L'd^2U_2$ so
that $L = L'$. The exit pupil may be thought of as a source with luminance
equal to the true source.

$$h_{iN} = \frac{|h_c(x, y)|^2}{|h_c(0, 0)|^2}$$

which is dimensionless. Let us write the convolution relationship as
$s_i(x, y) = \alpha\, o_i(x, y) * h_{iN}(x, y)$ and calculate coefficient α.

For this purpose let us assume the object has constant luminance L
and a surface area of S. The spread of the effective beam is $S\dfrac{S_p}{D^2}$ and

the flux is $LS\dfrac{S_p}{D^2}$.

The image has constant illuminance of $E = L\,\dfrac{S_p}{D^2}$.

By applying convolution we must find:

$$E = \alpha L * h_{iN}(x, y) = \alpha L \iint_{-\infty}^{+\infty} \frac{|h_c(x, y)|^2}{|h_c(0, 0)|^2}\, dx\, dy$$

with $\dfrac{|h_c(x, y)|^2}{|h_c(0, 0)|^2} = \dfrac{\left| P\left(\dfrac{x}{\lambda D}, \dfrac{y}{\lambda D}\right)\right|^2}{|P(0, 0)|^2}$ $P(u, v)$ being the F.T. of the pupil (chapter III, equation (5)).

By putting $\dfrac{x}{\lambda D} = u$, $\dfrac{y}{\lambda D} = v$ we have

$$E = \alpha \, L \, \lambda^2 \, D^2 \iint_{-\infty}^{+\infty} \frac{|P(u, v)|^2}{|P(0, 0)|^2} \, du \, dv$$

but $P(0, 0) = \displaystyle\iint_{-\infty}^{+\infty} p(x, y) \, dx \, dy = S_p$ since $p(x, y)$ is the pupil function.

Moreover $\displaystyle\iint_{-\infty}^{+\infty} |P(u, v)|^2 \, du \, dv = \iint_{-\infty}^{+\infty} |p(x, y)|^2 \, dx \, dy$ (this is called Parseval's equation).

This quantity also expresses S_p, the surface area of the pupil.

Therefore $E = \alpha \, L \, \lambda^2 \, D^2 \, \dfrac{S_p}{S_p^2} = \alpha \, L \, \dfrac{\lambda^2 D^2}{S_p}$.

By comparing the two results we obtain $\boxed{\alpha = \dfrac{S_p^2}{\lambda^2 D^4}}$ (6)

2. Transmittance, reflectance and optical density

Incident flux and transmitted flux can no longer be equal once any absorbant and (or) reflecting material has been placed in the path of the beam.

Figure IV.4.a shows an elementary beam. Part of the flux is absorbed, a further part is reflected and the remaining part is transmitted.

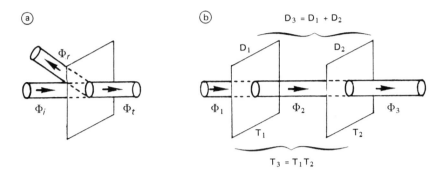

Fig.IV.4 - a) Transmittance and reflectance of a small element of a surface:

$$T = \frac{\Phi_t}{\Phi_i} \quad R = \frac{\Phi_r}{\Phi_i}(R + T \leq 1).$$ Optical   density

(transmission): $D_t = \log_{10} \frac{1}{T} = -\log_{10}T.$ Optical   density

(reflection): $D_r = \log_{10} \frac{1}{R} = -\log_{10}R,$ b) where two surfaces are in the beam path, the transmittances are multiplied and the densities are added.

The *transmittance* (or "transparency" or "optical transmission") of the small surface area of material in the path of the beam is defined by the following equation:

$$\boxed{T = \frac{\Phi_t}{\Phi_i}} \qquad (0 \leq T \leq 1) \qquad\qquad (7)$$

The *reflectance* of this same small surface area is defined by:

$$\boxed{R = \frac{\Phi_r}{\Phi_i}} \qquad (0 \leq R \leq 1) \qquad\qquad (8)$$

Note that absorption means we generally have $\Phi_i \geq \Phi_t + \Phi_r$ and therefore $R + T \leq 1$.

Optical transmission density is defined by the quantity:

$$D_t = \log_{10} \frac{1}{T} = -\log_{10} T \qquad (9)$$

Similarly *optical reflection density* is given as:

$$D_r = \log_{10} \frac{1}{R} = -\log_{10} R \qquad (10)$$

Let us work with transmission and place two surfaces in succession in the path of the beam (fig.IV.4.b). Equations $\Phi_2 = T_1 \Phi_1$ and $\Phi_3 = T_2 \Phi_2 = T_2 T_1 \Phi_1$ show [2] that the system as a whole behaves like a single surface with a transmittance of $\boxed{T_3 = T_1 T_2}$ and therefore with transmission density of $\boxed{D_3 = D_1 + D_2}$. Transmittances are multiplied together and densities are summed.

B. The photographic process

1. Physicochemical phenomena [8, 9]

Suppose we wish to preserve the image of an object formed by an optical system. We place a photographic plate or film at the image plane in question and in so doing allow the light to fall on it for a certain length of time.

A photographic film (fig.IV.5) is composed of a gelatine emulsion on a base. The emulsion contains particles of silver salts (silver halides, usually iodide, bromide or chloride) which are light-sensitive because of their interstitial Ag^+ ions.

a) *Exposure*

Light is allowed to fall on the film in a manner which varies according to the point being illuminated. In other words the transmitted luminous flux or photon flux per unit surface area depends on the point concerned.

- the first photon to reach a particle (or grain) with enough energy to create an electron-hole pair triggers the following reactions:

$$Ag^+ + e^- \rightarrow Ag : \text{silver atom}$$

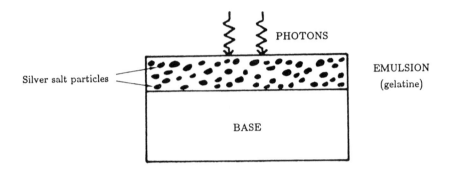

Fig.IV.5 - The composition of a photograhic film.

$$Ag\ Br + hole\ ->\left\{\begin{array}{l} Br : \text{bromine atom} \\ Ag^+ : \text{generated ion} \end{array}\right\}$$

- in the same conditions the second photon will produce the same reactions and the following will be created:
  • a molecule of bromine Br_2 which is eliminated from the lattice
  • a molecule of silver Ag_2 which is incorporated into the lattice.

The same happens with the third and fourth photons, and so on.
- if a large number of photons are received, the silver so formed blackens the whole film, which takes on a metallic appearance.
- if the process is halted when a grain has received say four photons, nothing is visible but the grain has become a *seed* allowing the process to be continued by chemical methods (the development phase). This means that exposure has created a *latent image*.

b) *Development*

The chemical developer has an effect on the grains like an amplifier with a gain proportional to grain surface. This gain is enormous (in the order of 10^6) enabling many molecules of metallic silver to be obtained.

c) *Fixing*

This phase eliminates the grains which were not dissociated during during exposure. In fact it is impossible to eliminate them all, and the grains which are left behind create a "fog level" with a density of around 0.04.

To sum up, the more an area of film is exposed, the darker it will appear. This creates a negative image. To obtain a positive, another photograph of the negative is taken by shining light through it.

In reality we shall see (section D) that not all photons, even those which are sufficiently energetic, will produce an atom of silver. The process is random, and the probability of a reaction is governed by the quantum efficiency of the emulsion. This varies considerably according to the emulsion type (0.3 to 10^{-4}).

2. Characteristic curve of an emulsion

- Illumination or exposure

This is defined by

$$\mathcal{E} = E.t \qquad (11)$$

This is the product of multiplying the illuminance received by the exposure time. It is expressed in lux-seconds and is proportional to the number of photons received per unit surface area.

Where exposure times are neither too long nor too short, the density of the developed film depends only on the exposure, that is the product of E.t, not on the quantities of E and t taken separately. This is called the *reciprocity law*.

- Hurter and Driffield's curve

This is the characteristic emulsion curve expressed by the function

$$D = f (\log_{10}\mathcal{E}) \qquad (12)$$

where D is the density obtained after development (fig.IV.6).

The residual density for very weak exposures is the *fog level*. The position of the exposure *threshold* defines the *sensitivity* or *speed* of the film, which is often expressed in ASA units. The more sensitive the film, the lower its light threshold. If more than a certain quantity of light is received, density does not continue to increase (because of the saturation effect) and even tends to decrease (this effect is difficult to explain). Between these two values lies a range which defines the dynamics or *latitude* of the emulsion, and in which density D increases as a function of $\log_{10}\mathcal{E}$ in a virtually straight line. A correctly exposed film which faithfully reproduces the received variations in illuminance is used in this range. The slope of the linear part, or rather the slope as far as the shoulder of the curve, is the *gamma* of the film:

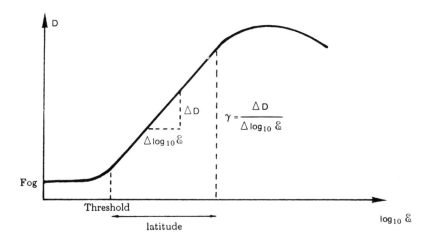

Fig.IV.6 - Characteristic curve of a photographic emulsion (or Hurter and Driffield's curve): $D = f(\log_{10}\mathcal{E})$. $\mathcal{E}$ is the illumination (or exposure): $\mathcal{E} = E.t$ (E = illuminance, t = time).

$$\gamma = \frac{\Delta D}{\Delta\log_{10}\mathcal{E}} \qquad (13)$$

The gamma characterises the *contrast*. It is said that a high gamma refers to a hard emulsion and a low gamma to a soft emulsion.

Another important characteristic which we shall examine in section C is the resolution of the film. This refers to the ability of the film to reproduce high spatial frequencies. It is related to grain size, so that a fine-grain film has higher resolution than a coarse-grain film.

Generally speaking, all these characteristics are to a greater or lesser extent mutually conflicting, in accordance with the following rules: [8, 9]

- high resolution   : fine grains, emulsion fairly thin
- high sensitivity   : coarse grains, emulsion fairly thin
- high maximum density : thick emulsion
- high contrast (i.e. little latitude)   : fine grains

Most of the time (fig.IV.7) a low-contrast emulsion will be sensitive (coarse-grained): curve {1}. On the other hand a high-contrast emulsion will have low sensitivity (fine-grained): curve {2}.

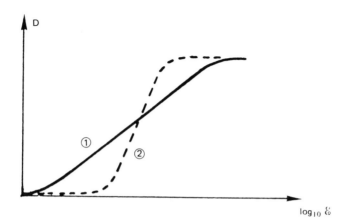

Fig.IV.7 - Generally speaking a sensitive emulsion will have low contrast (curve 1)
whereas a high-contrast emulsion will have low sensitivity (curve 2).

The emulsion chosen will be a compromise depending on the application intended. In addition, for any given film the development conditions have an effect on the characteristic curve.

C. Resolution and modulation transfer function

In the sections which follow it will be assumed that exposure time t is constant. The value on the abscissa of the characteristic curve becomes $\log_{10}E$.

1. One stage model (fig.IV.8)

This model assumes the following:
a) low-dynamic illuminances, in other words "weak signals". Around the mean operating point we can say that the characteristic curve $D = f(\log_{10}E)$ is linear. According to $D = -\log_{10}T$ absolute variations in density are associated with relative variations in transmission by

$$dD = -\log_{10}e \frac{dT}{T} = -0.43 \frac{dT}{T}$$

b) chemical effects associated with proximity during development are ignored (they will be introduced in the three stage model). Since this model is linear we may define a transfer function using input values of $\log_{10}E$ and output values of optical density D. If we accept that the photographic process is isotropic, that is unaffected by rotation, there is no need to invoke either of the spatial frequencies u and v. We shall therefore introduce a one-dimensional transfer function which will be a function of the single variable $w = \sqrt{u^2 + v^2}$.

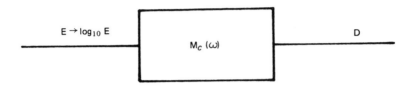

Fig.IV.8 - Single-stage model of a photographic film, valid for low-dynamic illuminances and ignoring chemical effects associated with proximity during development. This is a linear system with one transfer function (for contrast)
$M_c(\omega) = \gamma M(\omega)$ where $M(\omega)$ is the modulation transfer function (abbreviation
MTF).

Let us assume a one-dimensional sinusoidal test object (fig.IV.9), in other words a illuminance of

$$E(x) = E_0 (1 + a \cos 2\pi wx)$$

Under the weak signals hypothesis we are assuming that $a \ll 1$ and therefore

$$\log_{10}E(x) \simeq \log_{10}E + 0.43\, a \cos 2\pi wx$$

(if $x \ll 1, \ln(1 + x) \simeq x$).

If the photographic process transmitted all frequencies without attenuation it would be observed that density $D(x) = D_0 + 0.43\gamma a \cos 2\pi wx$ where γ is the slope of the tangent to the characteristic curve at the point for $\log_{10}$ coordinates E_0 and D_0.

The ratio of output contrast to input contrast for the system in figure IV.8 would then equal γ. In reality there is observed attenuation of contrast which is directly in proportion to the frequency ω of the test pattern. This feature can be explained by scattering of the light within the sensitive layer when the film is exposed, consisting of:
- geometrical scattering due to the finite thickness of the emulsion
- physical scattering across the silver salt grains.

The resulting density is then:

$D(x) = D_0 + 0.43 \; \gamma \; M(\omega) \; a \cos 2\pi\omega x$ $0 \le M\omega \le 1$

Function $\gamma M(\omega)$ which represents the ratio of output contrast to input contrast is called [8] the *contrast transfer function* and written $M_c(\omega)$. $M(\omega)$ is called the *modulation transfer function* of the film and is abbreviated to M.T.F.

The relationship between these two functions is expressed by:

$$M_c(\omega) = \gamma \; M(\omega)$$ (14)

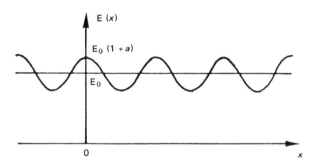

Fig.IV.9 - Function $M_c(\omega)$ can be measured using a sinusoidal test pattern to produce an illuminance of $E(x) = E_0(1 + a \cos 2\pi\omega x)$ with a $\ll$ 1. $M_c(\omega)$ equals the contrast ratio between the density created and the decimal logarithm of the illuminance received.

Up to a point on the characteristic curve γ is fixed. If this operational point is changed then γ is modified (it is at its maximum at the shoulder of the curve where the gamma of the film is defined). It is therefore possible to plot function $M_c(\omega)$ as a function of variables ω and $\log_{10}E$ (figure IV.10.a).

Figure IV.10.b gives the shape of a M.T.F. Note that $M(\omega)$ is a real quantity (no phase shift) which decreases with frequency. Unlike the optical transfer function it has no cut-off point. The rate of decrease changes in direct proportion to emulsion thickness and grain size.

Figure IV.11 shows examples of the M.T.F. for two films, Pan-X and Plus-X, with their spatial frequencies in mm^{-1}. Since the M.T.F. also depends on the wavelength of the exposing light, curves R, G and B correspond to red, green and blue light respectively (from

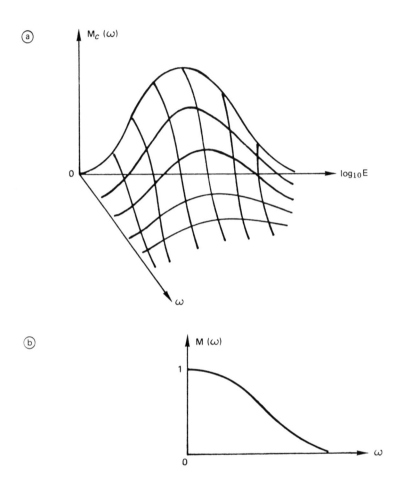

Fig.IV.10. - a) Changes in $M_c(\omega)$ as a function of ω and the logarithm of the illuminance received by the emulsion, b) the shape of the MTF for an emulsion (ω is the spatial frequency of the received illuminance).

J.C.Dainty and R.Shaw). [8]

It is also worthwhile remembering figure I.26, which shows how the M.T.F. affects reproduction of a periodic test pattern composed of stripes.

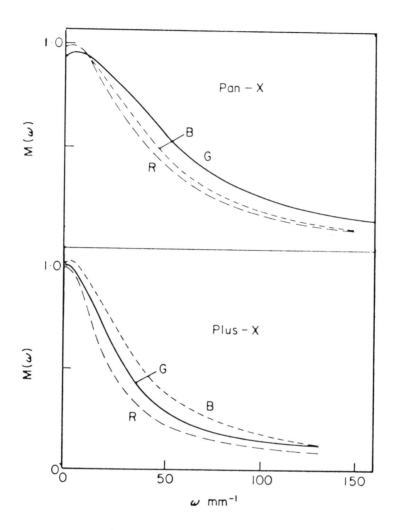

Fig.IV.11 - Specimen modulation transfer functions: a) Pan-X film, b) Plus-X film. Since the MTF depends on the wavelength of the exposing light, curves R, G and B correspond to red, green and blue light respectively (from J.C.Dainty and R.Shaw). [8]

2. Two stage model

As before, this model ignores proximity effects during development, but is more confined to small variations in illuminance. It leads us to place a linear filter in a cascade with a non-linearity (fig.IV.12).

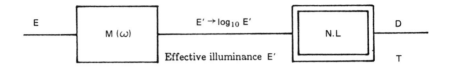

Fig.IV.12 - Two-stage model of a photographic film. The linear filter characterised by MTF $M(\omega)$ expresses the optical scattering which occurs in the photographic layer during exposure. The non-linearity is the response to effective
   illuminance E'; the output quantity is optical density D (or transmittance T)
   created subsequent to formation of the latent image and development.

As in the previous model, the linear filter represents the optical scattering of light in the sensitive layer during exposure. We know that M.T.F. $M(\omega)$ is the transfer function for this process, and that the output quantity is the *effective illuminance* E' produced by the process.

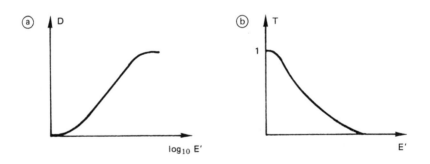

Fig.IV.13 - a) Non-linear characteristic $D = f(\log_{10}E')$ deduced from Hurter and
   Driffield's curve (figure IV.6), b) non-linear characteristic $T = f(E')$.

The transition from this illuminance, or more accurately the transition from $\log_{10}E'$ to the created density, is expressed by Hurter and

Driffield's non-linear curve (fig.IV.13.a). If transmittance T is taken as the output, the non-linearity corresponding to it is the characteristic $T = f(E')$ (fig.IV.13.b).

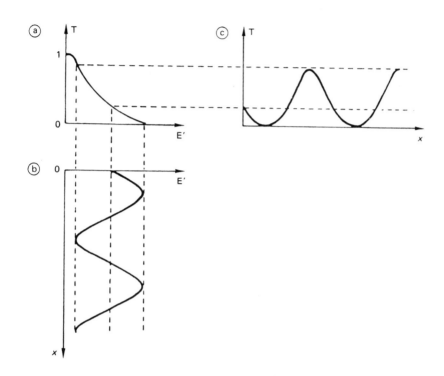

Fig.IV.14 - Two stage model: if non-linearity characteristic $T = f(E')$ is known, it is possible to measure the MTF using a sinusoidal test object E(x). Starting with the transmittance T(x) obtained as output (which is non-sinusoidal) it is possible to work back to the effective sinusoidal illuminance E'(x). M(ω) equals the contrast ratio between E' and E.

With this model we can measure the M.T.F. using highly contrasted sinusoidal test patterns with an illuminance of:

$$E(x) = E_0 (1 + a \cos 2\pi\omega x)$$

The corresponding effective illuminance $E'(x)$ is represented in figure IV.14.b.

The characteristic $T = f(E')$ (fig.IV.14.a) produces an output transmittance T which is no longer sinusoidal (fig.IV.14.c). Since the non-linearity is known, it is easy to work back from the measurement for T to the effective illuminance E'. As illuminance E is known it can be used to deduce the value of the M.T.F. for every frequency.

3. Three stage model (Kelly's model)

This model takes chemical effects into account. These are proximity effects due to migration of reaction products during processing (development and fixing).

As a first approximation they are assumed to be linear. The corresponding transfer function $M_1(\Omega)$ expresses the transition from latent image to the final created density.

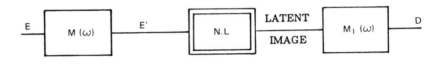

Fig.IV.15 - Three-stage model of a photographic film. Chemical proximity effects which arise during processing (development and fixing) are assumed to be linear and represented by a filter with a transfer function of $M_1(\omega)$.

Among other things it is worth mentioning the *Eberhard effect*. This is an edge effect which accentuates the contrast of fine details.

The broken lines in figure IV.16 represent three straight-sided latent images. One of them is wide (1), one is medium-sized (2) and the third is fine (3). Their corresponding densities are also shown.

In fact chemical effects depend very much on conditions at the time of development (time taken, ambient temperature, amount of stirring). Such considerations place a serious limit on the usefulness of the model.

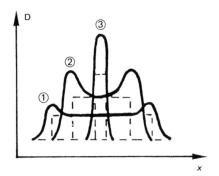

Fig.IV.16 - A special kind of proximity effect: the Eberhard effect. This is an edge effect. The finer the detail the more it accentuates the contrast: (1) "wide" detail, (2) medium detail, (3) fine detail.

D. Granularity and fluctuations in the density of film

So far it has been assumed that the quantities E (illuminance), D (optical density) and T (transmission) are fully known and free from fluctuations. This approximation is valid only for large, uniformly illuminated ranges observed on a "macroscopic" scale. In reality we are interested in density or transmission values measured over "small" surfaces, as we saw in the definitions of these quantities. But in this case, even if the illuminance appears to be uniform we observe that quantities E, D and T differ from point to point on the negative. These quantities are random or statistical in nature, and in a moment we shall see why. But first we must remind ourselves of a few things about statistics, that is to say how to calculate probabilities.

1. Probability calculation [11]

a) Random variables

A random variable (r.v) is a quantity which can take certain values. These values may be discrete or continuous, and it is not possible to choose between them in advance because they depend on the outcome of a random event. We are able to define only the *probabilities* of the various possible occurrences.

• *discrete* random variable X: can take only discrete values in the range $x_1 \ldots x_n$, each occurrence x_k having a probability of p_k. We say that p_k is the probability of r.v X taking the value x_k and we write $P[X = x_k] = p_k$.

Naturally $\displaystyle\sum_{k=1}^{n} p_k = 1$ or, if an infinite number of occurrences is

possible: $\displaystyle\sum_{k=-\infty}^{+\infty} p_k = 1.$

- *continuous* random variable X: as it can take any value in a continuous set, such as any value between $-\infty$ and $+\infty$, we define the probability of X taking a value between x and the very close value $x + \mathrm{d}x$ and we write:

$$P(x \le X < x + \mathrm{d}x) = p(x)\,\mathrm{d}x$$

$p(x)$ is called the probability density of X and the generalised case is written as:

$$\int_{-\infty}^{+\infty} p(x)\,\mathrm{d}x = 1$$

The *mean value* of X is written as $\langle X \rangle$ and is the sum of the possible occurrences weighted by their respective probabilities.

- in the case of discrete values: $\qquad \langle X \rangle = \displaystyle\sum_{k=-\infty}^{+\infty} x_k\, p_k$

- in the case of continuous values: $\qquad \langle X \rangle = \displaystyle\int_{-\infty}^{+\infty} x p(x)\,\mathrm{d}x$

It would be possible to define the mean value of X^n in the same way. For instance $\langle X^2 \rangle = \displaystyle\int_{-\infty}^{+\infty} x^2\, p(x)\,\mathrm{d}x$ in the case of continuous

values.

A quantity often used to define mean fluctuations about a mean value is the *standard deviation* σ which is the square root of the *variance* $V = \langle [X - \langle X \rangle]^2 \rangle$

Squaring we find: $\sigma^2 = \langle X^2 \rangle - 2\langle X \rangle^2 + \langle X \rangle^2$ giving: $\sigma^2 = \langle X^2 \rangle - \langle X \rangle^2$ which often proves to be a useful formula.

An example of a discrete random variable is the *Poisson distribution.*

The possible occurrences are all non-negative integers k from zero up.

$$P(X = k) = \frac{m^k}{k!} e^{-m} m \text{ is parameter of the law.}$$

It can be shown that $\langle X \rangle = m \; \sigma = \sqrt{m}$

An example of a continuous random variable is the *Gaussian distribution.*

It can be shown that Poisson's law is limited to cases where m is not large. The discrete law then tends towards a continuous law.

$$p(x) = \frac{1}{\sigma\sqrt{2\pi}} e^{-\frac{(x-x_0)^2}{2\sigma^2}}$$

$\langle X \rangle = x_0$. σ is the standard deviation for the law, shown as the familiar "bell-shaped curve".

b) Random functions

A random function is one which appears disordered and unpredictable, and able to take different forms depending on the outcome of a random event. In this way it is possible to use scanning to determine the density values of a line on a series of N negatives which have been printed uniformly in the same conditions. By this means we obtain N functions $D_1(x)$, $D_2(x)$, ... $D_N(x)$ and these are all functions of the x abscissa which differ from one negative to another. This set of functions constitutes the occurrences of a random function $D(x)$.

• *Mean value*

For a given x it is possible to calculate the mean value of occurrences $D_1(x)$, ... $D_N(x)$ which are written $\langle D(x) \rangle$.

If x varies the mean obtained is generally different. $\langle D(x) \rangle$ is therefore a function of variable x.

It is also possible to calculate more complicated means, such as $\langle D^2(x) \rangle$, $\langle D(x) \; D(x - x_0) \rangle$ where x_0 is a given deviation. The latter mean is generally a function of the two variables x and x_0.

• *Invariant random function*

If the calculated means do not depend on the chosen x abscissa we say that we have an invariant random function.

In this case $\langle D(x) \rangle = \langle D \rangle$ = constant. $\langle D(x) \, D(x - x_0) \rangle$ depends only on x_0. This quantity is then called the autocorrelation function of $D(x)$ and we write:

$$C(x_0) = \langle D(x) \, D(x - x_0) \rangle$$

If we define the standard deviation in the way we would for a random variable we have $\sigma_2 = \langle D^2 \rangle - \langle D \rangle^2$ = constant.

• *Ergodic random function*

The definitions given so far refer to statistical means calculated at a given point over the whole range of possible occurrences. But it is also possible to calculate the spatial mean for a given occurrence, for example the mean density of the line on the k'th negative $D_k(x)$ by calculating the mean of all values of x for the line.

If it so happens that the same result is obtained regardless of the negative used, in other words if $\overline{D_1(x)} = \overline{D_2(x)} = \overline{D_N(x)}$ it is possible to ask whether the spatial mean is equal to mean $\langle D \rangle$.

A random function for which the answer to this question is yes is called ergodic. In this case *statistical means* and *spatial means* may be taken as the same and it is possible to argue from a single occurrence. This is particularly the case with invariant functions. These too are ergodic, as may have been intuitively noticed.

2. Signal-to-noise ratio and equivalent quantum efficiency

• *The random nature of the illuminance* received on a small area of the negative surface: even with "uniform" illumination we observe fluctuations in illuminance E because of the fact that light is composed of particles.

In fact E is proportional to the number of photons per unit surface area per second. But this number is not a constant. It differs from one point on the negative to another, fluctuating about a mean value in accordance with Poisson's law. Let us more accurately call Q_s the random variable representing the number of photons received on surface area S during exposure of the negative:

$$P(Q_s = q) = \frac{(q_s)^q}{q!} \, e^{-q_s}$$

Mean value $\langle Q_s \rangle = q_s$

Standard deviation $\sigma_Q = \sqrt{q_s}$

An input *signal-to-noise ratio* (SNR)$_e$ for the photographic process may be defined as follows:

$$(SNR)_e = \frac{q_s}{\sigma_Q} = \frac{q_s}{\sqrt{q_s}} = \sqrt{q_s}$$

$$\boxed{(SNR)_e = \sqrt{q_s}} \qquad (15)$$

• *The random nature of the photographic process* itself (exposure and development). Leaving aside poorly understood chemical effects which can occur during development (and which in general are non-invariant and non-reproducible) we have seen that the process of creating a latent image has a statistical nature. The probability of creating an atom of silver with an incident photon is the *quantum efficiency* ϵ of the emulsion.

If grain-size variations in the developed silver are ignored and it is assumed that the number of grains developed varies only as a result of ϵ, it is easy to calculate an output signal-to-noise ratio (SNR)$_s$.

It turns out that the number of silver grains obtained on surface area S is a random variable N$_s$. This too has a Poisson distribution. Its mean value $n_s = \epsilon q_s$ and its standard deviation $\sqrt{n_s} = \sqrt{\epsilon q_s}$. Therefore:

$$(SNR)_s = \frac{\epsilon q_s}{\sqrt{\epsilon q s}} = \sqrt{\epsilon q s}$$

The ratio of squares of the input and output S.N.R. is called the *equivalent quantum efficiency* (E.Q.E.) of the emulsion.

Thus:

$$\boxed{EQE = \frac{(SNR)_s{}^2}{(SNR)_e{}^2} = \epsilon} \qquad (16)$$

The E.Q.E. equals the quantum efficiency. It expresses the extent to which fluctuations in illuminance are degraded to produce the density fluctuations observed. It is therefore an emulsion quality indicator.

Let us calculate standard deviation σ_D for the observed density. To do this let us express (SNR)$_s$ by introducing the number of input photons into the numerator and denominator.

$$(SNR)_s = \frac{q_s}{\sigma_D \dfrac{dq_s}{dD}} = \frac{q_s}{\sigma_D} \frac{dD}{dq_s}$$

but $\dfrac{dD}{dq_s}$ is easily expressed as a function of the γ of the emulsion.

$$\gamma = \frac{dD}{d \log_{10} E} = \frac{dD}{0.43 \dfrac{dE}{E}} = \frac{dD}{0.43 \dfrac{dq_s}{q_s}} = \frac{q_s}{0.43} \frac{dD}{dq_s}$$

this gives $\qquad \dfrac{dD}{dq_s} = \dfrac{0.43\gamma}{q_s} \quad$ and $\quad (SNR)_s = \dfrac{0.43\gamma}{\sigma_D}$

from which we derive

$$\sigma_D = \frac{0.43\gamma}{(SNR)_s} = \frac{0.43\gamma}{\sqrt{\epsilon}\,(SNR)_e}$$

so that:

$$\boxed{\sigma_D = \frac{0.43}{\sqrt{\epsilon}\sqrt{qs}}} \qquad (17)$$

σ_D characterises the granularity of the film
σ_D decreases if quantum efficiency ϵ increases.
    The minimum value for σ_D would correspond to a perfect photographic plate which would introduce no additional fluctuations and would transmit only the fluctuations occurring in the input photons. Thus

$$\sigma_D = \sigma_Q \frac{dD}{dq_s} = \sigma_Q \frac{0.43\gamma}{q_s} = \frac{0.43\gamma}{\sqrt{q_s}} \quad \text{giving} \quad \epsilon = 1$$

A perfect emulsion would have an E.Q.E. = 100%

3. Selwyn's law

The number of photons q_s received for a given illuminance is proportional to the surface area S.

Equation (17) shows that σ_D varies with $\dfrac{1}{\sqrt{S}}$

This is known as Selwyn's law:

$$\sigma D \propto \dfrac{1}{\sqrt{S}}$$ (18)

• **Nutting's formula.** This formula makes it possible to express an approximation of mean density D measured as a function of n_s, S and the mean surface area s of a grain of silver.

This means we can write:

$$T = \frac{\text{undarkened surface}}{\text{total surface area S}} = 1 - \frac{\text{darkened surface}}{\text{total surface area S}} = 1 - \frac{n_s \bar{s}}{S}$$

Therefore

$$D = -\log_{10}T = -\log_{10}\left(1 - \frac{n_s \bar{s}}{S}\right) = -0.43 \ln\left(1 - \frac{n_s \bar{s}}{S}\right)$$

If we assume $\dfrac{n_s \bar{s}}{S} \ll 1$ (which means that we are nowhere near maximum density on the characteristic curve) we can deduce

$$\ln\left(1 - \frac{n_s \bar{s}}{S}\right) \simeq -\frac{n_s \bar{s}}{S} \quad \text{and} \quad \boxed{D \simeq 0.43 \,\frac{n_s \bar{s}}{S}}$$ (19)

This is known as Nutting's equation, and it enables us to find Selwyn's law even when the situation is nowhere near saturation.

If we still assume that fluctuations are entirely due to variations in the number of grains, and the standard deviation is $\sqrt{n_s}$, we have:

$$\sigma_D = 0.43 \,\frac{\bar{s}}{S}\,\sqrt{n_s} = \sqrt{0.43}\,\sqrt{\frac{\bar{s}}{S}}\,\sqrt{D}$$

giving:

$$\sigma_D = 0.66 \,\frac{\sqrt{\bar{s}}}{\sqrt{S}}\,\sqrt{D} \quad \text{and therefore} \quad \sigma_D \propto \frac{1}{\sqrt{S}}$$

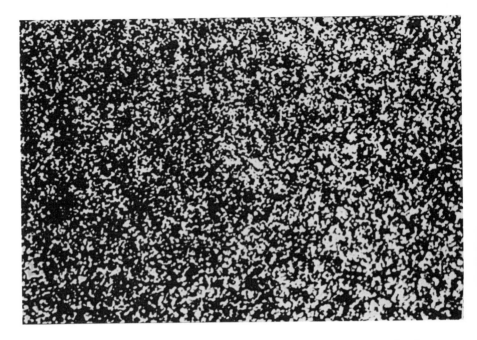

Fig.IV.17 - the grainy appearance of a photographic emulsion as seen under the
microscope. Single silver grains and accumulations of grains are clearly visible.

Notes:
 1. To characterise the granularity of a film regardless of the area of
observation, Selwyn proposed the *granularity coefficient* $S = \sigma_D \sqrt{2S}$.
 2. Equation (19) shows that granularity increases with density and
mean grain size, at any rate for so long as $\dfrac{n_s \bar{s}}{S} \ll 1$. In section 5 we
shall see the effect when this condition is not met.

4. Gaussian model

If surface area S is large enough for n_s to be very high, we can assume
that Poisson's law for random variable N_s is tending towards a Gaussian law. It can be shown that density fluctuations observed when this
is so are Gaussian also. This is a consequence of a statistical theorem
known as the central limit theorem. This explains why the characteristics of Gaussian distribution make their appearance whenever a feature is being observed at the macroscopic level. It results from adding
together a very large number of independent elemental contributions

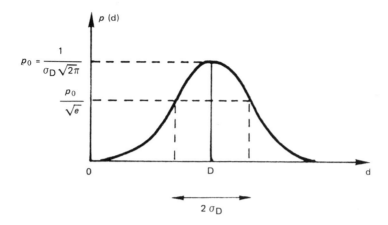

Fig.IV.18 - Theoretical Gaussian fluctuations in density about a mean value D. Density d is the density measured over a small area of surface (such as the analysis aperture of the digitizer): It is a random quantity with a probability density of $p(d) = \dfrac{1}{\sigma_D \sqrt{2\pi}} \, e^{-(d-D)^2/2\sigma_D^2}$ is the standard deviation).

governed by the same law.

The probability density of the observed density is then

$$p(d) = \frac{1}{\sigma_D \sqrt{2\pi}} \, e^{-\dfrac{(d-D)^2}{2\sigma_D^2}} \qquad (20)$$

where D is the mean value and σ_D is the standard deviation.

Figure IV.17 shows the grainy appearance of a photographic emulsion as seen under the microscope. Single silver grains and accumulations of grains are clearly visible. If the area of observation is very large, a Gaussian distribution prevails (fig.IV.18). This can be shown by digitizing the image and plotting the histogram of the digital data (see chapter VI, fig.VI.17).

Such Gaussian fluctuations due to granularity can be taken into account by adding Gaussian "noise" of mean zero and standard devia-

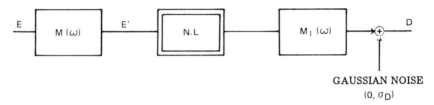

Fig.IV.19 - The three stage model can be completed by adding Gaussian noise to
its output. This would have a mean of zero and a standard deviation of σ_D to
express the observed density fluctuations.

tion σ_D to the output from a perfectly deterministic model of the photographic process, such as Kelly's model (fig.IV.19). [3]

5. Binary model

If quantity $\dfrac{n_s \bar{s}}{S}$ representing the darkened portion of the measured surface is near 1, Nutting's formula is no longer valid. This comes about when surface area S is small or when the situation is close to saturation density. It can be shown, however, that Selwyn's equation remains valid as long as S is greater than the surface area of a grain.

If S is smaller than the surface area of a grain, the quantity 1 - T is a binary variable which equals 0 where there is no grain and 1 where a grain is encountered (fig.IV.20.a).

Therefore

$$T^2 = T \quad \text{and} \quad \sigma_T^2 = \langle T^2 \rangle - \langle T \rangle^2 = \langle T \rangle - \langle T \rangle^2 = \langle T \rangle (1 - \langle T \rangle)$$

The curve (fig.IV.20.b) shows that the fluctuations reach their maximum for a mean transmission of 0.5.

Note that a situation such as this is rare, because for many reasons (coherence of the light among others) it is difficult to determine an area of observation which is smaller than an elementary grain size ($<1\mu^2$ for example).

- *Note:* Close to saturation a phenomenon known as "clamping" occurs, where the grains accumulate together in groups. Consequently an area of observation S which is larger than a grain may be smaller than the surface area of a clamping group and conditions become those of the binary model. It will be seen that fluctuations pass through a maximum as density increases.

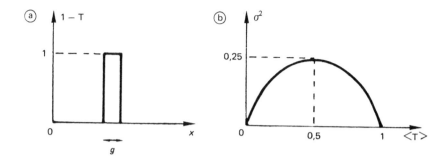

Fig.IV.20. - a) When density is close to saturation or when the area of observation is very small (about the same size as a grain) the observed transmittance is a succession of binary objects with a width of g (where g is the mean diameter of the grains), b) the observed variance is a maximum for a mean transmittance of 0.5.

E. Interference effects when measuring the density of a negative

1. Callier effect [5, 8]

To measure the density of a small area of negative we need to measure how much light has passed through it (fig.IV.21). But the finite thickness of the layer causes scattering and some light is lost. The measured density D is thus greater than the true density D_0. This is known as the Callier effect.

$$\boxed{D = q\, D_0}\qquad(21)$$

$q > 1$ is the *Callier coefficient*.

For instance, light falls on the zone from an illuminating objective and is captured using an analysis objective. If the capture angle is wide (fig.IV.22.a) the *diffuse density* is said to be measured. If both angles are narrow (fig.IV.22.b) it is the larger, *specular density* which is measured.

It can be shown that q depends symmetrically on the angles of illumination α and of analysis β (fig.IV.23.a) and is at its maximum for

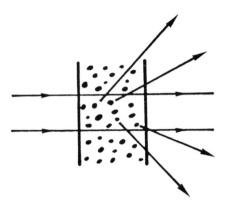

Fig.IV.21 - Explanation of the Callier effect: light scattering by the photographic
layer at the point under analysis causes measured density to exceed true density.

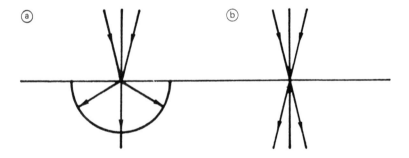

Fig.IV.22 - a) Measuring diffuse density, b) measuring specular density.

$\alpha = \beta$.

Figure IV.23.b gives the shape of function $q(\alpha, \beta)$.

The Callier coefficient also depends on the measured density and
the contrast of the film. It increases with γ and for any given γ it
passes through a maximum as D increases (fig.IV.24).

Note: expressed as a transmittance, equation (21) becomes:

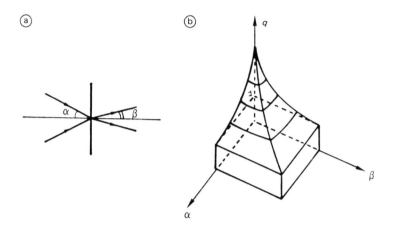

Fig.IV.23 - The Callier coefficient q(>1) depends symmetrically on aperture angles
α and β of the illumination and analysis beams; a) definition of α and β, b)
the surface of the variation law of q.

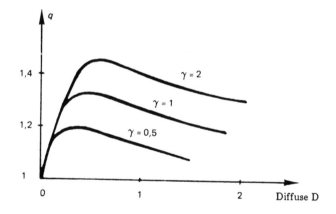

Fig.IV.24 - The Callier coefficient varies as a function of the measured density
and of film contrast.

$$T = T_0^q$$

2. 'Microdensitometer' effect

a) If a uniform density range is measured, the value obtained is independent of area of analysis S.

Let us assume in fact that S is divided up into n domains, each with a surface area of s which is large by comparison with grain size, so that $S = ns$ (fig.IV.25).

- the transmittance measured on each elementary domain is:

$$T_j = T_{0j}^q = \left(\frac{s'_i}{s}\right)^q = \left(\frac{s'}{s}\right)^q$$

and $s'_j = s'$ is the notation for the undarkened surface. This gives the mean for the n domains as:

$$\langle T \rangle = \frac{1}{n} \sum_{j=1}^{n} T_j = \frac{1}{ns^q} \sum_{j=1}^{n} s'^q = \frac{ns'^q}{ns^q} = \left(\frac{s'}{s}\right)^q$$

- the transmittance measured directly on surface S is:

$$T = T_0^q = \left(\frac{ns'}{S}\right)^q = \left(\frac{ns'}{ns}\right)^q = \left(\frac{s'}{s}\right)^q = \langle T \rangle$$

It therefore makes no difference which area of analysis is chosen.

b) The same is no longer true if density is variable. We shall now show that this is a consequence of the Callier effect.

- if there were no Callier effect, we would have $q = 1$ and therefore $T_j = T_{0j} = \frac{s'_i}{s}$ (s'_j is the undarkened surface of the j'th domain).

This gives:

$$\langle T \rangle = \frac{1}{n} \sum_{j=1}^{n} T_j = \frac{1}{ns} \sum_{j=1}^{n} s'_j = \frac{1}{S} \sum_{j=1}^{n} s'_j$$

The direct measurement at S:

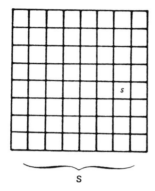

Fig.IV.25 - The "microdensitometer" effect: measuring variable density at the area
of analysis depends on the area selected. The density measured at S will not
equal the mean of the values obtained for the elementary surfaces s.

$$T = T_0 = \frac{\sum_{j=1}^{n} s'_j}{S} = \langle T \rangle$$

- if there is a Callier effect

$$T_j = (T_{0j})^q = \left(\frac{s'_j}{S}\right)^q$$

giving

$$\langle T \rangle = \frac{1}{n} \sum_{j=1}^{n} T_j = \frac{1}{n} \sum_{j=1}^{n} \frac{s'^q_j}{s^q} = \frac{1}{ns^q} \sum_{j=1}^{n} s'^q_j$$

The direct measurement at S:

$$T = T_0^q = \left[\frac{\sum_{j=1}^{n} s'_j}{S}\right]^q = \frac{\left[\sum_{j=1}^{n} s'_j\right]^q}{n^q s^q} \neq \langle T \rangle$$

It has been shown that T exceeds $\langle T \rangle$, therefore $D < \langle D \rangle$. This microdensitometer effect increases with the size of the area of analysis but partially compensates for the Callier effect.

3. Schwarzschild-Villiger effect

With all image analysers, especially digitizers, it is necessary to illuminate a larger area of negative than that required for study. The silver grains scatter the light in the illuminating beam causing the measured density to be influenced by the density of nearby regions (fig.IV.26).

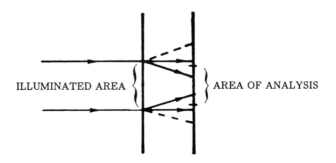

ILLUMINATED AREA   AREA OF ANALYSIS

Fig.IV.26 - The Schwarzschild-Villiger effect: The silver grains scatter the light causing the density measured at the area of analysis to depend on the densities of nearby illuminated regions.

If the illuminated area is not much larger than the area of analysis, as in digitizers of the two-slit microdensitometer type (chapter V, section E.4.b.) this effect may be ignored. On the other hand if the illuminated area is much larger, the proximity effect can be troublesome. This can happen for instance when observing a small, dark detail surrounded by a very bright region, and is particularly true of digitizers with no lighting aperture where the whole of the negative or scene is illuminated as in a video camera. Equipment of this sort gives reasonable image reproduction but is not suitable for the purpose of accurate photometric measurement.

This scattering effect also acts as a low-pass filter. The larger the illuminated surface area the more high frequencies will be cut out of the image. Thus figure IV.27 shows the analysis of a line 70μ wide with an area of analysis 5μ wide and increasingly large areas of illumination: a) 7μ b) 20μ c) 40μ d) 80μ e) the whole negative.

Figure IV.28 shows further demonstration of this effect. The larger the surface under illumination the more high frequencies are clipped from the "noise" caused by fluctuations in measured density. The standard deviation σ_D is therefore seen to decrease (see Wiener's spectrum in section F.3.).

Fig.IV.27 - The Schwarzschild-Villiger effect - 1. Measuring a line 70μ wide with an analysis slit 5μ wide and increasingly wide illumination windows: a) 7μ, b) 20μ, c) 40μ, d) 80μ e) unrestricted window size.

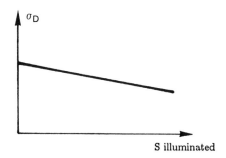

Fig.IV.28 - The Schwarzschild-Villiger effect - 2. The standard deviation of density fluctuations decreases as the surface area under illumination increases.

F. Autocorrelation and power spectrum of granular 'noise'

1. Granular 'noise': random invariant and ergodic process.

Earlier in this chapter, in section D, we examined fluctuations in measured density at a given surface of a uniformly printed negative when the location of the surface is changing, as for example when the negative is being scanned. We therefore treated this density as a random variable D, and were able among other things to determine with accuracy the mean value D_0 of this variable as well as its standard deviation σ_D. These mean values are calculated over the entire range of occurrences by measuring D at every possible location. It can thus be seen that statistical means are in this instance actually spatial means, in which spatial variable x is, say, the length of surface which has been scanned from the image origin (see figure V.1). It is therefore possible to consider a function $D(x)$ which is a random function for the negative under examination (see section D.1.b). If there were a series of identical negatives, all exposed in identical conditions, it would be possible to examine this random function fully. In fact it is usually accepted that the random function is invariant and ergodic. As we have seen, this means we can argue on the basis of a single occurrence, and it makes no difference whether we use the statistical or the spatial mean.

All the results shown in section D are therefore still valid for random function $D(x)$, enabling us to examine various models, to introduce

$$\overline{D(x)} = D_0, \ \sigma_D^2 = \overline{D^2(x)} - (\overline{D(x)})^2 = \overline{D^2} - D_0^2, \text{ etc.}$$

Similarly we shall now introduce the autocorrelation function of $D(x)$.

2. The autocorrelation function

We shall consider density fluctuations in relation to the mean density value, which is the random function:

$$\Delta D(x) = D(x) - D_0$$

By definition the autocorrelation function of $D(x)$ is:

$$C(x_0) = \overline{\Delta D(x) \ \Delta D(x - x_0)}$$

(the spatial mean for the whole negative).

In particular its value at the point of origin equals σ_D^2.

In fact $C(0) = \overline{\Delta D^2(x)} = \overline{(D(x) - D_0)^2} = \overline{D^2(x)} - D_0^2 = \sigma_D^2$

Moreover $C(-x_0) = C(x_0)$

The area of observation S may be large in comparison with the surface area of a grain. For instance we may be using a square with sides which measure $a \gg g$ (where g is the grain diameter). In such circumstances we find the type of autocorrelation function shown at figure IV.29.a. It is triangular in shape with a value of zero at a distance of $x_0 = a$. Distance a is called the *correlation distance*. As a is increased the triangle becomes wider and flatter since the height equals $\sigma_D^2 \propto \dfrac{1}{S} = \dfrac{1}{a^2}$ (Selwyn's law).

If we now decrease a to a point where it becomes smaller than g, we find a more or less fixed triangle (fig.IV.29.b). Its height of σ_D^2 is constant (see section D.5, binary model) and the correlation distance is equal to grain diameter g.

We can assume that this autocorrelation function is characteristic of the photographic medium itself, since the observed function for $a \gg g$ is derived from the medium after the low-pass filtering of the analysis aperture.

If it were possible to make an infinitely narrow aperture we could obtain the autocorrelation function for a film of microscopic grain size $g = 0$. It can be seen that this function would actually be a Dirac signal $\delta(x_0)$. It is known as the *microscopic correlation function* (fig.IV.29.c).

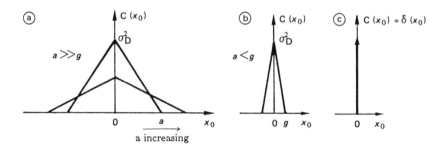

Fig.IV.29 - The autocorrelation function for photographic granularity (assumed to be one-dimensional); a) large area of observation compared with grain size, such as a square with sides measuring a >> g, b) area of observation smaller than grain size, c) microscopic correlation function (infinitely fine aperture and grain size).

Figure IV.30 shows how $C(x_0)$ alters as measured density D increases:

a) If $a \gg g$ (fig.IV.30.a) the correlation distance does not change but σ_D increases (see note 2, section D.3), at least provided conditions are not too close to saturation.

b) If $a < g$ the correlation distance increases with density because the grains group together due to clamping. In addition σ_D passes through a maximum, as we saw in the case of the binary model (fig.IV.30.b). The same situation occurs when $a \gg g$ as conditions approach saturation (see note, section D.5).

3. Power spectrum or Wiener's spectrum

Just as sinusoidal signal $D = D_0 \cos 2\pi wx$ has a mean power $\overline{D^2} = D_0^2 \frac{2}{2}$

$\left(\text{being the square of effective value } \frac{D_0}{\sqrt{2}} \right)$, it can be shown that

random signal $D(x)$ has a mean power:

$$\overline{D^2(x)} = \overline{[D_0 + \Delta D(x)]^2} = D_0^2 + 2D_0 \overline{\Delta D(x)} + \overline{\Delta D^2(x)}$$

but $\overline{\Delta D(x)} = 0$ and $\overline{\Delta D^2(x)} = \sigma_D^2$

therefore $\overline{D^2(x)} = D_0^2 + \sigma_D^2$

D_0^2 represents the mean power of the continuous component D_0 (mean 2 value) and σ_D^2 is the mean power of the fluctuations (noise).

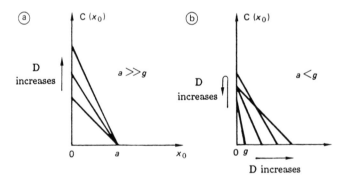

Fig.IV.30 - How the autocorrelation function varies with measured mean density; a) when a >> g correlation distance does not change and remains equal to a; the standard deviation increases with D while conditions are not too close to saturation, b) when a < g (or when conditions are close to saturation) correlation distance increases with D because of clamping; the standard deviation passes through a maximum (see figure IV.20).

To see how this power is distributed in the frequency domain, we resort to the concept of *spectral power density*, also called power spectrum (or Wiener's spectrum) $W(\omega)$. This is by definition the F.T. of the autocorrelation function $C(x_0)$.

$$W(\omega) = F \ (C(x_0)) = \int_{-\infty}^{+\infty} C(x_0) \ e^{-2\pi j \omega x_0} \ dx_0$$

Conversely

$$C(x_0) = \int_{-\infty}^{+\infty} W(\omega) \ e^{2\pi j \omega x_0} \ d\omega$$

If we put $x_0 = 0$ we find $C(0) = \int_{\infty}^{+\infty} W(\omega) \ d\omega$

But $C(0) = \sigma_D^2 = $ mean power.

$W(\omega)$ is in fact a spectral power density. The surface area of the spectrum represents the mean noise power, with $W(\omega)d\omega$ being the mean power in frequency band $(\omega, \omega + d\omega)$.

In practice, if small enough areas of measure are used Wiener's spectrum for an emulsion appears as in fig.IV.31.a. It holds good up to frequencies of the order of $\frac{1}{g}$. The corresponding correlation function does not quite take on the triangular appearance of figure IV.29.b. The spectrum corresponding to the microscopic correlation function shown in figure.IV.29.c is in fact the "*white noise*" spectrum in figure IV.31.b. A very fine grain emulsion will give a "*pink noise*" (fig.31.c).

Figure IV.32 gives examples of Wiener's spectra for colour films (unbroken lines: fast film; broken lines: medium-fast film). They do not exhibit "flat" spectra because they are not fine-grain films. The effect of a change of density can also be seen. It alters the autocorrelation function (see fig.IV.30) and therefore the spectrum.

Similarly it is also possible to talk of Wiener's spectrum for the input noise of photons entering the photographic process. It can be shown that it is a flat spectrum (perfect white noise). This noise is filtered by the photographic process, for instance by the linear filter of

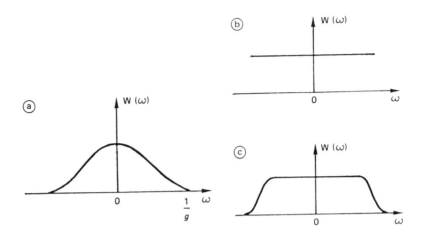

Fig.IV.31 - Wiener's spectrum for a photographic emulsion. This is the Fourier transformation for the autocorrelation function. a) the appearance of the spectrum, b) "white noise" spectrum (or microscopic correlation noise; see figure IV,29.c), c) "pink noise" spectrum.

transfer function $M_c(\omega)$ using the one stage model (fig.IV.8). It can be shown statistically [11] that Wiener's spectrum for the output noise is equal to the input spectrum multiplied by the square of the transfer function. Output will therefore be seen to exhibit a spectrum which is proportional to $|M_c(\omega)|^2 = \gamma^2 |M(\omega)|^2$ and therefore $W(\omega) = k |M(\omega)|^2$.

This means that providing the areas of analysis are small, Wiener's spectrum is another way of deriving the M.T.F. By finding the modulus of its measured value we are in fact finding the M.T.F. itself [8].

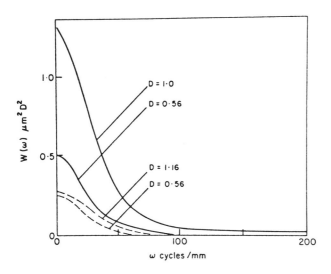

Fig.IV.32 - Specimen Wiener's spectra for colour films (unbroken lines: fast film; broken lines: medium-fast film). Such films do not exhibit flat spectra. The effect of a change of density can also be seen. It alters the autocorrelation function (see fig.IV.30) and therefore the spectrum (from J.C.Dainty and R.Shaw). [8]

5

Digitizing and reconstructing images

A. Process of digitizing and reconstruction

1. Digitizing

Before an analogue image can be processed by computer it must first be digitized, or expressed as an array of numbers. The digitizing process can be divided into three phases:

a) The image area is *scanned* by an aperture or spot. By definition this is finite in size, and simultaneously acts as a low-pass *prefilter* (attenuating the higher spatial frequencies). As often as not scanning is of the X - Y type, whereby the image is described line by line. Thus in figure V.1 a small square aperture of side a is being moved across lines which are a apart.

b) Spatial *sampling* takes place in two-dimensions. It means accepting from the aperture only those values which describe a series of points forming the nodes of a network. This is usually an orthogonal grid with the same interval gauge in both x and y.

In the above example this means that an interval equal to the side of the square aperture divides the image into a mosaic of small adjoining squares (figure V.2). Each square is called a picture element or "*pixel*". It is assigned a value equal to the aperture response for the position concerned. On this principle figure V.3 shows a sampled image with adjoining square pixels, and illustrates the effect of decreasing the number of elements.

c) *Quantization*: the value of each pixel represents, say, the mean transmittance (or optical density) measured across the aperture area concerned. It is convenient to express this continuous value as a numeric value which is usually a whole number, using a convention (or

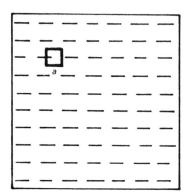

Fig.V.1 - Digitizing an image means
scanning it with a spot or aperture
which may be square in shape and is
finite in size.

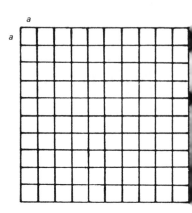

Fig.V.2 - Image sampling involves
capturing the transmission or density
values reported by the aperture in the
previous figure.Sampling points usually
form a regularly spaced orthogonal
grid. If the sampling interval equals
the side of the "aperture", pixels are
adjacent. They then form a mosaic of
small, uniformly grey squares.

coding rule) with a finite number of levels. It is usual to ensure that
these levels are equidistant.

Figure V.4 shows how a transmittance T is quantized in this way. T
= 0 for black, T = 1 for white (perfect transparency). Figure V.4.a
uses a quantizer with ten equidistant levels. By this convention T = 0
is coded as 0 and T = 1 is coded as 9. Similarly a quantizing scale with
256 equidistant levels represents T = 0 as 0 and T = 1 as 255 (closely
similar levels have not been represented in the diagram). In the first of
the above instances a computer can distinguish ten levels of grey in
the image and in the second example 256 levels (always assuming that
no other inaccuracies arise during measurement, as we shall see
below).

Figure V.5 shows the array of numbers which is obtained by quantizing the 16 x 16 pixels image in figure V.3.d across 16 levels (0 to
15).

In practice operations b) and c) above are often performed at one
and the same time by an analogue-to-digital converter which carries
out a conversion every time the spot crosses a sampling point. An

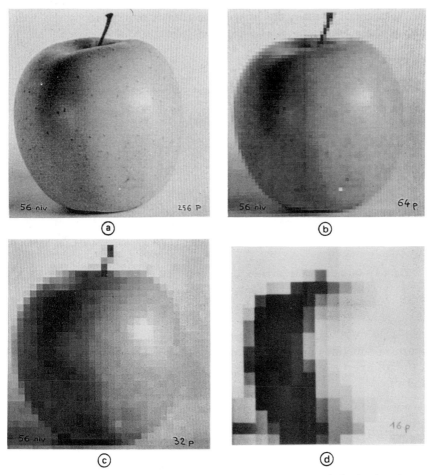

Fig.V.3 - Examples of image sampling using adjacent square pixels showing the effect of reducing the number of elements; a) 256 x 256 pixels, b) 64 x 64 pixels, c) 32 x 32 pixels, d) 16 x 16 pixels.

n-bit converter yields 2^n levels of grey.

2. Prefiltering

The finite dimensions of the scanning spot or aperture prefilter the image being digitized. This in effect means that whilst the intention is to digitize the transmittance values of a photographic negative, the outcome is actually a record of mean transmittance values across the aperture area. As we saw in chapter II, this operation is a convolution of the image in the spatial domain by the reversed aperture function.

In the spectral domain the image spectrum is multiplied by the aperture transfer function.

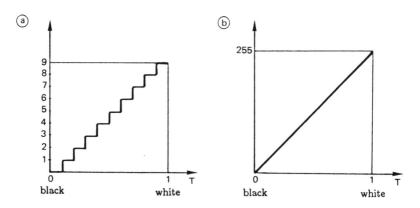

Fig.V.4 - Quantization involves coding the grey value of each pixel by assigning it
a numerical value which is usually a whole number; a) 10-level coding (0 to 9),
b) 256-level coding: the trend line is actually 255 steps.

Figure V.6 recapitulates the one-dimensional situation for the aperture functions and corresponding normalised transfer functions of a square aperture of side a (fig. a and b) and a Gaussian spot (fig. c and d).

3. Sampling

We shall base our reasoning on a one-dimensional signal $f(x)$ (fig. V.7.a). Regular sampling of $f(x)$ at interval T involves ignoring values of $f(x)$ unless they are at abscissa points which are multiples of T. The mathematical operation is to multiply $f(x)$ by the comb function

$$p(x) = \sum_{n=-\infty}^{+\infty} \delta(x - nT)$$

(fig.V.7.b) where T is the sampling interval.

This gives us the sampled function

0	0	0	0	0	0	0	1	5	0	1	1	1	1	1	1
0	0	0	0	0	0	1	2	5	1	1	1	1	1	1	1
1	1	1	1	3	6	8	10	5	4	3	1	1	1	1	1
1	1	3	9	9	12	13	12	10	9	7	5	2	1	2	2
1	2	11	14	15	14	12	10	9	7	6	5	4	2	2	2
1	8	12	15	15	14	11	9	8	6	5	4	4	3	2	2
2	10	13	15	14	13	11	8	7	5	2	3	4	4	3	3
4	10	13	14	13	12	10	8	6	5	2	3	4	4	4	4
5	11	12	13	13	12	10	8	7	6	5	4	4	4	4	4
5	11	12	13	13	12	11	9	7	6	6	5	5	5	4	4
5	10	12	12	13	12	12	9	8	7	6	5	5	5	4	4
6	9	12	12	12	13	12	9	8	8	6	5	5	4	4	4
9	8	12	12	12	12	12	10	9	8	7	6	5	4	4	4
8	8	10	12	12	13	12	10	9	9	7	6	4	4	4	4
10	10	10	11	12	12	12	11	9	9	8	4	4	4	4	4
8	8	9	10	12	12	12	10	9	7	5	4	4	5	5	5

Fig.V.5 - Array of numbers obtained by quantizing the 16 x 16 pixels image in figure V.3.d across 16 levels (0 to 15).

$$f_e(x) = \sum_{n=-\infty}^{+\infty} f(x)\, \delta(x - nT) \qquad \text{(fig.V.7.c)}$$

This may also be written $f_e(x) = \sum_{n=-\infty}^{+\infty} f(nT)\, \delta(x - nT)$.

Let us examine the equation $f_e(x) = f(x)\, p(x)$.

We know from chapter II, section C.2 that every multiplication in the spatial domain has a corresponding convolution in the frequency domain.

If we take the F.T. of each member, we obtain:

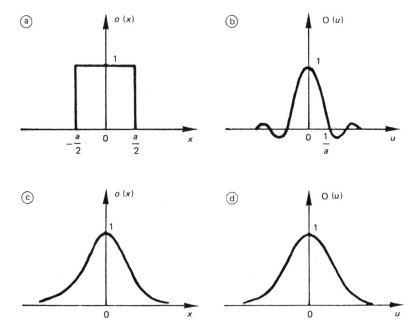

Fig.V.6 - The finite dimensions of the scanning spot or aperture prefilter the image being digitized. This operation is a convolution of the image by the aperture function o(x) (spatial domain) and a multiplication of the image spectrum by the aperture transfer function O(u) (frequency domain); a) aperture function for a square of side a, b) normalised transfer function of the square aperture, c) Gaussian spot, d) normalised transfer function of the Gaussian spot.

$$F_e(u) = F(u) * P(u)$$

But (see chap.I, equation 19): $P(u) = \dfrac{1}{T} \displaystyle\sum_{n=-\infty}^{+\infty} \delta\left(u - \dfrac{n}{T}\right)$

giving

$$F_e(u) = \frac{1}{T} \sum_{n=-\infty}^{+\infty} F(u) * \delta\left(u - \frac{n}{T}\right)$$

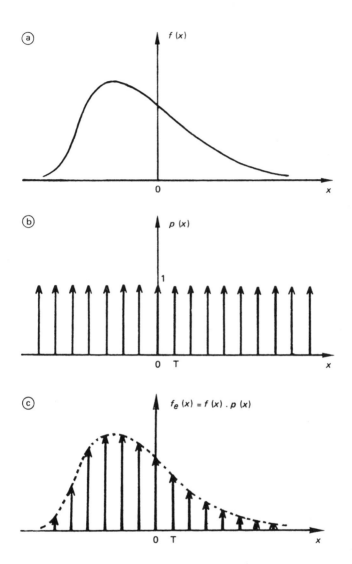

Fig.V.7 - Sampling a one-dimensional signal: a) Function to be sampled: f(x), b) sample comb with interval T: p(x), c) sampled function: $f_e(x) = f(x) \times f(x)$. Sampling a signal amounts to multiplying it by the comb function.

and we therefore obtain (see chap.II, section B, exercise 2):

$$F_e(u) = \frac{1}{T} \sum_{n=-\infty}^{+\infty} F\left(u - \frac{n}{T}\right) \qquad (1)$$

The spectrum of the sampled function can therefore be obtained to the nearest factor $\frac{1}{T}$ by repeating the spectrum of the function on the frequencies axis with an interval of $\frac{1}{T}$.

a) Let us assume that $F(u)$ cancels out beyond cut-off frequency u_0 (fig.V.8.a) and we choose a sampling interval such that $\frac{1}{T} \geq 2u_0$ (fig.V.8.b).

It can easily be seen in such an instance that periodic repetition will not alter the repeated component (fig.V.8.c).

To put it another way, even though the values of $f(x)$ lying outside the sampling points have been "ignored", it must be possible theoretically to retrieve the spectrum for $F(u)$ and thereby to reconstruct the continuous function $f(x)$ accurately. It is enough for example to use a perfect low-pass filter with a cut-off frequency of $\frac{1}{2T}$ (its shape is shown in dotted lines at figure V.8.c). This will allow only the central component of the spectrum to pass through. This problem will be considered in the next section. Frequency $2u_0$ is called the *Shannon frequency* and the condition shown here:

$$\frac{1}{T} \geq 2u_0 \qquad (2)$$

is called *Shannon's condition*. It is expressed as follows:
"To sample a bond-limited signal without loss of information, the minimum required sampling frequency is twice the highest frequency contained in the signal".

b) Let us assume by contrast that we are sampling $f(x)$ at a frequency where $\frac{1}{T} < 2u_0$ (fig.V.9). In such conditions the spectrum of the sampled function will be composed of overlapping components. Even if we try to isolate the central component by means of a low-

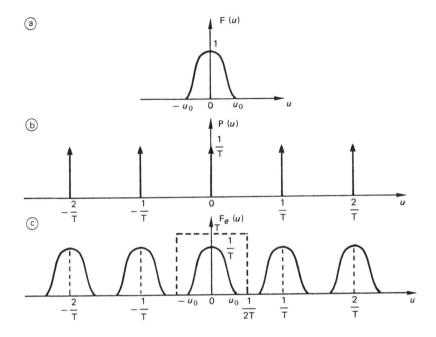

Fig.V.8 - Sampling a signal at a higher frequency than the Shannon frequency; a) spectrum of the function, maximum frequency u_0, b) spectrum of the sampling comb, interval T with $\frac{1}{T} > 2u_0$, c) spectrum of the function sampled: the components are separated; it is theoretically possible to isolate the central component and accurately reconstruct the signal which has been sampled.

pass filter with a cut-off frequency of $\frac{1}{2T}$, this component will be disrupted by the influence of overlapping frequencies from neighbouring components. Such spectral *aliasing* makes it impossible to reconstruct signal $f(x)$ accurately.

The same argument may be applied to images, which are two-dimensional signals [3]. Thus the spectrum of an image sampled in accordance with an orthogonal grid spaced at regular intervals of T on x and y will be derived by indefinitely repeating the spectrum $F(u, v)$ at intervals of $\frac{1}{T}$ on each of the Ou and Ov axes. This result can be found at once by treating this form of sampling as if it were multiplication by a brush function in the spatial domain, and therefore convo-

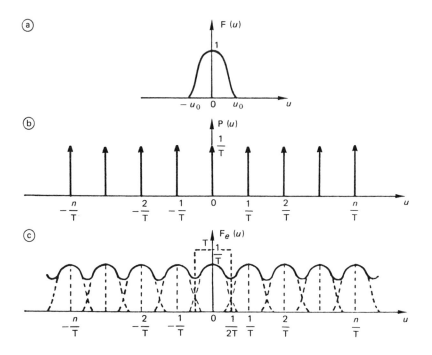

Fig.V.9 - Sampling a signal at a lower frequency than the Shannon frequency; a) spectrum of the function, maximum frequency u_0, b) spectrum of the sampling comb, interval T with $1/T < 2u_0$, c) spectrum of the function sampled: the components overlap (phenomenon known as aliasing); it is no longer possible to "retrieve" the central component and the sampled signal cannot be accurately reconstructed.

lution by a brush function in the frequency domain. Figure V.10 illustrates this operation in the case of an image which has a spectrum $F(u,v)$ with circular symmetry and a maximum frequency of u_0. It is being sampled with a frequency of $\frac{1}{T} > 2u_0$ in both directions. There is no overlapping of components.

Figure V.11 shows what happens when a square aperture is used to sample a radial test pattern (spatial frequencies are in units of $\frac{1}{r}$ where r is the distance from the centre). Spectral aliasing causes interfering frequencies n which give rise to "moiré" patterns in the image (fig.a). The larger the aperture the further from the centre the effect appears, and therefore the lower the spatial frequencies concerned. (Fig.b.).

4. Reconstruction

a) The purpose of the operation
Every image processing system is provided with a display device so that for instance it is possible to view the images obtained after different stages of processing. Suppose for the moment that we wish to display the "raw" digitized image. It is possible to use various kinds of *image reconstruction filter* which do the very opposite of a digitizer. They take the array of numbers in the digital image and convert it into an analogue image which is visible to the observer. For this purpose different kinds of device can be used, such as a cathode ray tube, photographic negative, paper printout, and so on. In every case, each digital image sample recreates another picture element. Each *new pixel* is in an appropriate form for reconstructing an image which is as close as possible to the image before digitizing, bearing in mind any errors introduced by the various operations (prefiltering, sampling, quantization, etc.).

On this basis figure V.3 used adjacent square pixels identical to the pixels in the digitization, but this is not a general rule.

b) The ideal reconstruction filter
Let us take another look at one-dimensional signals.

Let us examine a correctly sampled signal, that is, a bond-limited signal which has been sampled at a frequency no lower than the Shannon frequency. Spectrum $F_e(u)$ appears in figure V.8.c.

If a filter has a transfer function $G(u)$ which allows all of the central component to pass with a gain of T whilst completely cutting out the other components, it is able to reconstruct the signal perfectly. Such a filter is called an *ideal reconstruction filter*. It is shown on figure V.12 and its impulse response is $g(x) = 2u_1 T$ sinc $2\pi u_1 x$

for which:

$$\boxed{u_0 \leq u_1 < \frac{1}{T} - u_0}$$

(3)

It is possible in particular to choose $u_1 = \frac{1}{2T}$ and obtain the ideal reconstruction filter shown in figure V.8.c., with impulse response

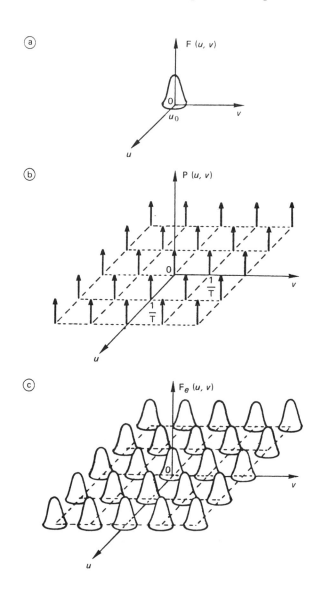

Fig.V.10 - Sampling a two-dimensional signal; a) spectrum $F(u,v)$ with circular symmetry and maximum frequency u_0. b) spectrum $P(u,v)$ for the brush function with a sampling frequency of $\frac{1}{T} > 2u_0$, c) spectrum $Fe(u,v)$ of the signal being sampled: there is no overlapping of components.

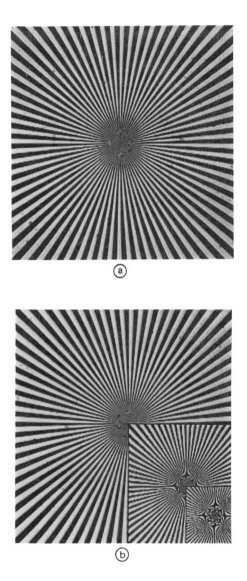

Fig.V.11 - Using a square aperture to sample a radial test pattern in which spatial frequencies increase in units of $\frac{1}{r}$ where r is the distance from the centre; a) spectral aliasing gives rise to "moiré" patterns, b) the larger the aperture the further from the centre the effect appears, and therefore the lower the spatial frequencies concerned.

$$g(x) = \text{sinc } \pi \frac{x}{T}.$$

The set of operations represented by prefiltering + sampling + ideal reconstruction is shown in the form of a diagram in figure V.13.

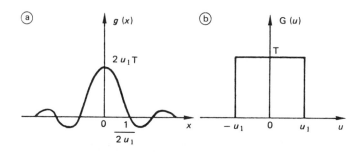

Fig.V.12 - Ideal reconstruction filter for reconstructing a signal sampled at a higher frequency than the Shannon frequency; a) the impulse response of the filter, b) the corresponding transfer function; u_1 must be chosen so that $u_0 \leq u_1 < \frac{1}{T} - u_0$ (u_0 is the maximum frequency in the signal being sampled), for instance $u_1 = \frac{1}{2T}$ as in figure V.8.c.

Because of prefiltering, signal $f(x)$ is different from the original signal $f_1(x)$. If $f(x)$ is sampled at a higher frequency than the Shannon frequency it is possible to reconstruct $f(x)$ but not $f_1(x)$. If the sampling rate is too low, reconstructed signal $f_r(x)$ is necessarily different from $f(x)$ because of aliasing.

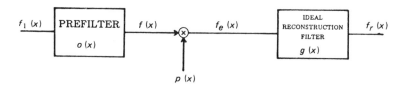

Fig.V.13 - Diagram of the prefiltering + sampling operation followed by an ideal reconstruction filter. If sampling is carried out at a frequency higher than the Shannon frequency, f(x) can be reconstructed (but not $f_1(x)$) since $f_r(x) = f(x) \neq f_1(x)$. If the sampling rate is too low, $f_r(x)$ is different from f(x) because of aliasing.

Unfortunately in practice it is impossible, even in the first instance, to reconstruct $f(x)$ with total accuracy. This is because the form of pixel corresponding to the impulse response in figure V.12.a is physically impossible to produce. There is no way of creating negative illuminances! The same problem arises with time-related signals, but not for the same reasons.

The ideal reconstruction filter therefore does not exist. We shall return to this problem in section C. We shall see that the filters actually used introduce yet further errors. [2, 3].

B. ERRORS DUE TO SAMPLING

1. Shannon's condition

In practice this condition is never fulfilled for a real image because of noise. True, the useful image may have a sharp cut-off frequency, as is the case with images formed by optical systems. Despite this there is always background noise of some kind, such as the granularity of the photographic medium. This noise includes higher spatial frequencies.

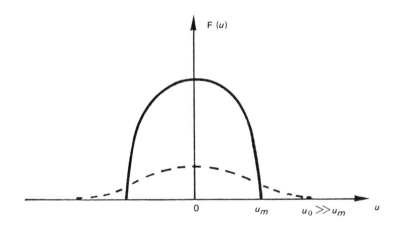

Fig.V.14 - Spectrum of a useful signal with a maximum frequency of u_m (unbroken line) and spectrum of the noise with a maximum frequency u_0 (dotted line). Generally $u_0 \gg u_m$. Even if Shannon's condition is observed for the signal, the presence of noise creates aliasing.

We can say that the spectrum of the image (fig.V.14) is the sum of the spectrum of a useful image with a maximum frequency u_m and the spectrum of a "noise" with a maximum frequency u_0. Frequency u_m is by and large equal to the reciprocal of the dimension of the smallest significant detail. Higher frequencies are unimportant. In general $u_0 \gg u_m$. Even if Shannon's condition is observed for the signal, the presence of noise creates aliasing. Interference frequencies are present within the spectrum of the signal. Figure V.15 shows how this problem applies to a two-dimensional spectrum. Since the spectrum of the useful signal is limited to the square with sides measuring $\frac{1}{T}$ and the noise spectrum is confined to the circular component, the four shaded areas correspond to the aliasing of neighbouring components within the square measuring $\frac{1}{T}$ along each side.

2. Prefiltering effect

We know that the finite size of the aperture or analysis spot acts as a low-pass image prefilter. The first consequence is a loss of resolution in the fine details, but there is also a favourable attenuation of high frequencies in the noise.

This has a beneficial effect with regard to the aliasing error. When we are free to choose the size of aperture we effect a compromise between loss of resolution and the aliasing error.

In order to compare different kinds of prefilter it is useful to set up a "perfect" prefilter as reference.

Let us examine the combination of a signal + a noise with a maximum frequency of u_m, sampled at a frequency of $\frac{1}{T}$.

If we had a perfect prefilter (but, like the perfect reconstruction filter, it is impossible in practice) with a cut-off frequency of $\frac{1}{2T}$ (fig.V.16.a) we could totally suppress the aliasing error without attenuating any of the frequencies below $\frac{1}{2T}$. In this fictitious situation, using the ideal reconstruction filter in figure V.12 with $u_1 = \frac{1}{2T}$ would make it possible to reconstruct all these frequencies accurately. Their spectrum is shown as a dotted line in figure V.16.a, and their corresponding maximum reconstructed signal energy is shown as E_{RM}.

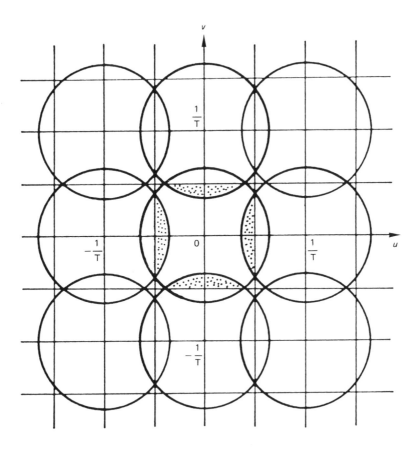

Fig.V.15 - Spectrum of a two-dimensional signal sampled at too low a rate: components overlap. The four shaded areas represent the aliasing of adjoining components within the square measuring $\frac{1}{T}$ along each side.

If we use a real prefilter, such as the one with its transfer function shown in figure V.16.b, it attenuates frequencies below $\frac{1}{2T}$ and the signal reconstructed by the ideal reconstruction filter has an energy $ER < E_{RM}$. If we ignore the energy derived from aliasing, we can write down the *resolution error* [3] introduced by this prefilter by calculating the relationship:

$$\epsilon_R = \frac{E_{RM} - E_R}{E_{RM}} \qquad (4)$$

(for the perfect prefilter $\epsilon_R = 0$ since $E_R = E_{RM}$).

In the same way, to find a notation for the aliasing error we continue to assume that the signal is being reconstructed by the ideal reconstruction filter, and we calculate the energy ER contributed by neighbouring components in frequency range $\left(-\frac{1}{2T}; \frac{1}{2T}\right)$ which is the range of the perfect prefilter (fig.V.17.a). This energy corresponds to the shaded areas in the diagram. If we assume that the contribution from the other components is negligible, it can easily be seen (fig.V.17.b) that this energy equals $E_0 0 - E_R$. $E_0 0$ is the total energy of the prefiltered signal and E_R is the energy of this signal corresponding to frequencies below $\frac{1}{2T}$, in other words the energy of the signal reconstructed by the ideal reconstruction filter.

We can find a notation for the aliasing error [3] from the relationship:

$$\epsilon_A = \frac{E_A}{E_0} = \frac{E_0 - E_R}{E_0} \qquad (5)$$

In the case of the perfect prefilter there is no aliasing: $(E_0 = E_R = E_{RM})$ and $\epsilon_A = 0$.

Figure V.18 makes it possible to compare resolution errors (fig.V.18.a) and aliasing errors (fig.V.18.b) for various kinds of prefilter. Calculations have been carried out for a signal with a Lorentzian spectrum, which is in the form $F(u) = \dfrac{A}{1 + \left(\dfrac{u}{u_c}\right)^2}$ The variable on the abscissa of the curves is $2Tu_m$ (where T is the sampling interval).

Curves {1} correspond to a circular lens with a cut-off frequency u_m, curves {2} are for a Gaussian spot with $\sigma = \dfrac{2}{u_m}$, and curves {3} refer to a square aperture of side $\dfrac{1}{u_m}$.

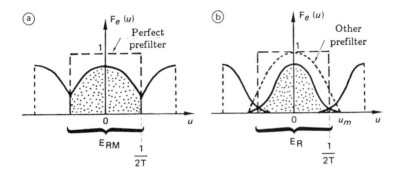

Fig.V.16 - a) A perfect prefilter with a cut-off frequency of $\frac{1}{2T}$ makes it possible to suppress the aliasing error without attenuating signal frequencies below $\frac{1}{2T}$; using the ideal reconstruction filter in figure V.12 with $u_1 = \frac{1}{2T}$ then makes it possible to reconstruct all these frequencies accurately; they correspond to E_{RM}, the maximum energy of the reconstructed signal, b) any other prefilter attenuates frequencies below $\frac{1}{2T}$ and the signal reconstructed by the ideal reconstruction filter has an energy $E\_R < E_{RM}$. The resolution error introduced by!this prefilter is derived from the equation $\epsilon_R = \dfrac{E_{RM} - E_R}{E_{RM}}$.

C. RECONSTRUCTION ERRORS

1. The ideal reconstruction filter

Let us re-examine the ideal reconstruction filter in figure V.8.c. Its impulse response is $g(x) = \text{sinc } \pi \frac{x}{T}$.

For a signal $f(x)$ sampled at a frequency of $\frac{1}{T}$, the reconstructed signal is $f_r(x) = f(x) = f_e(x) * \text{sinc } \pi \frac{x}{T}$.

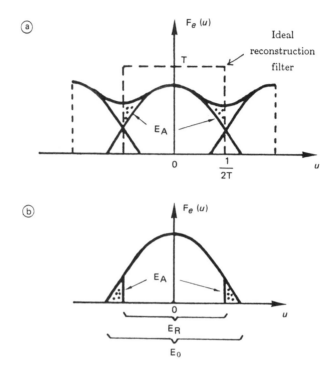

Fig.V.17 - a) The aliasing error obtained for a signal reconstructed by the ideal reconstruction filter corresponds to the frequencies in the shaded areas, with an energy of E_A. They are derived from adjoining components. The contribution from other components is assumed to be negligible. For two-dimensional situations see figure V.15, b)$E\_A = E_0 - E_R$:E_0 is the total energy of the prefiltered signal and E_R is the energy in this signal corresponding to frequencies below $\frac{1}{2T}$, being the energy of the signal reconstructed by the ideal reconstruction filter. The aliasing error is given by equation

$$\epsilon_A = \frac{E_A}{E_0} = \frac{(E_0 - E_R)}{E_0}.$$

$$= \sum_{n=-\infty}^{+\infty} f(nT)\, \delta(x - nT)) * \operatorname{sinc} \pi \frac{x}{T}$$

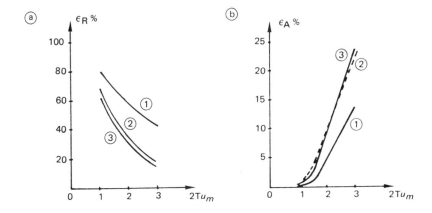

Fig.V.18 - Resolution error (figure a) and aliasing error (figure b) for various types of prefilter. The spectrum of the signal concerned is in the form

$$F(u) = \frac{A}{1 + \left(\dfrac{u}{u_c}\right)^2}$$

where T is the sampling interval; {1} circular lens with

cut-off frequency u_m, {2} Gaussian spot with $\sigma = \dfrac{2}{u_m}$ (see figure I.7), {3}

square aperture of side $\dfrac{1}{u_m}$.

$$= \sum_{n=-\infty}^{+\infty} f(nT) \left[\delta(x - nT) * \operatorname{sinc} \pi \frac{x}{T} \right]$$

giving

$$f(x) = \sum_{n=-\infty}^{+\infty} f(nT) \operatorname{sinc} \frac{\pi}{T}(x - nT) \qquad (6)$$

This operation is shown in diagram form in figure V.19. By summing samples $f(nT)$ weighted by sinc $\frac{\pi}{T}(x - nT)$ it is possible to reconstruct function $f(x)$ perfectly.

On this basis a constant signal equal to 1 leads to the equation:

$$1 = \sum_{n=-\infty}^{+\infty} \text{sinc } \frac{\pi}{T}(x - nT)$$

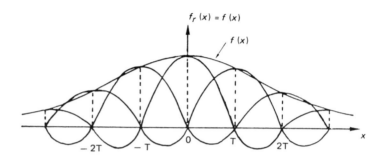

Fig.V.19   –   Ideal   reconstruction   of   signal   f(x)

$$f_{r(x)} = f(x) = \sum_{n=-\infty}^{+\infty} f(nT) \text{ sinc } \frac{\pi}{T}(x - nT).$$

Since it is physically impossible to produce the ideal reconstruction filter, we must examine filters of other kinds.

2. The zero-order blocking reconstruction filter

This filter produces an approximation of function $f(x)$ by a series of steps T wide, centred on sampling points nT. Its impulse response $r_0(x)$ is therefore a gate function T wide, and its transfer function is $R_0(u) = T \text{ sinc } \pi uT$. These are shown in figure V.20.

In two-dimensional situations this is the equivalent of reconstruction by adjoining square pixels.

3. Errors caused by a non-ideal reconstruction filter

Arguing from the zero-order blocking filter, it can be seen that a non-ideal reconstruction filter will introduce two kinds of fault:

a) a **loss of resolution**: the high frequencies in the signal will be smoothed by the impulse response, since there is a flat spot between two steps.

b) a **distortion** analogous to aliasing: frequencies not present in the original signal are produced, particularly the rapid transitions introduced by the steps. This may be thought of as an *interpolation error* between successive pixels, and generally shows on the image as frame lines. In the case of the zero-order blocking filter, frames can be seen around the actual pixels, and these do not exist on the original image.

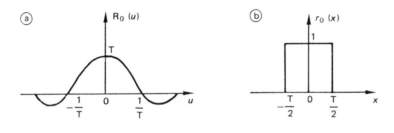

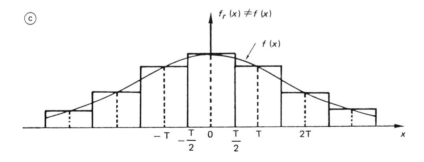

Fig.V.20 - Approximate reconstruction of a signal by a zero-order blocking filter: for an image this is the equivalent of reconstruction by adjoining square pixels; a) transfer function $R_0(u)$ for the filter, b) the corresponding impulse response $r_0(x)$, c) the reconstructed signal $f_r(x) \neq f(x)$.

A notation for these reconstruction errors can be developed by taking the example of a signal which is sampled at Shannon frequency

$\frac{1}{T} = 2u_0$. Spectrum $F_e(u)$ therefore consists of contiguous components (fig.V.21.a).

The ideal reconstruction filter with a transfer function of $G(u)$ makes it possible to retrieve total signal energy E_{RM} (the shaded area in figure V.21.a).

If another filter is used (fig.V.21.b) both the effects mentioned can be seen in the spectrum:

a) the useful frequencies $\left(< \frac{1}{2T}\right)$ are attenuated. From frequency range $\left(-\frac{1}{2T}; \frac{1}{2T}\right)$ it is possible to retrieve only energy $E\_R < E_{RM}$ shown by the shading. This gives a resolution error which can also be expressed [3] by the equation:

$$\epsilon_R = \frac{E_{RM} - E_R}{E_{RM}} \tag{7}$$

b) interference frequencies $\left(> \frac{1}{2T}\right)$ are introduced into the reconstructed signal spectrum from adjacent components. These components are represented by hatching in the figure, where it has been assumed that the filter has a cut-off frequency of $\frac{1}{T}$. By calling total reconstructed signal energy E_T, this interpolation error may be expressed [3] by the equation:

$$\epsilon_I = \frac{E_T - E_R}{E_T} \tag{8}$$

In the case of the ideal reconstruction filter $\epsilon_R = \epsilon_I = 0$.
For the zero-order blocking filter we find:
$$\epsilon_R = 26.9 \% \qquad \epsilon_I = 15.7 \%.$$

4. Other types of reconstruction filter

- some filters are of the *one-order blocking* or linear interpolation type. The reconstructed signal is obtained by joining successive sam-

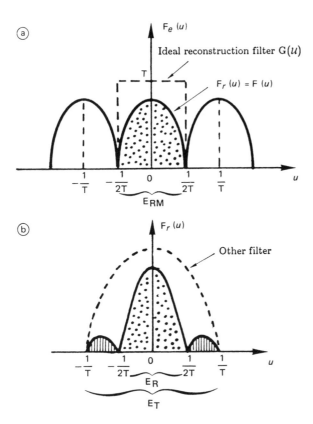

Fig.V.21 - Reconstruction of a signal which is sampled at Shannon frequency $\frac{1}{T} = 2u_0$: components are contiguous; a) ideal reconstruction: total signal energy E_{RM} is retrieved, b) actual reconstruction:

- useful frequencies ($\frac{1}{2T}$ are attenuated. Only energy $E_R < E_{RM}$ is retrieved (shaded area) giving resolution error $\epsilon_R = \dfrac{E_{RM} - E_R}{E_{RM}}$;

- in addition interference frequencies ($> \frac{1}{2T}$) are introduced into the reconstructed signal spectrum from adjacent components (shown as hatching in the figure, where it has been assumed that the filter has a cut-off frequency of $\frac{1}{T}$). By calling total reconstructed signal energy E_T, this interpolation error is

$$\epsilon_I = \dfrac{(E_T - E_R)}{E_T}.$$

ples with straight lines (fig.V.22.a). This corresponds to a saw-tooth impulse response of $r_1(x)$ (fig.V.22.c) and a transfer function of $R_1(u) = T \, (\text{sinc} \, \pi \, uT)^2$ (fig.V.22.b).

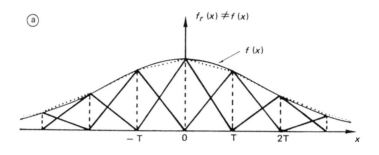

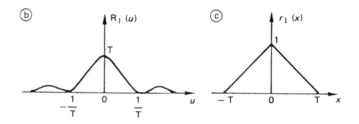

Fig.V.22 - Approximate reconstruction of a signal by a one-order blocking filter (or linear interpolator); a) reconstructed signal $f_r(x) \neq f_1(x)$, b) transfer function $R_1(u)$ of the filter, c) corresponding impulse response $r_1(x)$.

In this case reconstruction errors are as follows:
$$\epsilon_R = 44 \% \qquad \epsilon_I = 3.7 \%$$
- very often the filter has an impulse response which is *Gaussian* in shape. This is the situation for the spots on a cathode ray tube. If the Gaussian curve is defined by $\sigma = \dfrac{T}{2}$ we find:
$$\epsilon_R = 54.6 \% \qquad \epsilon_I = 2 \%$$
Quite apart from these objective error measurements, we have to take into account the response of the human eye. This can be very different depending on the appearance of the reconstructed image. As it turns out, the many short-duration, random incidents are "rubbed out" by the *eye's integrating effect* [6], which is very tolerant in such

situations. By contrast periodic frame effects are easily detected by the eye, which is good at spotting alignments and regular patterns. As for the "step" effect introduced by the reconstruction filter, we shall meet it again when we are looking at quantization. We shall find that in areas of turbulent contrast it is hardly noticeable, but where there is little variation it can create distracting "*density slicing*" effects due to *Mach's phenomenon* (see section D).

D. QUANTIZATION

We know that the intensity of each pixel is a continuous value which has to be expressed as a number. Quantization is usually carried out in conjunction with image sampling, by an analogue-to-digital converter which is instructed to carry out a conversion every time the spot crosses a sampling point. A simplified functional diagram for a digitizer is shown in figure V.23.

Let us assume for the sake of simplicity that quantization levels are equidistant. The less levels there are, the greater will be the degree of imprecision regarding the value to be attributed to each pixel. Quantization therefore introduces error, known as the *discretizing error*. This measurement error may be thought of as a source of noise, known as *quantizing noise*. It adds further noise to those present in the digitizer, and is distinct from errors arising during sampling. We shall be examining these sources of noise in section E. They determine measurement precision and what calculations can be carried out on the image.

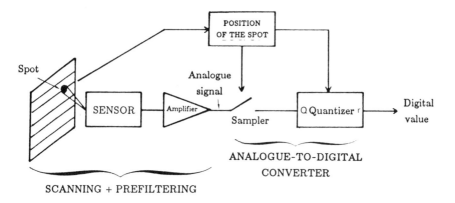

Fig.V.23 - Diagram of an image digitizer

During restoration pixels are similarly synthesised with the aid of digital-to-analogue converters (see chapter VIII). These take only a finite number of quantization levels into account. The most distracting effect which may be observed in an image displayed in this way is the creation of *false slices*. This phenomenon is hardly noticeable in areas of the image which have plenty of variety and contrasting detail. It occurs mainly in areas where the lighting intensity varies only gradually. Figure V.24 shows how the 256 x 256 pixels image in figure V.3.a is affected by decreasing the number of levels.

The explanation for this is *Mach's phenomenon* [6] which has the effect of emphasising transitions allowing the human eye to differentiate even very similar levels of grey if they are adjacent. Figure V.25 shows that it is possible to distinguish between 32 levels when they are contiguous, whereas it is no longer possible to distinguish between two of these very similar levels if a band of black is placed between them.

In practice digital-to-analogue converters working with 256 levels are generally adequate.

With respect to inaccuracies in calculation, it may be tempting to reduce the quantization error by using converters with a high number of levels, such as ten bits/1024 levels, or twelve bits/4096 levels. This is comparable to that other tempting possibility, over-sampling so as to minimise aliasing errors. But it is important to beware the volume of information which then has to be handled, as well as the calculation time which may be required.

- The *amount of information* contained in a digitized image.

A square image of N lines with N pixels per line, each pixel being coded over n bits, requires storage of N^2 x n bits.

By way of example let us suppose that we wish to digitize a 6 cm x 6 cm photograph at a sampling interval of 5 microns with a 12-bit converter. The number of pixels is then:

$$\left(\frac{60,000}{5}\right)^2 = 144 \text{ x } 10^6 \text{ pixels.}$$

Number of bits: 144 x 10^6 x 12 = 1.7 x 10^9 bits or 1.7 thousand million bits.

Remembering that a 2400-foot, 1600 bpi magnetic tape can hold around 320 million bits, it would take more than 5 magnetic tapes to store this photograph, which would be quite unreasonable. Since a limit is imposed on the quantizer, the sampling interval has to be increased. Consequently the size of the analysis spot needs to be selected taking into account the smallest size of detail to be observed.

Fig.V.24 - Quantizing the 256 x 256 pixels image in figure V.3.a: the effects of reducing the number of levels; a) 256 levels; b) 16 levels; c) 8 levels.

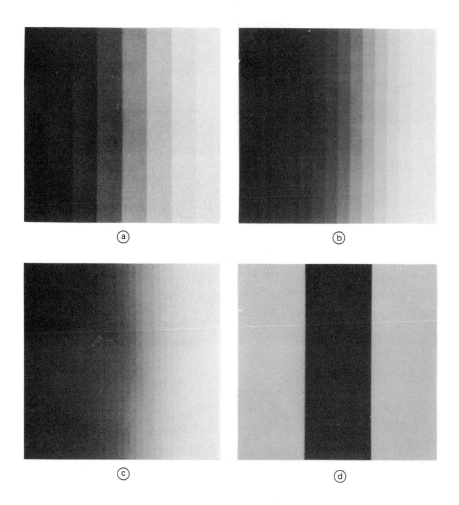

Fig.V.25 - Mach's phenomenon allows the human eye to differentiate even very similar levels of grey if they are adjacent. This is the phenomenon of transition emphasis (the edge effect); a) 8 levels, b) 16 levels, c) 32 levels, d) two of the very similar levels in figure c can no longer be distinguished if a band of black is placed between them.

E. THE DIGITIZING CHAIN

1. Measurement noise: sensor noise, electronic noise, quantization noise

The block diagram in figure V.26 corresponds to the functional diagram in figure V.23. The sensor is a photodetector which receives a flux of photons and delivers a signal which is integrated in the course of time constant. The analogue signal obtained is then amplified in an electronic measuring device. This is a linear channel for digitizing transmittance or a logarithmic channel for processing optical density. The analogue-to-digital converter then carries out its sampling and quantizing routine. The various "technological" measuring errors (not counting errors of principle related to sampling at too low a rate) have been shown as additional noises superimposed on the useful signal at various points in the chain: sensor noise, electronic noise and quantization noise.

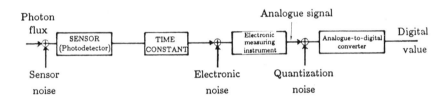

Fig.V.26 - Block diagram corresponding to the functional diagram in figure V.23. The various measuring errors have been shown as noises superimposed on the useful signal at various points in the measuring chain: noise inherent in the sensor (created mainly by "photon noise" in the case of a photomultiplier), noise from the electronics and quantization noise (due to the "step" height in the quantizer).

We can ignore electronic noise, as sensor noise and quantization noise are generally so much greater.

- *Important note:*

As we are now examining the digitizing chain, we are not bringing in any of the various noises which can exist on the object being measured. But these noises are important, and indeed may even exceed digitizer noise. When digitizing a photographic negative using a microdensitometer, for instance, granularity noise from the emulsion can often be the dominant effect (see chap.IV).

a) **Sensor noise**

Let us take the example of the *photomultiplier* (fig.V.27). The photon flux arrives at the photocathode, which outputs a current in proportion to the flux. This current is amplified by a system of dynodes connected in cascade and an anode current is received which is also proportional to the incident flux. This current is averaged by an integrating circuit which is often a simple RC circuit with terminals from which a voltage V is collected as the output signal.

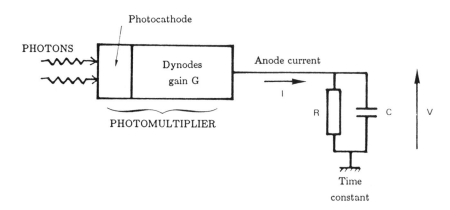

Fig.V.27 - Example of a sensor: the photomultiplier with its time constant. The signal is a voltage created by the anode current and generally collected at the terminals of the RC circuit.

To study the noise arising in this output signal let us consider the individual photons arriving at the photocathode (fig.V.28). They give rise to a random process which is a *Poisson process*. The number of photons N reaching the photocathode per second is a Poisson random variable such that:

$$P(N = n) = \frac{\lambda^n}{n!} e^{-\lambda}$$

$\lambda = \langle N \rangle$ the mean number of photons per second is called the *process density*.

The standard deviation of N is: $\sigma_N = \sqrt{\lambda}$.

As with a photographic emulsion, we define the *equivalent quantum efficiency* (E.Q.E.) of the photocathode. This is the probability r that a photon will create a photo-electron.

Thus the photocathode emits photo-electrons distributed evenly according to a Poisson process with a density of λr.

If N′ is the random variable representing the number of such photo-electrons emitted per second, we have: $P(N = n) = (\lambda r)^n \dfrac{e^{-\lambda r}}{n!}$ and $\langle N' \rangle = \lambda r$, $\sigma_{N'} = \sqrt{\lambda r}$.

Since each photo-electron has an elementary charge e, the derived mean photocathode current is $I_C = e\lambda r$.

By introducing frequency f it can be shown that these processes are perfect examples of "white noise". For example the spectral power density (or Wiener's spectrum) of the photocathode current is: $W_{I_C}(f) = e^2 \lambda r$.

If we assume that the process of amplifying the current by dynode gain G contributes no fluctuation, the anode outputs a current composed of packets of electrons, each carrying a charge Ge and distributed according to the same Poisson process with density λr.

Mean anode current is therefore: $I_a = eG\lambda r$ and its Wiener's spectrum is: $W_{I_a}(f) = e^2 G^2 \lambda r$.

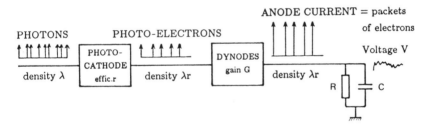

Fig.V.28 - To study noise in the output voltage of the photomultiplier, we must consider the Poisson distribution of the incoming photons, the photo-electrons at the photocathode and the packets of electrons comprising the anode current.

This current passes through the circuit RC and its terminals yield a voltage with a mean value of $V = RI_a = eG\lambda rR$. The transfer function for the circuit is $G(f) = \dfrac{R}{1 + 2\pi j f RC}$ and Wiener's spectrum for this voltage is therefore (see chap.IV, section F.3)

$$W_V(f) = W_{I_a}(f) \, |G(f)|^2 = e^2 G^2 \lambda r \, \frac{R^2}{1 + 4\pi^2 f^2 R^2 C^2}$$

The standard deviation for this noise is derived from the equations in chap.IV, section F.3.

$$\sigma_V^2 = \int_{-\infty}^{+\infty} W_V(f) \, df$$

We find

$$\sigma_V^2 = e^2 G^2 \lambda r \, \frac{R}{2C}$$

Giving:

$$\sigma_V = eG \sqrt{\lambda r \, \frac{R}{2C}}$$

The *signal-to-noise* ratio for output from the sensor is:

$$\boxed{SNR = \frac{V}{\sigma_V} = \sqrt{2 \, RC \, \lambda r}} \tag{9}$$

It has the following properties:
- it is independent of dynode gain G
- it increases with photocathode efficiency r
- it increases with the RC time constant selected (to the detriment, naturally, of measuring rate)
- it increases with the square root of the flux being measured: it is also possible to say that relative measurement accuracy $\frac{\sigma_V}{V}$ is inversely proportional to the square root of the flux or even that it varies by $\frac{1}{\sqrt{T}}$ when transmittance T is being measured.

- *Note:* it is easy to find the proportionality of SNR to $\sqrt{RC\lambda r}$ without Wiener's spectra. If we take it that RC represents measuring time, the number of packets of electrons emitted by the anode during this time is a Poisson random variable with mean value $RC\lambda r$ and standard deviation $\sqrt{RC\lambda r}$. Taking the signal-to-noise ratio to be proportional to the ratio $\frac{\text{mean value}}{\text{standard deviation}}$ the result shown above can be derived.

b) **Quantization noise**

If the quantization rate is designated P, it is possible to show statistically [11] that the measurement uncertainty created in this way corresponds to a noise Q with standard deviation such that $\sigma_Q^2 = \dfrac{P^2}{12}$ when P is small in proportion to the signal being measured.

This gives

$$\sigma_Q \simeq \frac{P}{3.5} \tag{10}$$

Since P is a constant, the resulting relative measurement accuracy varies by $\dfrac{1}{T}$ when transmittance T is being measured.

c) Resultant noise

As sensor noise and quantization noise have different physical origins they are not correlated. It can be shown in this case that the standard deviations are related quadratically [11] such that the resulting standard deviation σ is:

$$\sigma_T^2 = \sigma_V^2 + \sigma_Q^2 \tag{11}$$

Example 1:
Microdensitometer digitizer (fig.V.29).

The sensor is a photomultiplier. It is assumed that $\dfrac{\sigma_V}{V} = 3 \times 10^{-3}$ at maximum flux (T = 1). If the analogue-to-digital converter could work at an infinitely small rate, it would be possible to measure transmissions as small as 10^{-5} $\left(\text{at } T = 10^{-5}, \dfrac{\sigma_V}{V} \text{ would reach } 100 \%\right)$.

Assuming a quantizer with 10^4 levels, it becomes apparent that quantization noise is the dominant effect below $T = 10^{-3}$, and that this is the limiting factor on the measurement dynamics. For $T = 10^{-4}$ (= quantizer rate) we have $\dfrac{\sigma_Q}{Q} = 100 \%$, giving dynamics of 10^4.

A quantizer with 10^3 levels (or less) places serious limits on measurement accuracy and dynamics when using a sensor with the qualities of a photomultiplier.

Example 2
Video camera digitizer (fig.V.30).

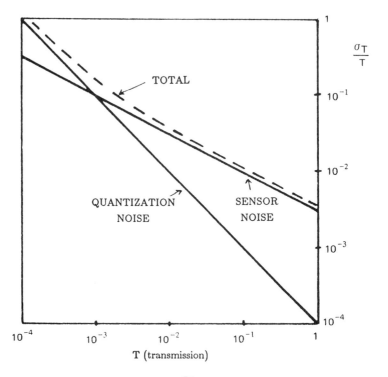

Fig.V.29 - Relative transmission error $\frac{\sigma_T}{T}$ as a function of T for a digitizer using a photomultiplier and a quantizer with 10^4 levels. Electronic noise is assumed to be negligible.

It can be shown that similar results are obtained. Sensor noise still varies in units of $\frac{1}{\sqrt{T}}$ but is much more significant. Assuming that

$\frac{\sigma_V}{V}$ = 3 x 10^{-3} at maximum flux, then even in conditions as optimistic as these, sensor noise is by and large the dominant effect, and there is no point in using quantizers with a large number of levels. Here we have assumed 256 levels, and this gives a dynamic range of 256.

Note 1. There is another reason in favour of using quantizers with a large number of levels. If calculations need to be carried out using several images, inaccuracies are summed and there is a risk that the results will be meaningless. Also we should recall the Mach phenomenon. Whilst it is accepted that the human eye cannot differentiate more than about forty levels of grey, it can perceive many more

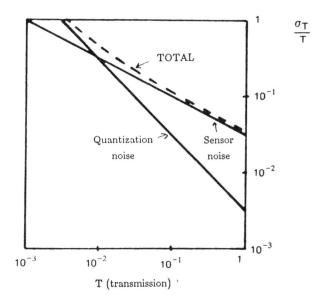

Fig.V.30 - Relative error $\dfrac{\sigma_T}{T}$ as a function of T for a video camera

digitizer with a quantizer operating on 256 levels.

(perhaps as many as 256) when they are adjacent.

Note 2. The dynamic range of a digitizer or restorer is still low compared to the total dynamic range of the human eye, which can adapt to ambient brightness spanning a total of six orders of magnitude (10^6). Its "instantaneous" dynamic range is estimated at two orders of magnitude, that is to say, around 100-fold range in brightness.

2. Other faults: photometric defects and geometric defects.

In addition to the measurement noises we have just examined, defects can arise from many sources to restrict the photometric or geometric accuracy of an image digitizer.

• **Photometric defects**

- Non-linear characteristics in the sensor, the electronics and the analogue-to-digital converter.

- drift of operating characteristics with time or temperature changes.

- the response time of the various elements in the chain.

- optical defects, such as geometric and chromatic aberrations, focussing errors, instability of the analysis spot.

- measurement errors detected in the photographic medium (Callier

effect, etc) particularly the proximity effect.
- the surface of the object being digitized fails to respond uniformly throughout.
   • **Geometric defects**
- inaccuracy in establishing and recalling the positions of sampling points.
- irregularities in the sampling grid (orthogonality defects, various kinds of distortion).

3. Essential characteristics of image digitizers

It is possible to draw a distinction between geometric and photometric characteristics [5].
   a) **Geometric characteristics**
- an upper limit to the size of image which can be digitized.
- spatial resolution: a lower limit to the scanning spot size, choice of sampling interval and resolution of the optics.
- the accuracy, reproducibility and linearity of the sampling grid.
- an upper limit to speed of spot movement.
   b) **Photometric characteristics**
- the quantity measured: transmittance or optical density by either transmission or reflection.
- measurement dynamic range = ratio of maximum signal to minimum signal.
- sensitivity: minimum detectable quantity (determined either by inherent sensor noise or quantization rate).
- the number of quantization levels.
- the signal-to-noise ratio or measurement accuracy (usually given for the maximum signal).
- linearity of response at a given point.
- photometric stability (with time and temperature).
- uniformity of response over the entire measured surface.
- response time.
- spectral response (wavelength of the light).
   By way of example, we give below the characteristics of the digitizer at the C.D.S.I. (Centre de Dépouillement et de Synthèse des Images) at Orsay. The device in question is a PDS 1010 G Perkin-Elmer type microdensitometer:
- maximum negative size: 20 x 20 cm
- minimum aperture 5 μ x 5 μ
- minimum sampling interval: 1 μ
- optical resolution: 1000 mm^{-1} at 200 x magnification in the object plane (see section 4.b)

- sampling grid accuracy: $\left\{\begin{array}{l} \text{reproducibility} \pm 1 \ \mu \\ \text{linearity} \pm 5 \ \mu \text{ in 20 cm} \end{array}\right\}$
- maximum rate of movement: 200 mm/s
- quantities measured: T and D (by transmission)
- measurement range: $\left\{\begin{array}{l} \text{T: 100 \% at } 2.5 \times 10^{-4} \\ \text{D: 0 to 4.} \end{array}\right\}$

- sensitivity: $\left\{\begin{array}{l} \text{T: } 2.5 \times 10^{-4} \\ \text{D: } 3 \times 10^{-3} \end{array}\right\}$
- number of quantization levels: 4096

- measurement accuracy: $\left\{\begin{array}{l} \dfrac{\Delta T}{T} = 3 \times 10^{-3} \text{ (for T = 1)} \\ \Delta D = 3 \times 10^{-3} \text{ (for D = 0)} \end{array}\right\}$

- photometric linearity: $\left\{\begin{array}{l} \text{T: } \pm 0.5 \ \% \\ \text{D: } \pm 0.02 \ D \end{array}\right\}$

- stability over time: $\left\{\begin{array}{l} \text{T: } \pm 1 \ \% \\ \text{D: } \pm 0.02 \ D \end{array}\right\}$ $\quad \begin{array}{l} \text{in 10 hours} \\ \text{after 45 min. warm-up} \end{array}$
- maximum measuring rate: 25,000 pixels/second
- frequency response of electronics: 30 μs.

4. Transfer function of a digitizer

We know that one of the basic characteristics of a digitizing system is the size of the scanning spot. It must be suited to the smallest detail needing to be scanned on the image, so as to avoid over-sampling. But a digitizer usually has an optical part with a certain magnification, so the dimensions and spatial frequencies *at the object plane* have to be taken into consideration. It is also necessary to take account, where appropriate, of measurement chain response time. This is generally the same as the integration time constant located at the sensor output (fig.V.27 and V.28). This time constant amounts to a widening of the spot, which moves slightly during the period in question. Here again it is necessary to base one's calculations on the object plane, taking the scanning rate into account.

We shall now give two examples showing how to go about reducing the transfer functions of the various linear elements in the chain to an overall transfer function of the digitizer expressed as a function of the spatial frequencies of the object [2].

a) *First example: digitizer = microscope + video camera* [2]

Let us consider the assembly in figure V.31.a, where a vidicon tube camera is placed in series with a microscope in order to observe objects (in this case cells) with a diameter of 1 μ in a field measuring 100 x 100 μ.

The linear part of this assembly can be illustrated by the sketch in figure V.31.b, where the three basic linear filters are the microscope, the scanning spot and the amplifier (the various measurement errors have been represented by adding a noise $b(x,y)$ to the useful signal).

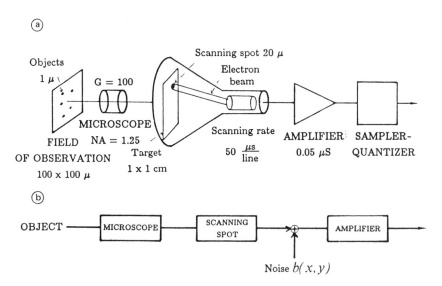

Fig.V.31 - Example of a digitizer consisting of a microscope + vidicon tube camera; a) operating principles, b) diagram of the linear part. The various measurement errors are represented by a noise b(x,y) added to the useful signal.

Figure   V.32   shows   the   spectrum   of   the   object

$\left(\text{with a cut-off frequency of } \dfrac{1}{(10^{-3} \text{ mm})} = 10^3 \text{ mm}^{-1}\right)$ and the

transfer functions of the three linear elements in figure V.31, where the spatial frequencies are those of the object plane:

- the O.T.F. of the microscope is determined by the cut-off frequency (assuming incoherent light)

$$f_c = \frac{2NA}{\lambda} = \frac{2 \times 1.25}{0.5 \times 10^{-3}} \text{ mm}^{-1} = 5 \times 10^3 \text{ mm}^{-1}$$

(see chapter III, section C.4).
- when reduced to the object plane, the dimension of the scanning

spot (which is Gaussian) is $\frac{20\mu}{100} = 0.2 \, \mu$ being a frequency of

$\frac{1}{0.2 \times 10^{-3}} \text{ mm}^{-1} = 5 \times 10^3 \text{ mm}^{-1}$ at $\frac{1}{\sqrt{e}}$.

- the time constant of the amplifier ($0.05 \, \mu s$) corresponds to a distance

in the object plane of $\frac{100}{50} \times 0.05 \, \mu = 0.1 \, \mu$, which is therefore a spa-

tial frequency of 10^4 mm^{-1}.

It can be seen that the overall digitizer response, which basically is determined by the microscope O.T.F., is well suited to digitizing the objects in question.

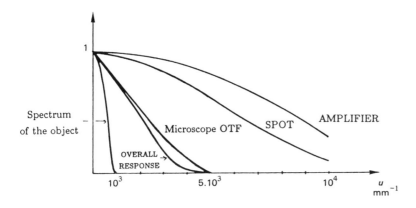

Fig.V.32 - Spectrum of the object and transfer functions of the three linear elements in figure V.31 (the spatial frequencies are those of the object plane). The overall transfer function is determined basically by the microscope O.T.F.

b) *Second example: the microdensitometer at the C.D.S.I.*
This device has two apertures, one for illumination and the other for scanning. A simplified diagram of its optical arrangement is shown at figure V.33. An illuminating microscope operating as a reducer is used to form the image of the illumination aperture in the plane of the negative being scanned. The image is captured by a scanning microscope of the same magnification. It acts as an enlarger and pro-

jects this image in the plane of a scanning aperture which is slightly smaller than the illumination aperture, in view of the Schwarzschild-Villiger effect (see chap.IV, section E.3). Thus the useful "spot" in the plane of the negative is this scanning aperture divided by the magnification.

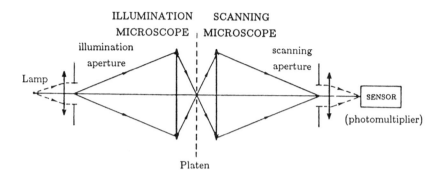

Fig.V.33 - Simplified optical diagram of a microdensitometer type of digitizer with twin illumination and scanning apertures. The illumination and scanning microscopes are shown symbolically as lenses.

The photocathode in the photomultiplier receives a flux of light which is proportional to the mean transmittance of this small area of the object. It is scanned by mechanical displacement of the platen. A more detailed diagram is shown in figure V.34. The optical fibre bundle makes it possible to observe the complete field of the instrument on the ground-glass screen. The illumination and scanning apertures are selected by rotating wheels. The red, green and blue filters are for scanning a three-colour image in three successive passes. The neutral filters are used for calibrating the equipment in order to operate at all times in the area of linear response of the photomultiplier.

Figure V.35 shows the microdensitometer and its control console.

Let us calculate the equipment transfer function. For this purpose we shall use figure V.36, showing a diagram of the scanning and measuring parts of the microdensitometer. We shall assume that we wish to scan a 10 μ object with a 5 μ square scanning aperture (the true aperture measures $5 \times 10^{-3} \times 200 = 1$ mm).

The spectrum of the object and the transfer functions of the linear system elements (aperture, scanning microscope and amplifier time constant) are shown in figure V.37, where it has been assumed that the scanning rate is 40 mm/s. At this speed the 30 μs time constant is

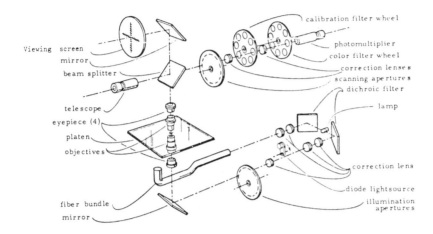

Fig.V.34 - Detailed optical diagram of the PDS 1010 twin aperture Perkin-Elmer microdensitometer. The optical fibre bundle makes it possible to observe the complete field of the instrument on the ground-glass screen. The illumination and scanning apertures are selected by rotating a wheel. The red, green and blue filters are for scanning a colour image (in three successive passes). The neutral filters are used for calibrating the equipment in order to operate in the area of linear response of the photomultiplier.

equivalent to an aperture in the plane of the negative with a width of $40 \times 30 \times 10^{-6}$ mm = 1.2×10^{-3} mm, which thus equates to a cut-off frequency of $\dfrac{1}{(1.2 \times 10^{-3} \text{ mm}^{-1})} = 8 \times 10^2$ mm^{-1}.

It is therefore the aperture transfer function which determines overall response. It would no longer be possible to ignore amplifier response at high scan speeds.

- *Note:* returning to expression (9) for the signal-to-noise ratio at the photomultiplier output, it might be thought possible to enhance this ratio by increasing time constant RC. Apart from the disadvantage mentioned above about reducing the measuring rate, it can be seen that this operation would also have the effect of widening the equivalent aperture in the plane of the negative. The overall transfer func-

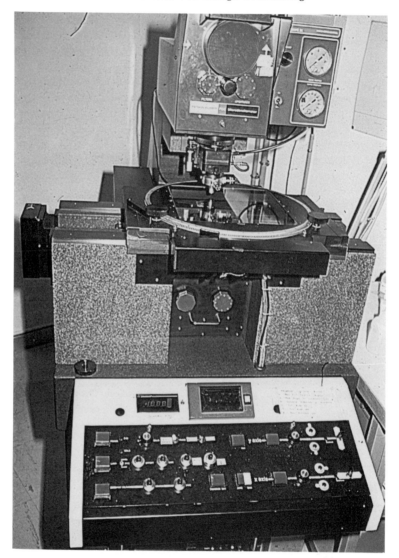

Fig.V.35 - The PDS 1010 microdensitometer and its control console.

tion of the equipment would no longer be that of the scanning aperture.

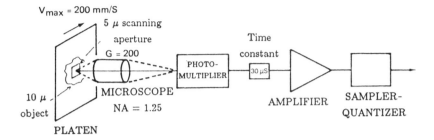

Fig.V.36 - Functional diagram of the scanning and measuring parts
of the microdensitometer digitizer.

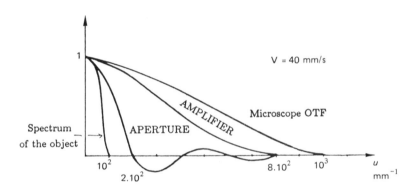

Fig.V.37 - Spectrum of the object and transfer functions of the linear system elements in figure V.36 (the spatial frequencies are those of the object plane). At
the scanning rate selected ($\frac{40 \text{ mm}}{\text{s}}$) overall system response is limited by the
aperture transfer function.

6

Basic techniques of digital image processing

A. Introduction

The term "basic techniques" is used to include all the *point operations* which can be carried out on an analogue or digital image.

A point operation is one which transforms an input image $A(x,y)$ into an output image $B(x,y)$ in accordance with a law f, which may or may not be linear and is consistent for the whole image:

$$B(x,y) = f[A(x,y)]$$

In the case of digitized images, each starting pixel is converted to another pixel at the same location which derives its grey level from the original pixel using law f. Such operations therefore handle *dynamic range* and *contrast*. For example the law for figure VI.1.a, which shows two trend segments with slopes less than and greater than one, will reduce the contrast in dull areas of the image and heighten contrast in light areas.

The operation illustrated in figure VI.1.b converts the image to binary giving only black or white. This is a *threshold operation*, in which all pixels below the threshold value turn black and all those above it turn white.

If we wish to consider how these operations alter the distribution of grey levels in the image without disturbing its geometry, it is useful to introduce the concept of the *histogram*.

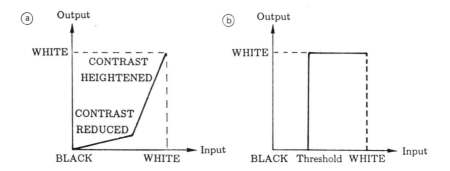

Fig.VI.1 - a) Manipulating image contrast, b) converting an image to binary with a threshold operation. All values below the threshold are converted to black, all those above are converted to white.

B. Histogram and cumulative histogram of an image

1. The continuous image [2]

Let us consider the image in figure VI.2, showing an object which increases in density towards the centre. Two curves of equal density, or *isodensity* curves, have been plotted for $D = D_1$ and $D = D_2 > D_1$.

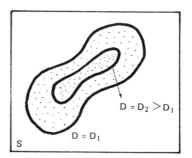

Figure VI.2 - In this image density D is assumed to be continuous and increases regularly towards the centre. Isodensity curves have been plotted for D_1 and $D_2 > D_1$.

Let S be the total surface area of the image. It may be useful to know the surface area of region S_1 lying outside the curve $D = D_1$, the surface area of region S_2 outside the curve $D = D_2$, and so on. In more general terms, it is possible to define a function S(D) which equals the surface area of image regions with density $\leq$ D. Surface area function S(D) increases with D and reaches maximum value S (being the total surface area of the image) for maximum density D = D_{max} (fig.VI.3.a).

The surface area of image regions with density values in the very narrow range D to D + dD is:

$$S(D + dD) - S(D) = S'(D) \, dD$$

where $S'(D)$ is the derivative of function S (D).

It is then said that $\boxed{S'(D) = h(D)}$ (1)

is the *histogram* of the image (fig.VI.3.b).

Conversely S(D) is the primitive of $h(D)$ and cancels out for D = 0. It is called the *cumulative histogram* of the image.

$$\boxed{\int_0^D h(D) \, dD = S(D)}$$ (2)

In this way we obtain $S_1 = \int_0^{D_1} h(D) \, dD$ shown by the shaded area

in the figure, and $S = \int_0^{D_{max}} h(D) \, dD$. The surface area of the histo-

gram equals the surface area of the image.

If D_{max} is not known we can still write:

$$S = \int_0^{+\infty} h(D) \, dD$$

Returning to figure VI.2, we can take it that the outline of the object is defined by the curve $D = D_1$, and that its surface area is:

$$S - S(D_1) = \int_{D_1}^{+\infty} h(D)\, dD$$

The analogy with calculating probabilities

$\dfrac{h(D)}{S}$ is analogous to a *probability density* and it is possible to write

$\dfrac{h(D)}{S} = p(D)$.

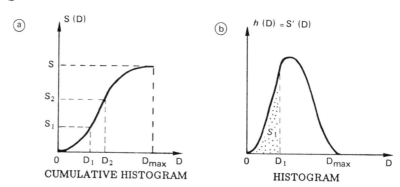

Fig.VI.3 - a) Surface area function S(D) of the continuous image with total surface area S in figure VI.2. S(D) represents the area of the image region(s) with
a density equal to or less than D, b) histogram h(D) is the derivative of the
surface area function. S(D) can therefore be interpreted as the primitive of
h(D) which cancels out for D = 0. It is the "cumulative histogram" of the
image, and is a function which increases from 0 to S.

In fact $p(D)\, dD$ is the proportion of points with densities in the
range D to D + dD, that is the probability of any point on the image
having a density in the following range:

$$P(D \leq \text{density} < D + dD) = p(D)dD$$

Similarly $\dfrac{S(D)}{S} = F(D)$ is analogous to a *distribution function* in
statistics, being the probability of a point having a density equal to or
less than D.

2. The discrete image

Let us assume that the image in figure VI.2 has been digitized, that is sampled into N pixels, each of which has been quantized into n levels in the range $d_0, d_1, ... d_{n-1}$.

The surface area function S(D) becomes $S(d_k)$ = the number of pixels with a level $\leq d_k$ and is written $H(d_k)$.

Similarly function $S'(D) = h(D)$ becomes:

$$h(d_k) = H(d_k) - H(d_{k-1}) = N_k$$

being the number of pixels with level d_k

so that

$$\boxed{h(d_k) = N_k}$$ (3)   histogram

and

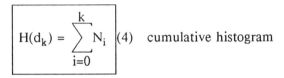

$$\boxed{H(d_k) = \sum_{i=0}^{k} N_i}$$ (4)   cumulative histogram

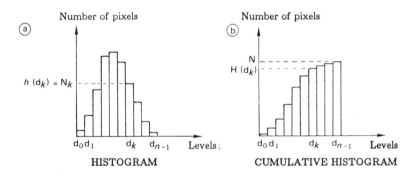

HISTOGRAM   CUMULATIVE HISTOGRAM

Fig.VI.4 - Discrete histograms of the image in figure VI.2 after digitization (sampled into N pixels, each of which has been quantized into n levels in the range $d_0, d_1, ... d_{n-1}$); a) histogram $h(d_k) = N_k$ the number of pixels of level d_k, b) cumulative histogram $H(d_k) = \sum_{i=0}^{k} N_i$ the number of pixels of level $\leq d_k$.

These are step functions (fig.VI.4.a and b). $H(d_k)$ increases from 0 to N, being the number of pixels in the image, since $\sum_{i=0}^{n-1} N_i = N$.

The analogy with calculating probabilities

$$\frac{h(d_k)}{N} = \frac{N_k}{N} = p_k$$
    the frequency of level d_k, or the probability of obtaining this level.

$$\frac{H(d_k)}{N} = F_k$$
    distribution function = probability of obtaining a level $\leq d_k$.

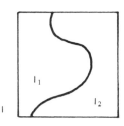

Fig.VI.5 - Image I broken down into two distinct sub-images I_1 and I_2.

Note: If an image I comprises two distinct areas or sub-images I_1 and I_2 (fig.VI.5) for which histograms $h_1(D)$ and $h_2(D)$ are known, it is clear that histogram $h(D)$ for image I is the sum of $h_1(D) + h_2(D)$. There is no difficulty in extending this property to any number of distinct areas.

3. Uses of the histogram [1,2]

There are many uses, but for the moment it is enough to indicate three important applications.

a) Digitization quality
The structure of the discrete histogram makes it possible to judge whether an image has been correctly digitized from the point of view of matching the dynamic range of its densities (D_{min} to D_{max}) to the dynamic range of the quantizer levels (d_0 to d_{n-1}).
- figure VI.6.a: the dynamic range is too narrow so that very few

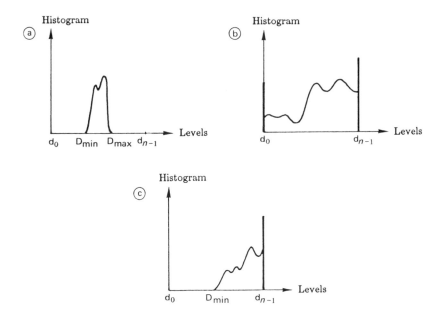

Fig.VI.6 - The histogram makes it possible to judge whether an image has been digitized with its dynamic range of densities (D_{min} to D_{max}) correctly matched to the dynamic range of the quantizer levels (d_0 to d_{n-1}); a) the dynamic range is too low and very few levels are shown, b) the dynamic range is too wide and overflows the high and low level dynamic range. Levels d_0 and d_{n-1} are "saturated" and densities outside these limits are lost, c) the dynamic range is off centre.

levels are shown. We have seen the disadvantage of using a limited number of levels from the point of view of calculation accuracy and displaying the image. In particular if we wish to heighten image contrast we are obliged to increase the distance between these levels whilst they remain the same in number, increasing the risk of false isocontours.

- figure VI.6.b: the dynamic range is too wide so that the high and low values are concentrated at two levels only, d_0 and d_{n-1}. Corresponding density values are therefore lost.

- figure VI.6.c: the dynamic range is off centre so that all high values have been lost.

Figure VI.7 shows an example of digitizing the density of a pale, poorly contrasted negative (fig.VI.7.a). The digitized image is practi-

(a)

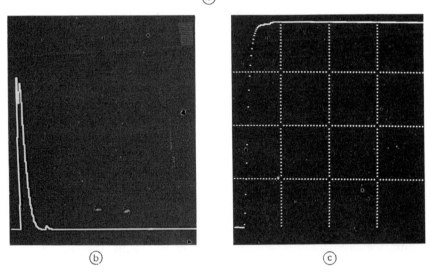

(b)   (c)

Fig.VI.7 - Histogram and cumulative histogram of a digitized image; a) the continuous image is a pale and poorly contrasted negative, b) The digitized image
and its histogram, mainly concentrated towards the low density values, c) the
corresponding cumulative histogram.

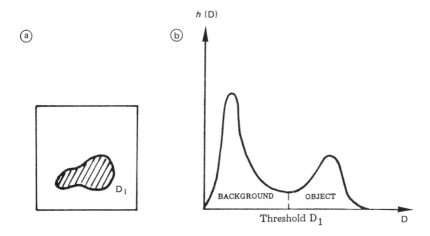

Fig.VI.8 - Using the histogram as an aid to choosing the
binary conversion threshold of an image.

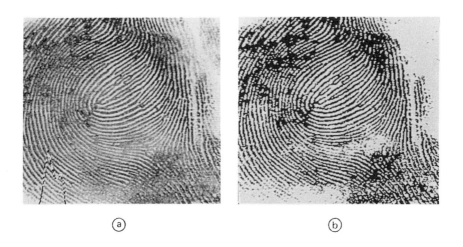

Fig.VI.9 - Binary conversion of an image by the threshold technique; a) the image
of a fingerprint and its double-peaked histogram, b) binary conversion of the
fingerprint by selecting the saddle of the histogram as the threshold.

cally invisible, since its histogram is concentrated too far towards the
low values of D (fig. VI.7.b). The corresponding cumulative histogram

is shown in figure VI.7.c (the abscissa has 256 quantization levels).

b) Choice of threshold for the threshold technique

Let the object be dark on a light background (fig.VI.8.a).

The histogram is helpful when choosing a threshold which will give the best possible definition of the outline of the object. There are two peaks in this histogram (fig.VI.8.b), one corresponding to the background and the other to the object.

It can be shown that the optimum choice of threshold is at abscissa D_1 of the histogram minimum, since that is the point at which surface area function S(D) varies most slowly and is therefore least sensitive to the choice of D.

An example of this will be found in figure VI.9, where a) shows the image of a fingerprint and its double-peaked histogram and b) shows conversion of the fingerprint into a binary image and selecting the saddle of the histogram as the threshold.

c) Mean grey level of an image or of an object contained within it.

Let the value for calculation be the mean density D of an image (or part of an image) which is continuous and of surface area S.

Instead of calculating the spatial mean

$$\overline{D} = \frac{1}{S} \iint_S D(x,y) \, dx \, dy$$

since the double integral applies to the whole surface of the image, it is easier to use histogram $h(D)$ and calculate the weighted mean of all density values encountered, that is the simple integral:

$$\overline{D} = \frac{1}{S} \int_0^{+\infty} Dh(D) \, dD \tag{5}$$

By applying the probabilities analogy, this amounts in fact to calculating the statistical mean $\overline{D} = \int_0^{+\infty} Dp(D) \, dD.$

Similarly if we wish to calculate, say, a mean value for the object in figure VI.8.a outlined by isodensity curve D_1 we write:

$$\overline{D}_{object} = \frac{\displaystyle\int_{D_1}^{+\infty} D h(D)\, dD}{\displaystyle\int_{D_1}^{+\infty} h(D)\, dD}$$

The analogous formulae for a discrete histogram are written:

$$\overline{D} = \frac{1}{N} \sum_{k=0}^{n-1} d_k\, N_k$$

$$\overline{D}_{object} = \frac{\displaystyle\sum_{k=k_1}^{n-1} d_k\, N_k}{\displaystyle\sum_{k=k_1}^{n-1} N_k}$$

4. Examples of histograms of simple images

a) **Circular image** with centre O and unit radius for which the density law is a hemisphere (fig.VI.10.a and b) giving

$$D^2 = 1 - r^2$$

The surface area function is $S(D) = \pi - \pi r^2 = \pi(1 - r^2) = \pi D^2$ therefore $h(D) = S'(D) = 2\pi D$ (fig. VI.10.c).

We find in fact

$$\int_0^{+\infty} h(D)\, dD = \pi = S$$

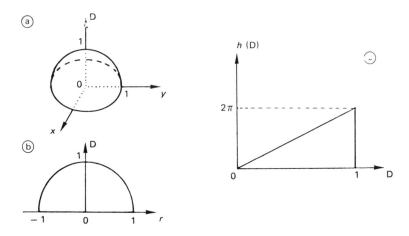

Fig.VI.10 - a) Circular image of centre O and unit radius with density varying in accordance with a spherical law (centre O, radius 1), b) cross-section of this density as a function of the radius, c) the corresponding histogram.

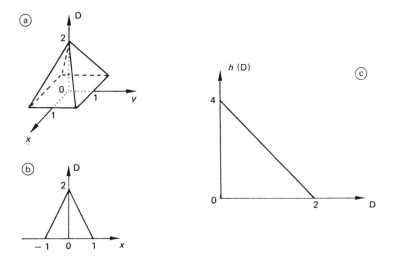

Fig.VI.11 - a) Square image centred on O of side 2, varying in density according to a law which has a pyramid structure centred on O of height 2, b) cross-section of this density in the vertical plane passing through Ox, c) the corresponding histogram.

being the surface area of the image.

b) **Pyramidal image** with square base (fig.VI.11.a and b)
The surface area function is $S(D) = 4 - (2 - D)^2$ therefore

$$h(D) = S'(D) = 2(2 - D) \qquad \text{(fig.VI.11.c)}$$

$$\int_0^{+\infty} h(D) \, dD = 4 = S$$

being the surface area of the image.

Let us assume that we are digitizing this image across $5 \times 5 = 25$ adjacent square pixels. The mean density values of each pixel are shown in figure VI.12.b. Using the 8-level quantization law for figure VI.12.a we obtain the array of numbers in figure VI.12.c. By counting the number of pixels at each level we construct the discrete histogram shown in figure VI.12.d. This histogram is very different from the continuous histogram, which is usual given the low numbers of pixels and levels used.

c) **Photographic film** which has been uniformly printed and digitized using an aperture much larger than the grain size. We can consider that fluctuations in density are Gaussian. Since the digitization is fine (256×256 pixels, 256 levels) we obtain a Gaussian histogram (fig.VI.17).

C. Point operations

1. Definition

A point operation is a law f which transforms an input image $A(x,y)$ into an output image $B(x,y) = f[A(x,y)]$ (fig.VI.13).

Law f may take any form (linear, non-linear, monotonic, non-monotonic etc.) but is consistent for all points on the image. Figure VI.14 gives two examples of strictly monotonic point operations transforming input density D_A into output density D_B.

a) non-linear law $D_B = f(D_A)$

b) linear law $D_B = a \, D_A + B$.

As we shall see, the applications of this principle are many. For instance:

- altering the contrast and (or) dynamic range of an image.
- correcting the non-linear response of a sensor or restorer, assuming that it is the same at all points on the image (the "decalibration"

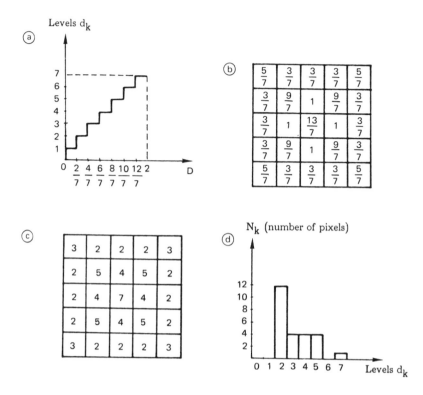

Fig.VI.12 - Digitizing the image in figure VI.11; a) 8-level quantization law, b) mean density values of the 5 x 5 = 25 adjoining pixels, c) array of digital values obtained following quantization, d) corresponding discrete histogram, very different from the continuous histogram in figure VI.11.c.

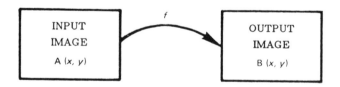

Fig.VI.13 - A point operation f transforming input image $A(x, y)$ into output image $B(x, y) = f[A(x, y)]$.

problem).

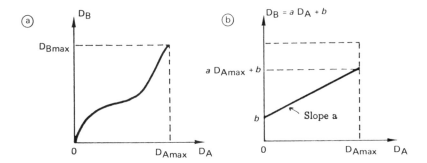

Fig.VI.14 - Examples of strictly monotonic point operations; a) non-linear law, b)
linear law $D_B = a D_A + b$.

- transition from a transmittance response to a density response
(logarithmic function) or vice versa (exponential function).

2. Transformation of the histogram [1,2]

a) Let us first assume that the law $D_B = f(D_A)$ is strictly monotonic, for instance that it is strictly increasing (fig.VI.15.a), so that it is
possible to define the reciprocal law $D_A = f^{-1}(D_B)$.

All points on the input image with densities between D_A and
$D_A + dD_A$ will give points on the output image with densities ranging
between D_B and $D_B + dD_B$. The surface areas $hA(D_A)dD_A$ and
$hB(D_B)dD_B$ are therefore equal:

$$h_B(D_B)\, dD_B = h_A(D_A)\, dD_A \quad \text{(fig.VI.15.b and c)}$$

giving $h_B(D_B) = \dfrac{h_A(D_A)}{dD_B/dD_A}.$

But $D_A = f^{-1}(D_B)$ and $\dfrac{dD_B}{dD_A} = f'(D_A)$ giving

$$h_B(D_B) = \frac{h_A(f^{-1}(D_B))}{f'(f^{-1}(D_B))}$$

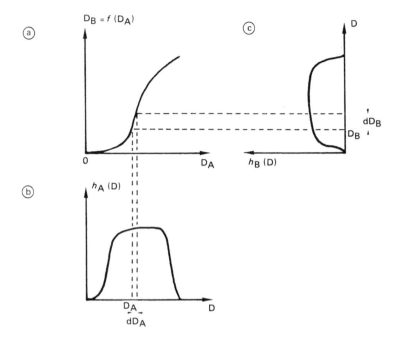

Fig.VI.15 - Transforming the histogram by a strictly monotonic point operation;
a) law $D_B = f(D_A)$, b) histogram of input image $h_A(D)$, c) histogram of

output image $h_B(D) = \dfrac{h_A[f^{-1}(D)]}{|df/dD|}$.

If f is strictly decreasing, f' becomes negative. The exact formula is
therefore:

$$h_B(D_B) = \frac{h_A(f^{-1}(D_B))}{|f'(f^{-1}(D_B))|} \qquad (6)$$

This is a classic result in probability calculations:

$$p_B(D) = \frac{p_A(f^{-1}(D))}{|df/dD|}$$

Example 1

Linear operation $D_B = f(D_A) = aD_A + b$ (fig.VI.16.a).

Therefore $D_A = f^{-1}(D_B) = \dfrac{(D_B - b)}{a}$ and $h_B(D) = \dfrac{1}{|a|} h_A\left(\dfrac{D - b}{a}\right)$.

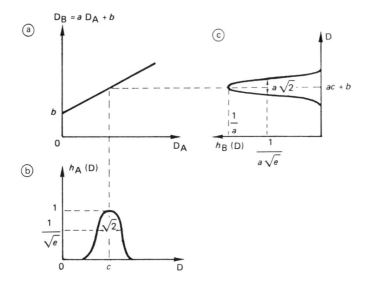

Fig.VI.16 - Example of a linear point operation; a) law $D_B = aD_A + b$, b) histogram of the Gaussian input image: $h_A(D) = e^{-(D-c)^2}$, c) histogram of the output image: Gaussian, centred on $D = ac + b$, of width multiplied by a and height divided by a.

It should be remembered that we obtain a Gaussian histogram by observing a uniformly printed photographic film with a scanning aperture which is very wide in comparison with mean grain size (fig.VI.17).

Let us assume a Gaussian input histogram $h_A(D) = e^{-(D-c)^2}$ (fig.VI.16.b).

We obtain: $h_B(D) = \dfrac{1}{|a|} e^{-\left(\frac{D-b}{a} - c\right)^2} = \dfrac{1}{|a|} e^{-\frac{(D-(ac+b))^2}{a^2}}$

(fig.VI.16.c).

The output histogram is also Gaussian, centred on density $ac + b$. It is widened if $|a| > 1$, narrowed if $|a| < 1$.

Fig.VI.17 - Example of a Gaussian histogram. The histogram of a uniformly
    printed film digitized using an aperture which is very large in comparison with
    mean grain size.

The case where $|a| > 1$ corresponds to an increase in image contrast.

Example 2

Quadratic operation $D_B = f(D_A) = D_A^2$ (fig.VI.18.a).

$$D_A = f^{-1}(D_B) = \sqrt{D_B}$$

$$f'(D) = 2D \quad f'(f^{-1}(DB)) = 2\sqrt{D_B}$$

If the input histogram is $h_A(D) = e^{-D^2}$ (fig.VI.18.b) then by virtue
of relation (6):

$$h_B(D) = \frac{e^{-D}}{2\sqrt{D}} \qquad \text{(fig.VI.18.c)}$$

b) Let us examine some cases where the f law *is not strictly monotonic*:

- a plateau of ordinate c creates a peak in the output histogram for $D = c$ (fig.VI.19.a and b).

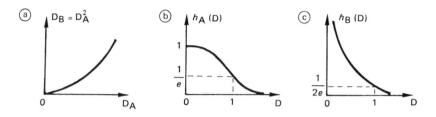

Fig.VI.18 - Example of a quadratic point operation; a) law $D_B = D_A^2$, b) input

histogram $h_A(D) = e^{-D^2}$, c) output histogram $h_B(D) = \dfrac{e^{-D}}{2\sqrt{D}}$.

- a vertical part (jump) between ordinates c and d creates a hole in the output histogram between densities c and d since the corresponding values are never reached (fig.VI.19.c and d).

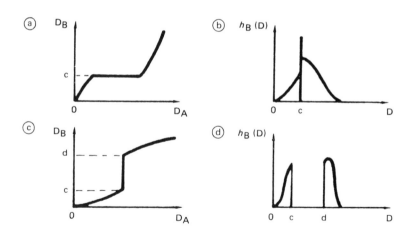

Fig.VI.19 - a) and b): A plateau of ordinate c in law $D_B = f(D_A)$ creates a peak of abscissa c in the histogram $h_B(D)$, c) and d): a vertical part between values c and d in law $D_B = f(D_A)$ creates a hole between abscissas c and d in the histogram $h_B(D)$.

- If the curve displays parts which are increasing and parts which are decreasing they are divided into monotonic intervals. The calculation shown above is possible for each interval. The decreasing parts reverse the image contrast.

Example

Let us consider the sawtooth law and the Gaussian histogram $h_A(D)$ shown in figure VI.20. The histogram $h_B(D)$ is a Gaussian half-curve since values for density $> c$ have been turned back on the interval $(0, c)$. The image regions corresponding to these densities have their contrast reversed due to the negative slope.

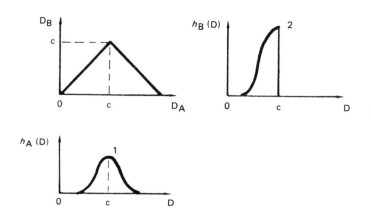

Fig.VI.20 - Example of non-monotonic law $D_B = f(D_A)$.

- *Exercises*: 1) The input image has a histogram represented in figure VI.21.a. It is transformed by means of law $D_B = (1 - D_A)^2$ (fig.VI.21.b)

Calculate $h_B(D)$.

$$h_A(D) = -2D + 2 \quad \text{if } 0 \le D \le 1$$
$$h_A(D) = 0 \quad \text{in other cases.}$$

$$D_A = f^{-1}(D_B) = 1 - \sqrt{D_B} \qquad f'(D) = 2D - 2$$

$$f'(f^{-1}(D_B)) = 2(1 - \sqrt{D_B}) - 2 = -2\sqrt{D_B}$$

giving

$$h_B(D) = \frac{-2(1 - \sqrt{D_B}) + 2}{|-2\sqrt{D_B}|} = \frac{2\sqrt{D_B}}{2\sqrt{D_B}} = 1 \qquad \text{if } 0 < D < 1$$

$$h_B(D) = 0 \text{ in other cases.}$$

Thus we obtain the flat histogram in figure VI.21.c.

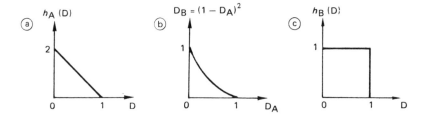

Fig.VI.21 - Example of transforming a histogram into a flat histogram; a) input histogram, b) law $D_B = f(D_A)$, c) output histogram.

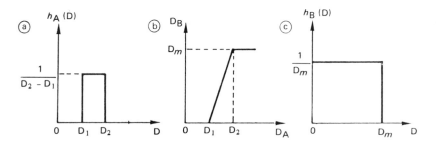

Fig.VI.22 - Increasing contrast image by stretching the dynamic range; a) input histogram, b) linear law $D_B = f(D_A)$, c) flat output histogram.

2) The input image has a flat histogram between D_1 and D_1 (fig.VI.22.a) and is transformed by the linear law between D_1 and D_2 (fig.VI.22.b).

$$h_A(D) = \frac{1}{D_2 - D_1} \quad \text{if} \quad D_1 \le D \le D_2$$

$h_A(D) = 0$ in other cases.

$$D_B = \frac{D_m}{D_2 - D_1}(D_A - D_1) \qquad D_1 \le D_A \le D_2$$

$$D_A = f^{-1}(D_B) = D_1 + \frac{D_2 - D_1}{D_m} D_B \qquad 0 < D_B < Dm$$

$$f'(D) = \frac{D_m}{D_2 - D_1}$$

giving
$$h_B(D) = \frac{D_2 - D_1}{D_m} \times \frac{1}{D_2 - D_1} = \frac{1}{D_m} \qquad 0 \le D \le Dm$$

The histogram obtained is still flat but the dynamic range of the image is now $(0, D_m)$ (fig.VI.22.c).

3. Applications [1,2,3]

a) **Manipulating contrast and dynamic range**
Since an image will have been digitized in less than ideal conditions, it can be useful to enhance its appearance in order to reveal required information and permit more effective processing. This can be done by manipulating contrast and dynamic range using point operations which modify the image histogram.

We should remember that in the case of digitized images such operations cannot increase the number of levels occupied, but simply change their distribution.

Great care must be taken when interpreting images derived by means of non-monotonic or non-continuous laws:
- horizontal plateaux (fig.VI.19.a and b) bring about a loss of information.
- vertical jumps (fig.VI.19.c and d) do not bring about any loss of information, but run the risk of causing breaks in the image. These show up as false contours or isolated point aberrations, since points of very similar density on opposite sides of the jump abscissa are found to exhibit very different densities. This is an example of an "artefact".
- negative slopes cause local contrast inversions which can be very distracting.

In view of these limitations, triangular or sawtooth functions are commonly used to reset regions of the image with very differing backgrounds to the same mean density. An example of this would be a very light patch and a very dark one.

b) **How to obtain a flat histogram**

This technique for equalizing the histogram gives the best possible dynamic range and strong contrast, in general making details more visible but giving the image a "hard" appearance (and in particular increasing the noise). The technique is often used when there is a need to compare two or more images or carry out joint operations on them.

•*The continuous case*

Let us find the appropriate point operation f (fig.VI.23.a) by arguing from the probability densities $p(D) = \frac{h(D)}{S}$ and the distribution functions $F(D) = \frac{S(D)}{S}$.

Input image $a(x,y)$ has probability density $p_1(a)$ (fig.VI.23.b) and distribution function $F_1(a)$ (fig.VI.23.d). We wish to obtain an output image $b(x,y)$ such that its density $p_2(b)$ is constant between 0 and D_m (fig.VI.23.c). Note that its distribution function $F_2(b)$ thus increases in a straight line from 0 to 1 (fig.VI.23.d).

Relation (6) is in fact written as

$$h_B(b) = \frac{h_A(a)}{|f'(a)|} \quad \text{or} \quad p_2(b) = \frac{p_1(a)}{|f'(a)|} = \frac{1}{D_m}$$

giving $|f'(a)| = D_m \, p_1(a)$ which gives by integration:

$$f(a) = D_m \int_0^a p_1(u) \, du = D_m \, F_1(a)$$

$$\boxed{f(a) = D_m \, F_1 \, (a)} \tag{7}$$

Thus as far as D_m, function f equals the distribution function of the input image. In other words, *transforming an image by its cumulative histogram gives an output histogram which is flat.*

Figure VI.24 compares the heightened contrast which can be obtained using a linear law and using the histogram equalization technique. The processed image is shown in figure VI.7.b. Figure a) shows the use of a linear function between the minimum and maximum image densities. This is the law shown in figure VI.22.b, and the histogram obtained is merely a stretched version of the original histogram. Figures b) and c) show the image obtained by histogram equali-

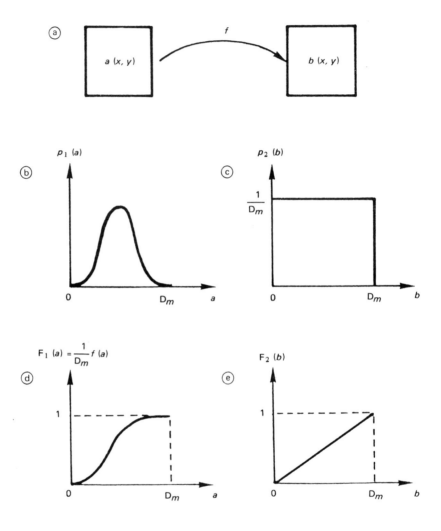

Fig.VI.23 - Equalizing the histogram; a) law $b(x,y) = f[a(x,y)]$, b) input histogram $p_1(a)$, shown as a probability density, c) flat output histogram $p_2(b)$, d) cumulative input histogram $F_1(a)$, increasing from 0 to 1 where $f(a) = D_m F_1(a)$ has been selected, e) linear cumulative output histogram $F_2(b)$.

zation using the cumulative histogram function in figure VI.7.c. The resulting histogram is far from being flat. We shall see why when we study the discrete case.

- *Example 1*: (fig.VI.25)

$$p_1(a) = -2a + 2 \quad\quad 0 \le a \le 1 \quad\quad\quad\quad \text{(fig.VI.25.a)}$$
$$p_1(a) = 0 \quad\quad\quad\quad \text{in other cases.}$$

The law being used is the following:

$$b = \mathrm{D}_m \, F_1(a) = F_1(a) = \int_0^a (-2a + 2) \, da = -a^2 + 2a \quad\text{(fig.VI.25.b)}$$

We can check that the histogram obtained is flat:

$$p_2(b) = \frac{p_1(a)}{|f'(a)|} = \frac{-2a + 2}{-2a + 2} = 1 \quad\quad\quad \text{(fig.VI.25.c)}$$

Comparing this with the previous exercise (fig.VI.21) we notice that law $b = (1 - a)^2 = a^2 - 2a + 1$ is different but also gives rise to a flat histogram.

This is not surprising since two different images can easily have the same histogram.

- *Example 2*: Return to the example in figure VI.22.
- *The discrete case*

We shall reason from discrete probabilities and distribution functions. For instance, let us assume an input image with $n = 64 \times 64 = 4096$ pixels quantized over 8 levels a_k ($a_0 = 0$, $a_1 = 1$, ... $a_7 = 7$).

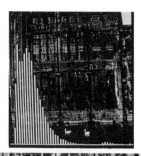

a) the image obtained using a linear function similar to the one in figure VI.22.b with the histogram superimposed on it,

b) the image obtained using the histogram equalization technique,

c) the "flat" histogram superimposed on the image.

Fig.VI.24 - Heightening contrast on the image in figure VI.7.b by stretching its dynamic range;

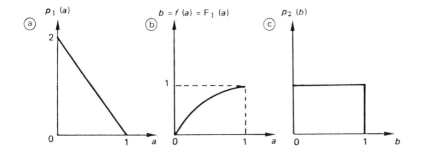

Fig.VI.25 - Example of histogram equalization; a) linear input histogram $p_1(a)$, b) law $f(a) = F_1(a)$ which was used, c) equalized output histogram $p_2(b)$.

The distribution law is as follows:

a_k	n_k	$p_1(a_k) = \dfrac{n_k}{n}$	$F_1(a_k)$
$a_0 = 0$	612	0.15	0.15
$a_1 = 1$	163	0.04	0.19
$a_2 = 2$	335	0.08	0.27
$a_3 = 3$	573	0.14	0.41
$a_4 = 4$	1186	0.29	0.70
$a_5 = 5$	613	0.15	0.85
$a_6 = 6$	614	0.15	1
$a_7 = 7$	0	0	1

Probability $p_1(a_k)$ is shown in figure VI.26.a and distribution function $F_1(a_k)$ is in figure VI.26.b.

To equalize the histogram we transform the original a_k levels according to the law $b_k = 7\, f(a_k) = 7\, F_1(a_k) = 7 \displaystyle\sum_{i=0}^{k} p_1(a_i)$ $\quad (7 = a_7$

takes the place of D_m).

The problem is that in general the calculation gives rise to values which do not correspond to an exact b_k level. We find, in fact, that $b'_k \neq b_k$ and the method involves choosing the nearest b_k level. Since this means that several a_k levels can give the same b_k, we assign this b_k level the sum of probabilities for the a_k levels from which it is derived.

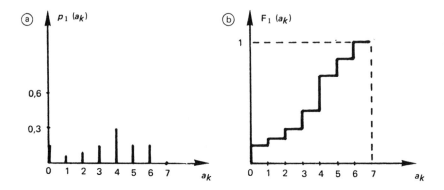

Fig.VI.26 - Discrete histograms of a digital image coded over 8 levels; a) histogram $p_1(a_k)$ considered as a probability, b) the corresponding cumulative histogram $F_1(a_k)$ is a function increasing in steps from 0 to 1.

The number of destination levels occupied is therefore equal to or less than the number of original levels and there are "holes" in the histogram. It can also be seen that the levels occupied are not filled equally, that is the histogram obtained is not perfectly flat (it is likely to be flatter as the number of quantization levels and pixels increases, that is the closer the approximation to a continuous image).

- *Example*: Let us consider the histogram in figure VI.27, corresponding to an image which has been quantized over 8 levels. The ideal flat histogram would have a probability of $\frac{1}{8}$ = 0.125 per level. From the law $p_1(a_k)$ it is possible to derive theoretical b'_k levels (fig.VI.27.b).

a_k	$P_1(a_k)$	$b'_k = 7\, f(a_k) = 7\, F_1(a_k)$
$a_0 = 0$	0.09	$b'_0 = 7 \times 0.09 = 0.63$
$a_1 = 1$	0.13	$b'_1 = 7 \times 0.22 = 1.54$
$a_2 = 2$	0.17	$b'_2 = 7 \times 0.39 = 2.73$
$a_3 = 3$	0.27	$b'_3 = 7 \times 0.66 = 4.62$
$a_4 = 4$	0.20	$b'_4 = 7 \times 0.86 = 6.02$
$a_5 = 5$	0.10	$b'_5 = 7 \times 0.96 = 6.72$
$a_6 = 6$	0.03	$b'_6 = 7 \times 0.99 = 6.93$
$a_7 = 7$	0.01	$b'_7 = 7 \times 1 \quad = 7$

Each b'_k is replaced by the b_k nearest, which is then assigned the sum of probabilities for the a_k levels from which it is derived.

$$b'_0 \rightarrow b_1 = 1 : p_2(b_1) = p_1(a_0) = 0.09$$
$$b'_1 \rightarrow b_2 = 2 : p_2(b_2) = p_1(a_1) = 0.13$$
$$b'_2 \rightarrow b_3 = 3 : p_2(b_3) = p_1(a_2) = 0.17$$
$$b'_3 \rightarrow b_5 = 5 : p_2(b_5) = p_1(a_3) = 0.27$$
$$b'_4 \rightarrow b_6 = 6 : p_2(b_6) = p_1(a_4) = 0.20$$

$$\left.\begin{array}{l} b'_5 \rightarrow b_7 = 7 \\ b'_6 \rightarrow b_7 = 7 \\ b'_7 = b_7 = 7 \end{array}\right\} \quad p_2(b_7) = p_1(a_5) + p_1(a_6) + p_1(a_7) = 0.14$$

It can be seen that levels b_0 and b_4 are blank. When the histogram obtained is compared to the histogram required we find:

b_k	$p_2(b_k)$ obtained	$p_2(b_k)$ required
$b_0 = 0$	0	0.125
$b_1 = 1$	0.09	0.125
$b_2 = 2$	0.13	0.125
$b_3 = 3$	0.17	0.125
$b_4 = 4$	0	0.125
$b_5 = 5$	0.27	0.125
$b_6 = 6$	0.20	0.125
$b_7 = 7$	0.14	0.125

The histogram obtained is shown in figure VI.27.c. It is far from being flat, as we saw with the one in figure VI.7.c.

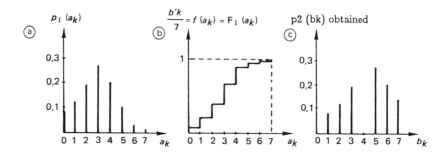

Fig.VI.27 - Example of discrete histogram equalization; a) input histogram $p_1(a_k)$,
b) law giving theoretical levels $b'_k = 7F_1(a_k)$, c) when b'_k values have been
replaced with the nearest true b_k levels an output histogram $p_2(b_k)$ is
obtained. This histogram will be flatter the more pixels and quantization levels
there are.

c) How to obtain a histogram of a given form

It is sometimes more useful to give the histogram a particular
structure, for instance to enhance certain density ranges for which
greater detail is required. We shall explain the principle of this technique in the case of a continuous image and then give an example of
performing calculations in the discrete case.

· *The continuous case*

Let us consider the possibility (fig.VI.28.a) of a fictitious image
$b(x,y)$ with a flat histogram being used as an intermediate stage.

We already know the first step in transforming image $a(x,y)$ with
histogram $p_1(a)$ (fig.VI.28.b) into an image $b(x,y)$ which has a flat
histogram $p_2(b)$ (fig.VI.28.c) and a linear distribution function $F_2(b)$
(fig.VI.28.f). This is done by using the law $f(a) = D_m F_1(a)$ where
$F_1(a)$ is the distribution function (i.e. cumulative histogram) of the
original image (fig.VI.28.e).

It would also be possible to work back from output image $c(x,y)$ to
$b(x,y)$ by the reciprocal operation g, letting $g^{-1}(c) = D_m F_3(c)$ giving

$g(b) = F_3^{-1}\left[\dfrac{b}{D_m}\right]$ where $F_3(c)$ is the distribution function of the des-

tination image (fig.VI.28.g). In fact we can check that the composition
of operations g and $D_m F_3(c)$ consists of the identical operator, since:

$$g[D_m F_3(c)] = F_3^{-1}\left[\frac{1}{D_m}D_m F_3(c)\right] = F_3^{-1}[F_3(c)] = c$$

All that remains to derive the global transformation

$$c(x,y) = g[b(x,y)] = g\{f[a(x,y)]\}$$

is to merge both operations:

$$\left\{ \begin{array}{l} b = f(a) = D_m F_1(a) \\ c = g(b) = F_3^{-1}\left[\dfrac{b}{D_m}\right] \end{array} \right\}$$

This gives

$$\boxed{c = g[f(a)] = F_3^{-1}[F_1(a)]} \tag{8}$$

from which D_m has disappeared.

Thus we obtain the required histogram $p_3(c)$ (fig.VI.28.d).

- *Example*: using the case shown in figure VI.29 the reader can check that it is possible to start from histogram a and obtain histogram c using the law which states:

$$c = F_3^{-1}[F_1(a)] = F_3^{-1}[-a^2 + 2a] = \sqrt{-a^2 + 2a}$$

It is possible to show by way of an exercise that the same result is obtained using the simpler law $c = 1 - a$ (since two different images can have the same histogram).

· *The discrete case*: The method is based on the continuous case and involves using functions F_1 and F_3^{-1}. Here again the histogram obtained will differ noticeably from the histogram required.

The detailed steps in the calculation with 8 levels are as follows:

a) "equalized" histogram $p_2(b_k)$ is calculated from source histogram $p_1(a_k)$ using the method shown earlier.

b) on the basis of required histogram $p_3(c_k)$ a calculation is performed to give the theoretical levels

$$b'_k = 7 \sum_{i=0}^{k} p_3(c_i) = g^{-1}(c_k)$$

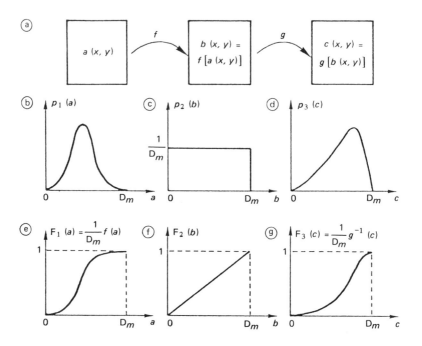

Fig.VI.28 - Obtaining a histogram of a given form; a) successive operations: $b(x,y) = f[a(x,y)]$, $c(x,y) = g[b(x,y)] = (g \circ f)[a(x,y)]$, b) input histogram $p_1(a)$, c) flat intermediate histogram $p_2(b)$, d) required output histogram $p_3(c)$, e) cumulative input histogram $F_1(a) = \dfrac{1}{D_m} f(a)$, f) cumulative intermediate histogram $F_2(b)$, g) cumulative output histogram $F_3(c) = \dfrac{1}{D_m} g^{-1}(c)$.

c) the reverse of the preceding law is applied to the b_k levels obtained at a) by taking the closest values of b'_k. Since this means that several b_k levels can give the same c_k, we assign to this level the sum of probabilities for the b_k levels from which it is derived.

- *Example*: we now return to the same histogram $p_1(a_k)$ reproduced in figure VI.30.a for which we have already calculated "equalized" histogram $p_2(b_k)$ (step a).

Let us assume that the required histogram $p_3(c_k)$ is the one in figure VI.30.b corresponding to the following table where b'_k levels have been calculated (step b) (fig.VI.30.c).

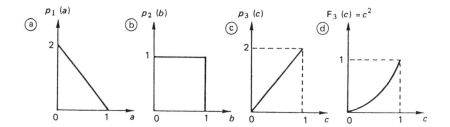

Fig.VI.29 - Example of obtaining a histogram of a given form; a) input histogram $p_1(a)$, b) flat intermediate histogram $p_2(b)$, c) required output histogram $p_3(c)$, d) cumulative output histogram $F_3(c)$.

c_k	$p_3(c_k)$ required	$b'_k = 7 \sum\limits_{i=0}^{k} p_3(c_i) = g^{-1}(c_k)$
$c_0 = 0$	0	$b'_0 = 0$
$c_1 = 1$	0.05	$b'_1 = 0.35$
$c_2 = 2$	0.10	$b'_2 = 1.05$
$c_3 = 3$	0.20	$b'_3 = 2.45$
$c_4 = 4$	0.30	$b'_4 = 4.55$
$c_5 = 5$	0.20	$b'_5 = 5.95$
$c_6 = 6$	0.10	$b'_6 = 6.65$
$c_7 = 7$	0.05	$b'_7 = 7$

Step c: let us consider the b_k levels in step a and their nearest b'_k levels. For each b'_k there is a c_k to which is assigned the sum of probabilities for the b_k levels from which it is derived.

$$b_0 \rightarrow b'_0 \rightarrow c_0 \ p_3(c_0) = p_2(b_0) = 0$$
$$b_1 \rightarrow b'_2 \rightarrow c_2 \ p_3(c_2) = p_2(b_1) = 0.09$$

$$\left. \begin{array}{l} b_2 \rightarrow b'_3 \rightarrow c_3 \\ b_3 \rightarrow b'_3 \rightarrow c_3 \end{array} \right\} \quad \begin{array}{l} p_3(c_3) = p_2(b_2) + p_2(b_3) \\ \qquad = 0.13 + 0.17 = 0.30 \end{array}$$

$$\left. \begin{array}{l} b_4 \rightarrow b'_4 \rightarrow c_4 \\ b_5 \rightarrow b'_4 \rightarrow c_4 \end{array} \right\} \quad \begin{array}{l} p_3(c_4) = p_2(b_4) + p_2(b_5) \\ \qquad = 0 + 0.27 = 0.27 \end{array}$$

$$b_6 \rightarrow b'_5 \rightarrow c_5 \ p_3(c_5) = p_2(b_6) = 0.20$$

$$b_6 \rightarrow b'_7 \rightarrow c_7 \quad p_3(c_7) = p_2(b_7) = 0.14$$

It can be seen that levels c_1 and c_6 are blank. This gives the histogram obtained (fig.VI.30.d).

c_k	$p_3(c_k)$ obtained
$c_0 = 0$	0
$c_1 = 1$	0
$c_2 = 2$	0.09
$c_3 = 3$	0.30
$c_4 = 4$	0.27
$c_5 = 5$	0.20
$c_6 = 6$	0
$c_7 = 7$	0.14

- *Note*: in most of the image processing systems on the market, histogram calculation and the preceding operations of equalization, specification etc. are carried out by standard programs which merely have to be called. For example in the case of stand alone workstations these functions are generally available from a *menu* and controlled from a keyboard.

4. Correcting a response from a sensor or display system [2,3]

If one or more non-linear elements are included by a digitizer or display system it is useful to correct these non-linear features (a problem also known as "decalibration"). The technique is simple when the non-linearity is the same for all points on the image.

a) **Correcting a non-linear digitizer**
Such a digitizer can be shown in model form (fig.VI.31) as an ideal digitizer delivering a linear image followed by a non-linear point operation leading to the real image.

An effort is made to correct this non-linear feature using a second point operation which will restore the output image to linearity.

We can call the linear image $a(x,y)$, the real image $b(x,y)$, the non-linear feature f, the law required g and the linear converted image $c(x,y)$, and our aim is to obtain $c(x,y) = a(x,y)$. But:

$$c(x,y) = g(b(x,y)) = g\{f(a(x,y))\}$$

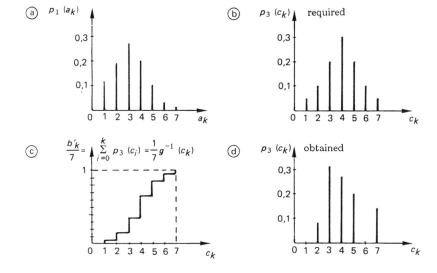

Fig.VI.30 - Obtaining a histogram of the required form in the discrete case; a) input histogram $p_1(a_k)$ (see figure VI.27.a), b) required histogram $p_3(c_k)$, c) intermediate theoretical levels calculated by: $b'_k = 7 \sum_{i=0}^{k} p_3(c_i) = g^{-1}(c_k)$.

The reverse transformation of g^{-1} is then applied to the "equalized" b_k levels obtained (see figure VI.27.c) by replacing each b_k with the closest b'_k and assigning to it a corresponding c_k, d) each b_k has a corresponding output c_k according to the $p_3(c_k)$ law.

giving $\boxed{g = f^{-1}}$.

Provided f is monotonic, g can be derived.

Example 1:

Let $b = f(a) = \alpha a^2 + \beta$ (quadratic characteristic). We find

$c = g(b) = f^{-1}(b) = \dfrac{\sqrt{b-\beta}}{\alpha}$

Example 2:

Figure VI.32 shows a simulated correction of non-linearity in a digitizer.

Figure a) shows an image which has been digitized in density mode on a microdensitometer, that is using a logarithmic type of non-linearity ($D = -\log_{10} T$). In figure b) this non-linearity has been corrected

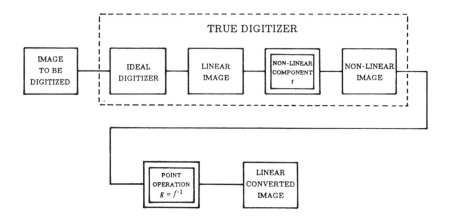

Fig.VI.31 - Model of a true digitizer with a non-linear characteristic and correction of the non-linearity f by a point operation $g = f^{-1}$ (problem of decalibration).

by a program which has created an exponential type of point operation.

Figure c) is the result of digitizing the original image in transmission mode, that is using a linear law. Image b) and image c) are indistinguishable.

b) **Correcting non-linearity in a display system**

The principle is identical. The digital image is corrected using a point operation. This carries out the g^{-1} operation which is the reciprocal of non-linear feature g in the display.

Notes

If the non-linearity is pixel-dependent, a point operation is not enough to correct it. This is the case with the non-linear response of a video camera, which is dependent on the point within the field. A correction of the above type is then required for individual pixels, which involves storing considerable amounts of information.

If it is simply a question of correcting a non-uniform response to take into account, say, background variations in different parts of the negative, or differences in sensor response, we shall see in the next chapter that it is possible to use a simple *algebraic operation* between the image and a "correcting image". For this purpose we can subtract the non-uniform background where known, and multiply each point

a) image digitized in density mode on a
microdensitometer, that is using a
logarithmic type of non-linearity
$(D = - \log_{10} T)$,

b) this non-linearity has been corrected
by a program which creates an exponential
type of point operation,

c) the result of digitizing the same image
in transmission mode, that is using a linear
law. Image b and image c are indistinguishable.

Fig.VI.32 - Example showing simulated correction of a non-linearity;

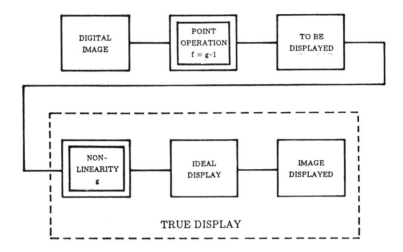

Fig.VI.33 - Model of a true display with a non-linear characteristic and correction of the non-linearity g by a point operation $f = g^{-1}$.

on the image by the "reverse" image obtained from the point sensitivity of the sensor.

7

Algebraic operations between images

This chapter considers certain basic algebraic operations (addition, multiplication etc.) which are commonly carried out between two or more images. These also are point operations, since the value attributed to each pixel in the output image depends solely on the point with the same coordinates in each of the images in question, without regard for neighbouring pixels. After examining the effect these operations have on histograms, we shall consider some classic applications and gain an insight into some simple and frequently used logical operations.

A. Effect on histograms

1. Histogram of the sum of two images

Let us base our reasoning on continuous images and assume that we are adding together corresponding points on two images $A(x,y)$ and $B(x,y)$. This gives us the new image

$$C(x,y) = A(x,y) + B(x,y)$$

We should immediately notice two special cases:
- If $B(x,y) = K$ (constant) we have $C(x,y) = A(x,y) + K$. This operation is simply a shift of the mean image level.
- If $B(x,y) = A(x,y)$ we have $C(x,y) = 2A(x,y)$. These two cases are identical to some of the point operations already studied in the last chapter.

In the general case, $A(x,y)$ and $B(x,y)$ have histograms $h_A(D)$ and $h_B(D)$ respectively.

In order to calculate histogram $h_C(D)$ we shall introduce the concept of a two-dimensional histogram $h_{AB}(D_A, D_B)$ or the histogram of a pair (A, B).

The quantity $h_{AB}(D_A, D_B)\, dD_A\, dD_B$ represents the total number of pairs of pixels which correspond to one another in the following manner: the first pixel in the pair is from image A with a density in the range D_A to $D_A + dD_A$ and the second pixel is from image B with a density in the range D_B to $D_B + dD_B$.

Consequently we derive the histogram $h_A(D)$ by integrating

$$h_{AB}(D_A) = \int_{-\infty}^{+\infty} h_{AB}(D_A, D_B)\, dD_B$$

and similarly

$$h_B(D_B) = \int_{-\infty}^{+\infty} h_{AB}(D_A, D_B)\, dD_A$$

Here too we see the analogy with probability calculations where we define the probability density $\rho(x, y)$ of the pair of random variables (x, y) by:

$$\rho(x, y)\, dx\, dy = P\,(x \leq X < x + dx \ \text{ and } \ y \leq Y < y + dy)$$

By writing $p(x)$ and $q(y)$ for the probability densities of variables X and Y considered separately, we have:

$$p(x) = \int_{-\infty}^{+\infty} \rho(x, y)\, dy \ \text{ and } \ q(y) = \int_{-\infty}^{+\infty} \rho(x, y)\, dx.$$

It can be then shown that the probability density of the summation variable $Z = X + Y$ is given by:

$$p_z(z) = \int_{-\infty}^{+\infty} \rho(z - y, y)\, dy$$

Similarly we have the following relation for the histograms:

$$h_C(D_C) = \int_{-\infty}^{+\infty} h_{AB}(D_C - D_B, D_B)\, dD_B$$

These relations simplify when the variables or images are said to be *independent*. Both random variables X and Y are *independent* if and only if $p(x,y)$ is equal to the product of $p(x)\, q(y)$

$$p(x,y) = p(x)\, q(y)$$

The relation becomes:

$$p_Z(z) = \int_{-\infty}^{+\infty} p(z - y)\, q(y)\, dy = p(z) * q(z)$$

Similarly we can say that images A and B are independent, if the two-dimensional histogram is equal to the product of the histograms of A and B:

$$h_{AB}(D_A, D_B) = h_A(D_A)\, h_B(D_B)$$

then

$$h_C(D_C) = \int_{-\infty}^{+\infty} h_A(D_C - D_B)\, h_B(D_B)\, dD_B$$

giving

$$\boxed{h_C(D_C) = h_A(D) * h_B(D)} \tag{1}$$

The histogram of the sum of two independent images is equal to the convolution product of the histograms of each image.

Example 1: Let A and B be two independent images with the following Gaussian histograms:

$$\left\{ \begin{array}{l} h_A(D) = e^{\displaystyle -\frac{(D-\mu_A)^2}{2\sigma_A^2}} \\[2em] h_B(D) = e^{\displaystyle -\frac{(D-\mu_B)^2}{2\sigma_A^2}} \end{array} \right\}$$

We know that the convolution of two Gaussians gives a Gaussian (see chap.II, section C.2, exercise 2). Knowing this we derive:

$$h_C(D) = \sqrt{2\pi}\,\sigma_A\,\sigma_B\;e^{\displaystyle -\frac{(D-\mu_C)^2}{2\sigma_C^2}}$$

with $\left\{ \begin{array}{l} \mu_C = \mu_A + \mu_B \\ \sigma_C^2 = \sigma_A^2 + \sigma_B^2 \end{array} \right\}$

- The mean value of the summation image is equal to the sum of mean values, and this is always so.
- The standard deviations are summed quadratically because both images are independent.

Example 2: Figure VII.1.a shows an image A and its density histogram consisting of three peaks. There is a peak at level 0 (for the black parts of the holes in the film), a wide peak around the mean level 100 and a narrow peak in the region of level 150. Figure VII.1.b shows an image B which is independent of A and has a histogram with a single symmetrical peak centred on level 50. Figure VII.1.c shows the sum of both images and the resulting histogram with its three peaks. The first of these, centred on level 50, comes from the convolution of the peak in B with the level 0 peak in A. The second, wider peak, is centred on level 150 and comes from convolution with the second peak in A (100 + 50 = 150). The third peak is centred on level 200 (= 150 + 50).

2. Histogram of the difference between two images

We can derive the relation $C(x,y) = A(x,y) - B(x,y)$ (assuming that $A(x,y) > B(x,y)$ in order to avoid negative values, shifting the mean level of A or B as necessary before carrying out the subtraction).

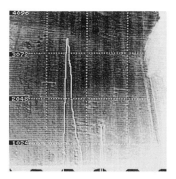

a) image A and its histogram,

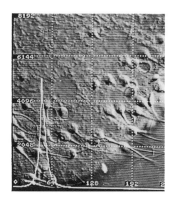

b) image B and its histogram,

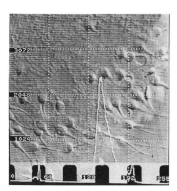

c) image A+B and its histogram, being
   the convolution of both the above histograms.

Fig.VII.1 - Histogram of the sum of two independent images.

a) image A and its histogram,

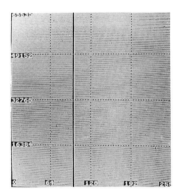

b) image B (continuous background)
   and its histogram,

c) image A-B and its histogram, being the
   convolution of both the above histograms.
   We find in fact that this is simply a
   shifted version of the histogram of A.

Fig.VII.2 - Histogram of the difference between two independent images. An
example of subtracting a continuous background.

a) image A,

b) image A shifted slightly with
respect to O.x,

c) the difference between both the
above images gives an approximation
of the partial derivative $\dfrac{\partial A}{\partial x}$.

Fig.VII.3 - Deriving an approximation of the derivative in a given direction from
the difference between an image and its likeness shifted in the same direction.

a) If A and B are independent we can derive, by the method that was used for the sum:

$$h_C(D_C) = h_A(D) * h_B(-D)$$ (2)

Example: Figure VII.2 shows straightforward subtraction of a constant image equal to D_0 (continuous background). Then:

$$h_B(-D) = \delta(-D - D_0) = \delta(D + D_0) \text{ and } h_C(D) = h_A(D + D_0)$$

The histogram is simply shifted to the left by quantity D_0.

b) By contrast let us assume that A and B are two nearly identical images. Image B, say, is the same as image A but shifted slightly by quantity Δx.

$$B(x,y) = A(x + \Delta x, y)$$

$$C(x,y) = A(x,y) - A(x + \Delta x, y) \simeq \frac{\partial A(x,y)}{\partial x} \Delta x$$

where ∂x is the partial derivative of A with respect to x, with a histogram of $h_{A'}(D)$. Therefore $h_C(D) = \Delta x \, h_{A'}\left(\dfrac{D}{\Delta x}\right)$

The difference between the two images gives a good approximation of the partial derivative of the image with respect to the direction of shift. This gives a first example of a directional derivative which discloses transitions perpendicular to the direction of shift.

Example: Figure VII.3 shows this result for the partial derivative with respect to x.

B. Principal applications

1. Subtraction of images

– subtracting a background
It is sometimes possible to obtain an image of the background alone by using, say, a microscope. This image is then subtracted, possibly after adding a realignment constant in order to avoid negative overflow. This makes it possible to correct for variations in the background itself or in sensor response.

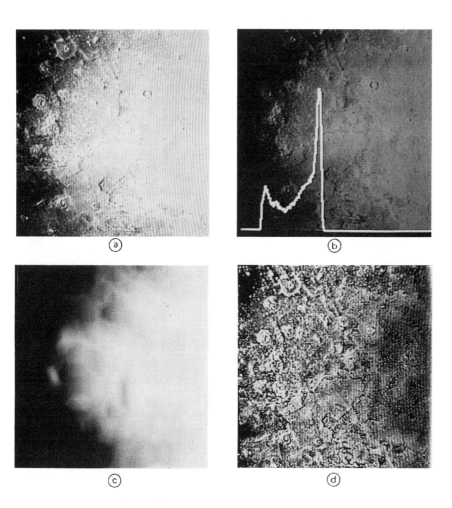

(a)

(b)

(c)

(d)

Fig.VII.4 - Correcting a background which is not uniform throughout; a) the planet Mars: the illumination is very weak on the left and very strong on the right, making it difficult to distinguish detail over the negative as a whole, b) the image and its histogram, c) the background derived from repeatedly smoothing the image, d) the processed image, obtained by subtracting background c) and adding a resetting constant. It is now possible to distinguish detail clearly throughout the entire image.

There is often only a single image available, which may have been taken with uneven illuminance. Figure VII.4 shows a view of the planet Mars taken in such conditions. Increasing the effective contrast in one part of the image makes the other parts totally black or totally

a) chess set: view A,

b) chess set: view B. One piece
  has been moved,

c) the realigned difference between both the
  above images: only the piece which was moved
  is still showing, in its original position.

Fig.VII.5 - Detecting movement by subtracting two images.

white. To bring out detail all over the picture it is possible to subtract a mean background derived by repeatedly smoothing the image until only the low frequencies are left. Figure d) shows the final result.

– detecting movement [2]

Figure VII.5 shows how it is possible to detect a chess-piece which has been moved. After realigning the difference between images a) and b), only the piece which was moved is still showing, as a light patch in the position it originally occupied. The edges of the squares and the other chess-pieces can also be seen because of the slight spatial displacement of one image with respect to the other.

– detecting edges and contours [1, 3]

It should be remembered that the partial derivatives with respect to x and y are easily derived by finding the difference between images which have been shifted slightly in the x and y directions. This is a good way of detecting edges which are perpendicular to the displacement. An effective contour detector is the length of the gradient vector:

$$\overrightarrow{\mathrm{grad}}\, f(x,y) = \vec{i}\,\frac{\partial f}{\partial x} + \vec{j}\,\frac{\partial f}{\partial y}$$

where $\vec{i}$ and $\vec{j}$ are the unitary vectors of the Ox and Oy axes.

$$\left|\overrightarrow{\mathrm{grad}}\, f\right| = \sqrt{\left(\frac{\partial f}{\partial x}\right)^2 + \left(\frac{\partial f}{\partial y}\right)^2}$$

An approximation to this expression is often found by taking the simpler expression

$$\left|\frac{\partial f}{\partial x}\right| + \left|\frac{\partial f}{\partial y}\right|$$

or even

$$\mathrm{sup}\left(\left|\frac{\partial f}{\partial x}\right|, \left|\frac{\partial f}{\partial y}\right|\right)$$

2. Averaging to reduce noise [2,11]

Let us assume we have n images of the same scene. Each image $M_i(x,y)$ consists of the same useful signal $S(x,y)$ to which the same noise $B_i(x,y)$ has been added:

$$M_i(x,y) = S(x,y) + B_i(x,y) \qquad i = 1, 2, \ldots n$$

$B_i(x,y)$ may represent noise from the digitizer, the photographic film grain or some other such source. The following assumptions are made:
- the noise is a stationary and ergodic random process with a mean value of zero and a standard deviation of σ
so that

$$\left\{ \begin{array}{l} \langle B \rangle = \overline{B_i} = 0 \\ \text{and } \langle B^2 \rangle = \overline{B_i^2} = \sigma^2 \end{array} \right\} \begin{array}{l} \text{statistical and spatial} \\ \text{means are treated the same}^. \end{array}$$

- occurrences of noise B_i constitute n occurrences of this process. If n is fairly large the following approximation is used:

$$\frac{B_1 + B_2 + \ldots + B_n}{n} = \langle B \rangle = 0$$

- it is assumed that occurrences of noise $B_i(x,y)$ are not mutually correlated. The mathematical notation for this condition is:

$$\overline{B_i(x,y)\, B_j(x,y)} = \overline{B_i(x,y)} \cdot \overline{B_j(x,y)} \; (i \neq j) \qquad \text{so in this case}$$

$$\overline{B_i B_j} = 0$$

Strictly speaking, non-correlation is not the same as independence. It can be shown that independence causes non-correlation, but the reverse is not true. We shall not dwell upon this subtle distinction at the moment.

For each image it is possible to define a signal-to-noise ratio for the point (x,y): $\left(\dfrac{S}{B} \right)_i = \dfrac{S(x,y)}{\sigma}$. It is therefore the same for all n images.

We can find the arithmetic mean of the n images and calculate the resulting signal-to-noise ratio.

$$M(x,y) = \frac{1}{n} \sum_{i=1}^{n} (S(x,y) + B_i(x,y)) = S(x,y) + B(x,y)$$

where

$$B(x,y) = \frac{1}{n} \sum_{i=1}^{n} B_i$$

It can be seen that:
- the signal is unchanged
- noise $B(x,y)$ has a standard deviation σ_B such that:

$$\sigma_B^2 = \overline{\left(\frac{1}{n} \sum_{i=1}^{n} B_i \right)^2} - \left(\overline{\frac{1}{n} \sum_{i=1}^{n} B_i} \right)^2$$

Since the second term of this expression remains zero, we are left with:

$$\sigma_B^2 = \overline{\left(\frac{1}{n} \sum_{i=1}^{n} B_i \right)^2} = \frac{1}{n^2} \overline{\left(\sum_{i=1}^{n} B_i^2 + \sum_{i \neq j} B_i B_j \right)}$$

$$= \frac{1}{n^2} \overline{\left(\sum_{i=1}^{n} B_i^2 \right)} + \frac{1}{n^2} \overline{\left(\sum_{i \neq j} B_i B_j \right)}$$

$$= \frac{1}{n^2} \sum_{i=1}^{n} \overline{B_i^2} + \frac{1}{n^2} \sum_{i \neq j} \overline{B_i B_j} = \frac{1}{n^2} \sum_{i=1}^{n} \sigma^2 = \frac{1}{n^2} n\sigma^2 = \frac{\sigma^2}{n}$$

giving

$$\sigma_B = \frac{\sigma}{\sqrt{n}} \tag{3}$$

The new signal-to-noise ratio (S.N.R.) is $\dfrac{S}{B} = \dfrac{S(x,y)}{\dfrac{\sigma}{\sqrt{n}}} = \sqrt{n}\left(\dfrac{S}{B}\right)_i$

$$\boxed{\; SNR = \sqrt{n}\;\left(\dfrac{S}{B}\right)_i \;}$$

(4)

We can say that the noise is divided by $\sqrt{n}$ or that the signal-to-noise ratio is enhanced by a factor of $\sqrt{n}$.

Example: Figure VII.6 shows the enhancement obtained by averaging the noise arising in the photographic grain.

3. Multiplication and division of images [3]

- These operations can be used to correct for a variation in sensor response at different points on the image. The array of values for correcting this non-uniform sensor characteristic is handled like an image and multiplied by or divided into the image being processed.
- when an image is multiplied by a purely binary image in which some regions take the value 0 and others take the value 1, a masking effect is created.
- image division is also used for processing multispectral images in the course of remote sensing, where it is necessary to compare various bands of the spectrum in order to arrive at a standard or compensated lighting intensity factor. An important defect of this process is that it accentuates the quantization error associated with each image. It can be shown that it is better to use the logarithms of the ratios rather than the ratios themselves.

4. Other operations

Many other operations are also used.
- pixel-by-pixel comparison of two images, putting say 0 if $A < B$ and 1 if $A \geq B$. This can be used for constructing a mask.
- logical operations, such as inclusive OR, exclusive OR, AND, complementation and logical contour rotation.
- reduction of an image by averaging the points in question.
- enlarging an image by linear interpolation between points. For example, reducing an image several times in succession and then re-enlarging it by the same amount is the same as a very powerful smo-

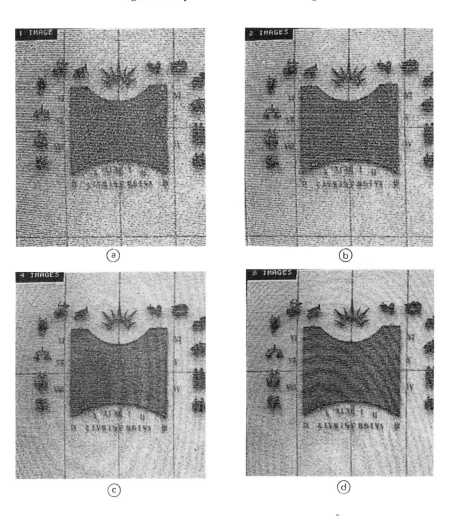

Fig.VII.6 - Enhancing the signal-to-noise ratio by a factor of $\sqrt{n}$ by averaging a series of n images of the same scene each exhibiting noise which is not mutually correlated (in this case the noise is arising in the photographic grain); a) any image in the series, b) the mean of two images, c) the mean of four images, d) the mean of eight images.

othing operation allowing only low-frequency components through.

8

Coloured images

So far we have thought of an image in terms of variations in illuminance (also called luminance or light intensity) distributed within a plane. This is the point of view of photography or black and white television, which use panchromatic images devoid of colour information.

There is often a requirement to deal with *trichromatic images*, such as colour photographs or television pictures. Colour information contained in such images enriches interpretation by the human eye in an obvious way. Such images are represented in what is called "true colour" mode.

Another case which is frequently encountered is that of *multispectral images*. Views of the same scene are taken in different wavelength bands. Some of these may even be beyond the spectral response of the human eye, such as infra-red or ultra-violet. Each band can then be assigned a colour, selected purely in accordance with a convention, to make the corresponding image visible for purposes of interpretation. In a moment we shall see the advantage of this display method, known as "false colour" mode.

Thirdly, it can be helpful to display even a monospectral image in colour. It often conveys more meaning, since the eye is very sensitive to colours. Whereas we know that the eye can see a difference between only some tens of shades of grey, it can distinguish between thousands of different shades of colour. This being so, it is possible to assign a conventionally agreed colour to each level of grey. This is called "pseudo-colour" mode.

A. 'True colour' mode

This representation mode attempts to display a coloured view of a scene keeping as faithfully as possible to the colours in the original. For this purpose we use the classic breakdown (or analysis) into primary components. These components are then used in the reconstruction (or synthesis) of the coloured image [1, 3, 9].

In the *additive process* any colour of the spectrum can be reproduced by mixing the three additive *primary colours, red, green and blue,* in the appropriate proportions. This is done by adding light together and is what happens when we observe, say, a colour slide or a picture on a colour television screen.

Mixing equal proportions of red, green and blue light gives white light of a certain intensity (actually a pale shade of grey). A mixture of red and green light gives yellow, red and blue give magenta, blue and green give cyan. Yellow, magenta and cyan are called the *secondary colours* of the additive process:

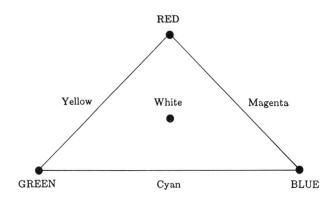

Even so it can be shown that certain colours cannot be reproduced by this process. We shall not go into the principles of colorimetry in detail here, but refer the reader to specialised works on the subject.

Figure VIII.1 shows the principles of displaying a trichromatic digital image in "true colour" mode on a television screen. The method uses the additive process. Each red, green and blue primary additive colour in the image has been digitized separately, by placing for instance red, green and blue filters in the analysis beam of a microdensitometer (chapter V). It is therefore given a bit code of a certain value (5 bits in the example shown in the figure, being $2^5 = 32$ levels). These bits are applied to the input of a digital-analogue converter which in turn controls the intensity of the corresponding electron gun in the colour monitor.

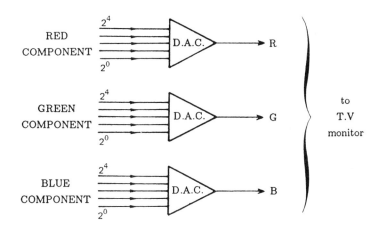

Fig.VIII.1 - Displaying a trichromatic digital image in "true colour" mode. Each red, green and blue primary additive colour in the image is given a bit code of a certain value (5 bits in this example, being $2^5 = 32$ levels). These bits are applied to the input of a digital-analogue converter. Each output signal controls the corresponding electron gun in the colour monitor.

By contrast the *subtractive process* involves observation by reflection, in which the colour obtained depends on the absorbed proportions of the red, green and blue components in the illuminating white light. This applies to painted or printed pictures, that is images formed of coloured pigments. The primary colours for pigments are therefore the secondary colours of the additive process:
- pigment which absorbs blue light reflects red and green in equal amounts, and as a result appears *yellow*;
- pigment which absorbs green light reflects a mixture of red and blue in equal proportions, and therefore appears *magenta*;
- pigment which absorbs red light gives a mixture of green and blue in equal amounts, and therefore appears *cyan*.

Here, too, all hues are obtained by mixing appropriate proportions of these three pigments. Mixing equal proportions of yellow, magenta and cyan gives black of a certain intensity (or rather, a deep shade of grey). An equal mixture of yellow and cyan gives green, and so on.

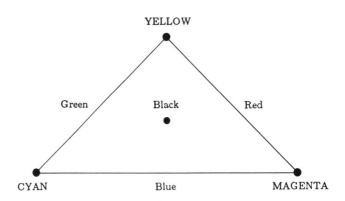

B. 'FALSE COLOUR' MODE

This representation mode attempts to display "in colour" several views of the same scene taken in different bands of the spectrum. This mode is very commonly used for multispectral images taken from remote sensing satellites, using sensors which operate in what are known as band 4 (green), 5 (red), 6 (infra-red 1) and 7 (infra-red 2). The system uses the same principle as for true colours (fig.VIII.1) but by convention one band is assigned to red, another to green and a third to blue.

This display method makes certain details, such as areas of vegetation, stand out more clearly by displaying them in a different colour from the usual one or by making use of the physiological characteristics of the eye. For instance the eye is very sensitive to the luminance in green, to faint contrasts in blue, and so on.

C. 'Pseudo-colour' mode

This representation mode is not to be confused with false colours. It starts from a purely monochrome image, taken either in white light or in any single band of the spectrum.

After digitization, therefore, this image is a distribution of grey levels. A colour is selected from a colour range agreed by convention and assigned to each grey level. To this end the system uses colour look-up tables (there is a table for red, another for green and a third for blue). Each look-up table is located ahead of the corresponding digital-analogue converter (fig.VIII.2) and assigns a weighting to the primary red, green or blue component.

Thus the range of colours available is in general very extensive. In practice the user can alter the selection of colours by amending the look-up tables through a keyboard or a system such as a "track-ball".

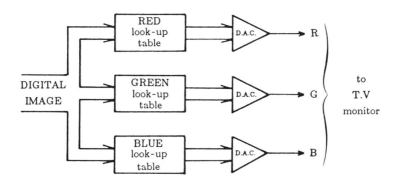

Fig.VIII.2 - Displaying a digital image in "pseudo-colour" mode. Each grey level in the image is converted into a colour chosen by convention using look-up tables. The output from each table controls the corresponding digital-analogue converter.

Figure VIII.3 gives an example of the rule for converting from a grey level to a pseudo-colour. Since the colour look-up tables assign the weights indicated in the figure to the three primary components, the result corresponds roughly to the colours of the visible spectrum (violet - indigo - blue - green - yellow - orange - red). With 256 levels of grey, level 0 is represented by deep violet and level 255 by bright red.

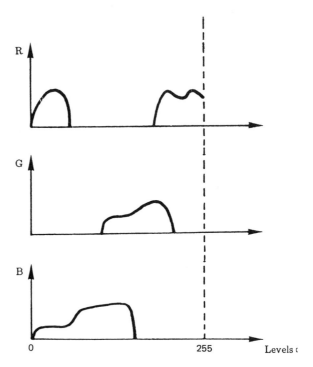

The result: Violet - blue - cyan - green - yellow - red

Fig.VIII.3 - Example of the law for converting a grey level to a pseudo-colour. Since the colour look-up tables assign the weights indicated in the diagram to the three primary components, the result corresponds roughly to the colours of the visible spectrum, ranging from deep violet for level 0 to bright red for level 255 (8-bit image coding).

Naturally, giving equal weight to the three primary components, for instance by taking a linear function of the level, will give a display in grey levels. This is shown schematically in figure VIII.4. Using 8 bits (256 levels) the display ranges from black for level 0 through to brilliant white for level 255.

The advantages of pseudo-colour representation stem from the fact that the eye is very sensitive to colour variation. This means that slight differences in grey levels can be emphasised by assigning them colours which are very different in character. Isodensity lines of particular interest can be highlighted and areas requiring special identification can be coloured artificially.

Sometimes a psychological link is made between colour and temperature. Blue and green are thought of as "cold" colours, whereas red is thought to be a "warm" colour.

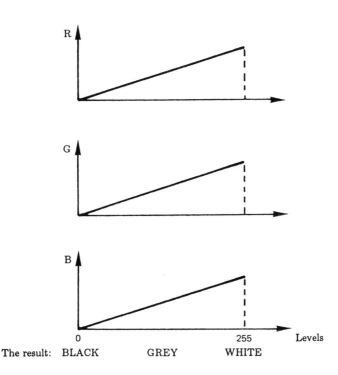

Fig.VIII.4 - Giving equal weight to each of the three colour components in the image by taking a linear function of the level will give a display in grey levels on the TV monitor, ranging from black for level 0 to brilliant white for level 255.

Figure VIII.5 is a digitized image of the solar corona displayed in grey levels. The same image, coded in pseudo-colours in accordance with the scheme in figure VIII.3, is shown in figure VIII.6. The red areas are the brightest parts of figure VIII.5, corresponding to the hottest regions of the corona.

Figure VIII.7.a shows an image obtained by thermography. This aerial photograph of a built-up area in the Meaux district was taken in infra-red.

This particular investigation (from the records of the Laboratoire National d'Essais - National Testing Laboratory) was undertaken to pinpoint leaks and losses from the pipes in the area heating system. When the contrast was enhanced, the red parts of the pseudo-colour display showed the warmest areas clearly. These probably corresponded to joints in the pipework (fig.VIII.7.b and c).

It is always wise to exercise caution when interpreting pseudo-colour images. Pseudo-colours can in fact produce artificial contours or mask genuine ones, emphasise noise peaks, accentuate density values of no special significance; in short, create "artefacts".

9

Linear processing of signals and images

A. Continuous domain: example of optical filtering

Figure IX.1 reminds us of the basic properties of a two-dimensional continuous linear filter, characterised by its impulse response $R(x, y)$ or its transfer function $G(u, v)$, both of which are Fourier transforms.

A filter of this kind carries out an operation in the spatial domain known as *convolution*, between the input signal $e(x, y)$ and the impulse response. The output signal is expressed as $s(x, y) = e(x, y) * R(x, y)$.

In the frequency domain it performs frequency *filtering* whereby the F.T. of the output signal $S(u, v)$ is equal to the F.T. of the input signal $E(u, v)$ multiplied by the transfer function of the filter:

$$S(u, v) = E(u, v) \cdot G(u, v)$$

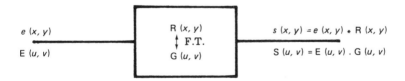

Fig.IX.1 - The properties of an "analogue" type of two-dimensional linear filter, characterised by its impulse response $R(x, y)$ or its transfer function $G(u, v)$, both of which are Fourier transforms.

We should remember that it is possible to perform continuous filtering by scanning with an aperture. The "reversed" aperture is then the system impulse response.

We also know that an optical system which is limited by diffraction in coherent light acts as a filter. To the nearest scale factor, the transfer function of this filter is the system exit pupil. It is therefore an easy matter to carry out any given real transfer function by placing a transmittance in the plane of this pupil equal to the the required transfer function $G(u, v)$. It goes without saying that this forbids any functions which are partly negative. Figure IX.2 reminds us how the system is assembled. The object is in the plane of the first lens and the optical filter is placed in front of the second.

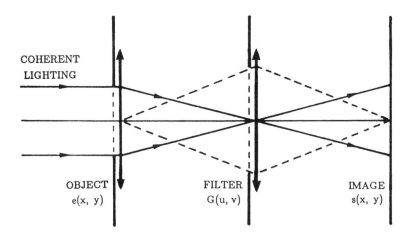

COHERENT LIGHTING

OBJECT
e(x, y)

FILTER
G(u, v)

IMAGE
s(x, y)

Fig.IX.2 - Two-dimensional analogue linear filtering can be easily carried out by an optical system using coherent lighting (see fig.III.12): $s(x, y) = e(x, y) * R(x, y)$.

Such a system has often been used to disclose directional trends in an image by letting through only the spatial frequencies which correspond to the directions in question. Thus a cross-shaped optical filter which admits frequencies in two directions at right-angles to each other has been used on an image of a rural area to show up the outlines of the Roman cadastral system seen in figure IX.3 (G. Chouquer and F. Favory: GIS "Techniques Nouvelles en Sciences de l'Homme", Besancon) [15].

Examples of optical filters [1, 7, 10]

   a) **The ideal low-pass filter**

   A filter of this type with circular symmetry and cut-off frequency u_0 has the transfer function $G(u, v)$ shown in figure IX.4.a. This has the cross-section, say, $G(u, O)$ (fig.IX.4.b).

   It is constructed in the form of a simple circular aperture.

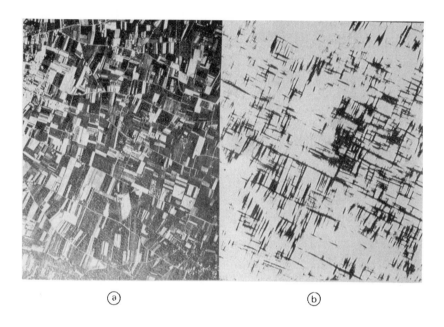

(a)   (b)

Fig.IX.3 - A directional optical filter is used to admit spatial frequencies in two
   right-angled directions from an image of a rural area; a) IGN aerial negative
   of the region to the east of Valence (Drôme), b) filtered negative revealing the
   directional outlines of the Roman cadastral system (from G.Chouquer and
   F.Favory)[15].

   b) **Butterworth's low-pass filter**
   Its transfer function is:

$$G(u, v) = \frac{1}{1 + (\sqrt{2} - 1) \, d(u, v)/D_0^{2n}} \text{ with } d(u, v) \ \sqrt{u^2 + v^2}$$

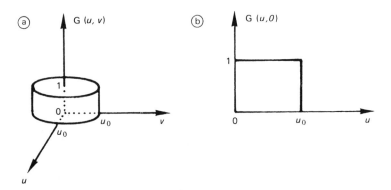

Fig.IX.4 - a) The transfer function of an ideal low-pass optical filter with a cut-off frequency u_0, made out of a simple circular aperture, b) the corresponding cross-section.

Taking for example $n = 1$ and $D_0 = (\sqrt{2} - 1)$ we obtain the filter in figure IX.5.a the cross-section for which is $G(u, O) = \dfrac{1}{1 + u^2}$.

Since this filter is semi-infinite it can be constructed in only approximate fashion.

c) Exponential low-pass filter

$$G(u, v) = e^{-(d(u,v)/D_0)^n} \quad \text{with} \quad d(u, v) \sqrt{u^2 + v^2}$$

With $n = 2$ and $D_0 = 1$ we obtain the filter in figure IX.5.b the cross-section for which is $G(u, O) = e^{-u^2}$. An approximation of this filter can be constructed.

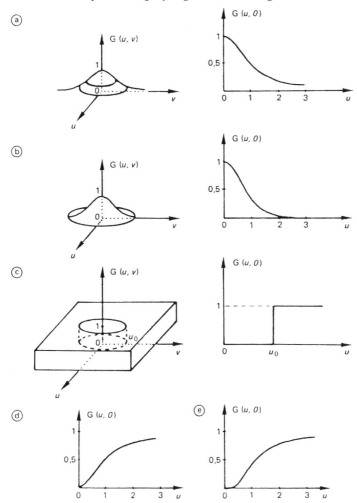

Fig.IX.5 - Transfer functions of various types for optically feasible filters; a) Butterworth's low-pass filter, with cross-section $G(u, O) = \dfrac{1}{1 + u^2}$, b) exponential low-pass filter, with cross-section $G(u, O) = e^{-u^2}$, c) ideal high-pass filter with cut-off frequency u_0, d) Butterworth's high-pass filter, with cross-section $G(u, O) = \dfrac{1}{1 + 1/u^2}$, e) exponential high-pass filter with cross-section $G(u, O) = e^{-(1/u^2)}$.

d) **The ideal high-pass filter**

$$\left\{ \begin{array}{l} G(u,\ v) = 1 \text{ if } d(u,\ v) \geq D_0 \\ G(u,\ v) = 0 \text{ if } d(u,\ v) < D_0 \end{array} \right\}.$$

This transfer function is shown schematically in figure IX.5.c.

e) **Butterworth's high-pass filter**

$$G(u,\ v) = 1/(1 + (\sqrt{2} - 1)\ (D_0/d(u,\ v))^{2n}$$

With $n = 1$ and $D_0 = (\sqrt{2} - 1)^{-\left(\frac{1}{2}\right)}$ we obtain the filter shown in figure IX.5.d the cross-section for which is $G(u,\ O) = \dfrac{1}{1 + 1/u^2}.$

f) **Exponential high-pass filter**

$$G(u,\ v) = e^{-(D_0/d(u,v))^n}$$

With $n = 2$ and $D_0 = 1$ we obtain the filter in figure IX.5.e the cross-section for which is $G(u,\ O) = e^{-(1/u^2)}$.

g) **Trapezoidal high-pass filter**
Figure IX.6.a shows this filter in perspective. Its cross-section is $G(u,\ O)$ such that:

$$\left\{ \begin{array}{ll} G(u,\ O) = 0 & \text{if } u < u_1 \\ G(u,\ O) = \dfrac{u - u_1}{u_0 - u_1} & \text{if } u_1 \leq u \leq u_0 \\ G(u,\ O) = 1 & \text{if } u > u_0 \end{array} \right\} \qquad \text{(figure IX.6.b)}$$

Figure IX.7 shows an example of analogue low-pass filtering using a microdensitometer with a square scanning aperture. The object for analysis is a test pattern measuring 1.3 x 1.3 mm (fig.IX.7.a). The test pattern is first filtered by an aperture of side 50 μ (fig. IX.7.b) and then an aperture of side 140μ (fig.IX.7.c). Smoothing due to high-frequency attenuation can be seen as well as contrast inversion caused by negative values of the transfer function (see chapter II, Fig.II.12.a).

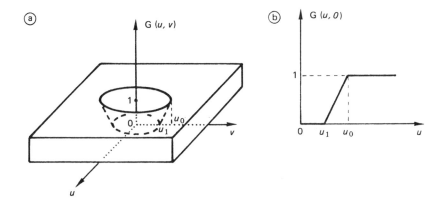

Fig.IX.6 - Trapezoidal high-pass filter; a) the filter viewed in perspective, b) the corresponding cross-section.

B. Digital domain

1. Discrete convolution in one and two dimensions [1,2,3]

a) **In one dimension**

We already know that the convolution of two analogue signals $e(x)$ and $R(x)$, where $R(x)$ represents, say, the impulse response of a continuous filter, is expressed by:

$$s(x) = e(x) * R(x) = \int_{-\infty}^{+\infty} e(x') \, R(x - x') \, \mathrm{d}x'$$

In the case of digital signals, that is of sampled signals, we are concerned only with the values of the signals at abscissa points in multiples of the sampling interval, say $e(\ell T)$. For the sake of simplicity we shall write these samples e_ℓ.

By analogy with continuous convolution, the discrete sum:

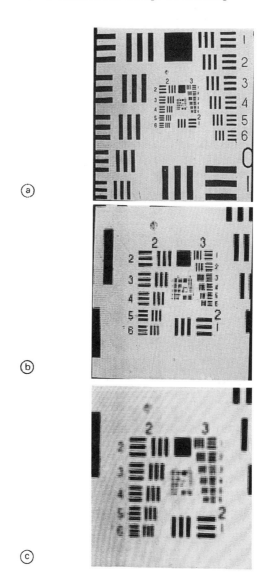

Fig.IX.7 - Analogue low-pass filtering using a scanning aperture of increasing size;
a) the object for analysis (measuring 1.3 x 1.3mm), b) smoothing with a
square aperture of side 50μ, c) smoothing with a square aperture of side 140μ.

$$s_\ell = e_\ell * R_\ell = \sum_{n=-\infty}^{+\infty} e_n \, R_{\ell-n} \tag{1}$$

is called the discrete convolution of discrete signals e_ℓ and R_ℓ.

To calculate each sample of the output signal it is therefore necessary to know every sample of the input signal and of the impulse response of the filter. There could theoretically be an infinite number of these.

In practice we shall assume that we are dealing with signals which contain a finite number only of samples arranged symmetrically with respect to $x = 0$.

- the input signal consists of $2m + 1$ samples ranging from e_{-m} to e_m $(e_{-m}, e_{-m+1}, \dots e_{-1}, e_0, e_1, \dots e_{m-1}, e_m)$
- the filter has $2k + 1$ samples from $R-k$ to R_k $(R_{-k}, R_{-k+1}, \dots R_{-1}, R_0, R_1, \dots R_{k-1}, R_k)$.

Let $k < m$.

Then $R_{\ell-n}$ is non-zero only when $\ell-n$ is such that:

$$-k \le \ell-n \le k$$

that is: $\ell-k \le n \le \ell+k$
giving the expression for samples $s\ell$:

$$s_\ell = \sum_{n=\sup(-m, \ell-k)}^{n=\inf(m, \ell+k)} e_n \, R_{\ell-n} \tag{2}$$

This can be explicated as follows:

This can be explicated as follows:

e		$-m-k$	$-m+k$	0	$m-k$	$m+k$
s_ℓ	0	$\displaystyle\sum_{n=-m}^{\ell+k} e_n R_{\ell-n}$	$\displaystyle\sum_{n=\ell-k}^{\ell+k} e_n R_{\ell-n}$	$\displaystyle\sum_{n=\ell-k}^{m} e_n R_{\ell-n}$		0

Example 1: (fig.IX.8.a)

$$k = m = 1 \quad e_{-1} = e_0 = e_1 = 1 \quad R_{-1} = R_0 = R_1 = 1$$

The above formula gives:

$$s_{-2} = 1 \quad s_{-1} = 2 \quad s_0 = 3 \quad s_1 = 2 \quad s_2 = 1$$

Example 2: (fig.IX.8.b)

$$k = 1 \quad m = 2 \quad e_{-2} = e_{-1} = e_0 = e_1 = e_2 = 1$$

$$R_{-1} = R_0 = R_1 = 1$$

From this we derive:

$$s_{-3} = 1 \quad s_{-2} = 2 \quad s_{-1} = s_0 = s_1 = 3 \quad s_2 = 2 \quad s_3 = 1$$

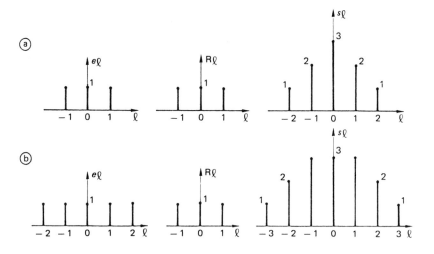

Fig.IX.8 - Illustrating the discrete convolution of two one-dimensional signals: $s_\ell = e_\ell * R_\ell$, a) e_ℓ and R_ℓ are limited to three samples of unity, b) e_ℓ has five samples, R_ℓ has three.

Note: discrete convolution can be written in the form of a product of matrices S = RE:

E is an input matrix in the form of a column of $2m + 1$ lines

R is a rectangular matrix of $2(m + k) + 1$ lines and $2m + 1$ columns. It is an *impulse response array*.

S is an output matrix in the form of a column of $2(m + k) + 1$ lines.

$$
\begin{pmatrix} s_{-m-k} \\ \vdots \\ s_{-m+k} \\ \vdots \\ s_\ell \\ \vdots \\ s_0 \\ \vdots \\ s_{m-k} \\ \vdots \\ s_{m+k} \end{pmatrix}
=
\begin{pmatrix}
R_{-k} & 0 & .. & .. & .. & .. & .. & .. & .. & .. & 0 \\
\boxed{R_k \ldots R_{-k}} & 0 & .. & .. & .. & .. & .. & 0 \\
0 & .. & \boxed{R_k \ldots R_{-k}} & 0 & .. & .. & .. & 0 \\
0 & .. & .. & .. & .. & .. & 0 & \boxed{R_k \ldots R_{-k}} \\
0 & .. & .. & .. & .. & .. & .. & .. & 0 & R_{-k}
\end{pmatrix}
\begin{pmatrix} e_{-m} \\ \vdots \\ e_{\ell+k} \\ \vdots \\ e_0 \\ \vdots \\ e_{\ell-k} \\ \vdots \\ e_m \end{pmatrix}
$$

Example 1 can therefore be written:

$$
\begin{pmatrix} s_{-2} \\ s_{-1} \\ s_0 \\ s_1 \\ s_2 \end{pmatrix}
=
\begin{pmatrix}
R_{-1} & 0 & 0 \\
R_0 & R_{-1} & 0 \\
R_1 & R_0 & R_{-1} \\
0 & R_1 & R_0 \\
0 & 0 & R_1
\end{pmatrix}
\begin{pmatrix} e_{-1} \\ e_0 \\ e_1 \end{pmatrix}
$$

$$
=
\begin{pmatrix}
1 & 0 & 0 \\
1 & 1 & 0 \\
1 & 1 & 1 \\
0 & 1 & 1 \\
0 & 0 & 1
\end{pmatrix}
\begin{pmatrix} 1 \\ 1 \\ 1 \end{pmatrix}
=
\begin{pmatrix} 1 \\ 2 \\ 3 \\ 2 \\ 1 \end{pmatrix}
$$

Similarly for example 2 we have:

$$\begin{pmatrix} s_{-3} \\ s_{-2} \\ s_{-1} \\ s_0 \\ s_1 \\ s_2 \\ s_3 \end{pmatrix} = \begin{pmatrix} R_{-1} & 0 & 0 & 0 & 0 \\ R_0 & R_{-1} & 0 & 0 & 0 \\ R_1 & R_0 & R_{-1} & 0 & 0 \\ 0 & R_1 & R_0 & R_{-1} & 0 \\ 0 & 0 & R_1 & R_0 & R_{-1} \\ 0 & 0 & 0 & R_1 & R_0 \\ 0 & 0 & 0 & 0 & R_1 \end{pmatrix} \begin{pmatrix} e_{-2} \\ e_{-1} \\ e_0 \\ e_1 \\ e_2 \end{pmatrix}$$

$$= \begin{pmatrix} 1 & 0 & 0 & 0 & 0 \\ 1 & 1 & 0 & 0 & 0 \\ 1 & 1 & 1 & 0 & 0 \\ 0 & 1 & 1 & 1 & 0 \\ 0 & 0 & 1 & 1 & 1 \\ 0 & 0 & 0 & 1 & 1 \\ 0 & 0 & 0 & 0 & 1 \end{pmatrix} \begin{pmatrix} 1 \\ 1 \\ 1 \\ 1 \\ 1 \\ 1 \end{pmatrix} = \begin{pmatrix} 1 \\ 2 \\ 3 \\ 3 \\ 3 \\ 2 \\ 1 \end{pmatrix}$$

Exercise: calculate the convolution of an input signal composed of unit samples with the impulse response R_ℓ shown in figure IX.8 (three samples of unity). a) e_ℓ has 15 samples from e_{-7} to e_7. The result is shown in figure IX.9.a. b) e_ℓ has 7 samples from e_{-3} to e_3. The result is shown in figure IX.9.b.

Very often the extent of the filter impulse response is low compared with the input signal, that is $k \ll m$ (as we shall see, this is true of images in particular). We can then confine our attentions to a single equation for calculating the discrete convolution, namely that for the "central zone".

$$s_\ell = \sum_{n=\ell-k}^{\ell+k} e_n R_{\ell-n} = e_{\ell-k} R_k + \ldots + e_\ell R_0 + \ldots + e_{\ell+k} R_{-k}$$

This equation, which is true for $-m+k < \ell < m-k$, is considered to be true for all cases. It will therefore be incorrect at each of the extremes, that is for $-m-k < \ell < -m+k$ and $m-k < \ell < m+k$, but this "*edge effect*" can be ignored.

Calculation of the discrete convolution can be considered as follows: to derive the value of each point s_ℓ the corresponding point e_ℓ in the input signal is read, along with neighbouring points $e_{\ell-k}, \ldots, e_{\ell+k}$. All these values are weighted by multiplying them by

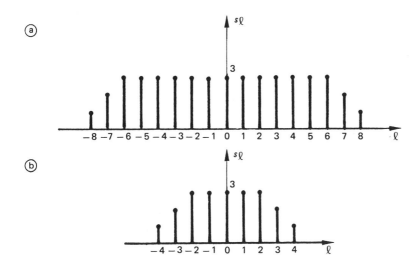

Fig.IX.9 - Convoluting an input signal e_ℓ composed of unit samples with the impulse response R_ℓ shown in figure IX.8; a) e_ℓ consists of 15 samples (ℓ: -7 to + 7), b) e_ℓ consists of 7 samples (ℓ: -3 to + 3).

R_k, ... R-k respectively:

$$
\begin{array}{ccc}
R_k & R_0 & R_{-k} \\
\downarrow & \downarrow & \downarrow \\
e_{\ell-k} & e_\ell & e_{\ell+k}
\end{array}
$$

The products so derived are then summed.

This corresponds to the product of the matrices:

$$
(s_\ell) = (R_k \ ... \ R_0 \ ... \ R_{-k}) \begin{pmatrix} e_{\ell-k} \\ . \\ . \\ e_\ell \\ . \\ . \\ e_{\ell+k} \end{pmatrix}
$$

The analogy with the convolution obtained by scanning with an aperture is at once apparent. It is as if an aperture, or window consisting of samples R_k ... $R-k$ from the impulse response, were being moved over the input signal in such a way that the samples falling within this window are averaged by the corresponding R_k coefficients. Here too it should be noted that the scanning window is not the impulse response itself, that is $R-k$, ... R_k, but the impulse response reversed. To put it another way, the impulse response is the reverse of the aperture (see chapter II).

b) In two dimensions

We shall restrict ourselves to square images. The two-dimensional discrete convolution of signals $e_{\ell\ell'}$ and $R_{\ell\ell'}$ is:

$$s_{\ell\ell'} = e_{\ell\ell'} * R_{\ell\ell'} = \sum_{n=-\infty}^{+\infty} \sum_{n'=-\infty}^{+\infty} e_{nn'} R_{\ell-n,\ell'-n'} \tag{3}$$

The first superscript is for the line, the second indicates the column. If the image $e_{\ell\ell'}$ is a square image of $(2m+1)$ lines and $(2m+1)$ columns, and if window $R_{\ell\ell'}$ is a square aperture of $(2k+1)$ lines and $(2k+1)$ columns with $k \le m$, $s_{\ell\ell'}$ is a square image of $2(m+k) + 1$ lines and columns.

The above equation becomes:

$$s_{\ell\ell'} = \sum_{n=\ell-k}^{\ell+k} \sum_{n'=\ell'-k}^{\ell'+k} e_{nn'} R_{\ell-n,\ell'-n'}$$

This equation only applies in the central zone:

$$\left\{ \begin{array}{l} -m+k \le \ell \le m-k \\ -m+k \le \ell \le m-k \end{array} \right\}$$

Ignoring the "edge effect", when $k \ll m$ it is assumed that the equation is true for all cases. These concepts are shown schematically in figure IX.10.a.

Note: the above equation may also be written in the form of a product of matrices

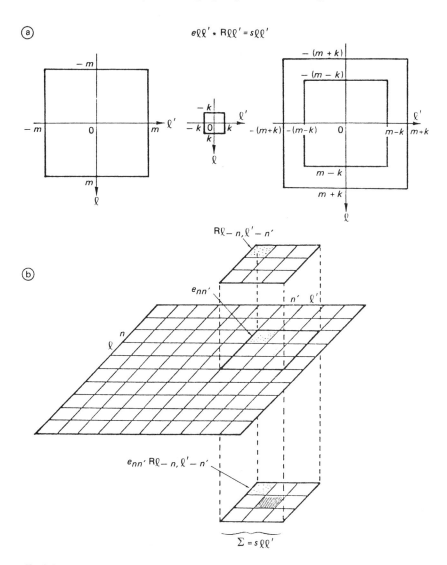

Fig.IX.10 - The two-dimensional discrete convolution of two square images $s_{\ell\ell'} = e_{\ell\ell'} * R_{\ell\ell'}$; a) if ℓ and ℓ' vary from $-m$ to $+m$ for $e_{\ell\ell'}$ and from $-k$ to $+k$ for $R_{\ell\ell'}$, then ℓ and ℓ' will vary from $-(m+k)$ to $m+k$ for $s_{\ell\ell'}$, with an "edge effect" between $-(m+k)$ and $-(m-k)$ and, symmetrically, between $m-k$ and $m+k$, b) the calculation explained for k=1. The 3 x 3 "window" $R_{\ell\ell'}$ is moved across the image $e_{\ell\ell'}$. Within this window each pixel $e_{nn'}$ of the image e is multiplied by the corresponding pixel $R_{\ell-n}$, $l'-n'$ of the image R. The sum of the results for the whole window gives $s_{\ell\ell'}$.

$$(s_{\ell\ell'}) = \left[\boxed{R_{kk}..R_{k\text{-}k}}\ ..\ \boxed{R_{0k}..R_{0\text{-}k}}\ ..\ \boxed{R_{\text{-}kk}..R_{\text{-}k\text{-}k}}\right]$$

$$* \begin{pmatrix} e_{\ell\text{-}k,\ell\ell'\text{-}k} \\ .. \\ e_{\ell\text{-}k,\ell\ell'+k} \\ .. \\ e_{\ell,\ell\ell'\text{-}k} \\ .. \\ e_{\ell,\ell\ell'+k} \\ .. \\ e_{\ell+k,\ell\ell'\text{-}k} \\ .. \\ e_{\ell+k,\ell\ell'+k} \end{pmatrix} \begin{matrix} \left.\vphantom{\begin{matrix}a\\a\\a\end{matrix}}\right\} & \text{line}\ \ell\text{-}k \\[2em] \left.\vphantom{\begin{matrix}a\\a\\a\end{matrix}}\right\} & \text{line}\ \ell \\[2em] \left.\vphantom{\begin{matrix}a\\a\\a\end{matrix}}\right\} & \text{line}\ \ell+k \end{matrix}$$

The method of calculation can be considered analogous to the method used for a one-dimensional signal: to derive each pixel $s_{\ell\ell'}$ the corresponding pixel $e_{\ell\ell'}$ of the input image is read, along with the pixels immediately next to it in the following window:

$e_{\ell\text{-}k,\ell'\text{-}k}$	...	$e_{\ell\text{-}k,\ell'}$	...	$e_{\ell\text{-}k,\ell'+k}$
...		...		...
$e_{\ell,\ell'\text{-}k}$		$e_{\ell\ell'}$		$e_{\ell,\ell'+k}$
...		...		...
$e_{\ell+k,\ell'\text{-}k}$		$e_{\ell+k,\ell'}$		$e_{\ell+k,\ell'+k}$

then each of these pixels is multiplied by the pixel which corresponds to it in the "reversed impulse response" window.

R_{kk}	...	R_{k0}	...	$R_{k\text{-}k}$
...		...		...
R_{0k}		R_{00}		$R_{0\text{-}k}$
...		...		...
$R_{\text{-}kk}$		$R_{\text{-}k0}$		$R_{\text{-}k\text{-}k}$

and finally all the derived products are summed.

For example where $k = 1$ the windows to be taken into account are the following 3 x 3 windows:

$e_{\ell-1,\ell'-1}$	$e_{\ell-1,\ell'}$	$e_{\ell-1,\ell'+1}$
$e_{\ell,\ell'-1}$	$e_{\ell\ell'}$	$e_{\ell,\ell'+1}$
$e_{\ell+1,\ell'-1}$	$e_{\ell+1,\ell'}$	$e_{\ell+1,\ell'+1}$

R_{11}	R_{01}	R_{-11}
R_{10}	R_{00}	R_{-10}
R_{1-1}	R_{0-1}	R_{-1-1}

This calculation is shown in the form of a diagram in figure IX.10.b, where window $R_{\ell\ell'}$ is shown being moved across the image $e_{\ell\ell'}$.

Example 1: let the images be represented by matrix notation [ ] and let us consider the convolution of two 3 x 3 images without ignoring the edge effect ($m=k=1$). We derive a 5 x 5 image:

$$
\begin{bmatrix} 1 & 1 & 1 \\ 1 & 1 & 1 \\ 1 & 1 & 1 \end{bmatrix} * \begin{bmatrix} 1 & 1 & 1 \\ 1 & 1 & 1 \\ 1 & 1 & 1 \end{bmatrix} = \begin{bmatrix} 1 & 2 & 3 & 2 & 1 \\ 2 & 4 & 6 & 4 & 2 \\ 3 & 6 & 9 & 6 & 3 \\ 2 & 4 & 6 & 4 & 2 \\ 1 & 3 & 3 & 2 & 1 \end{bmatrix}
$$

Example 2: the convolution of a 7 x 7 image with a 3 x 3 image ($m=k$, $k=1$). The edge effect is ignored. We calculate the resulting image for ℓ and ℓ' only between $-(m-k) = -2$ and $m-k = 2$, giving a significant image of 5 x 5.

$$
\begin{bmatrix} 0 & 0 & 0 & 10 & 10 & 10 & 10 \\ 0 & 0 & 0 & 10 & 10 & 10 & 10 \\ 0 & 0 & 0 & 10 & 10 & 10 & 10 \\ 0 & 0 & 0 & 10 & 10 & 10 & 10 \\ 0 & 0 & 0 & 10 & 10 & 10 & 10 \\ 0 & 0 & 0 & 10 & 10 & 10 & 10 \\ 0 & 0 & 0 & 10 & 10 & 10 & 10 \end{bmatrix} * \begin{bmatrix} 1 & 2 & 1 \\ 2 & 4 & 2 \\ 1 & 2 & 1 \end{bmatrix}
$$

$$= \begin{bmatrix} X & X & X & X & X & X & X \\ X & 0 & 40 & 120 & 160 & 160 & X \\ X & 0 & 40 & 120 & 160 & 160 & X \\ X & 0 & 40 & 120 & 160 & 160 & X \\ X & 0 & 40 & 120 & 160 & 160 & X \\ X & 0 & 40 & 120 & 160 & 160 & X \\ X & X & X & X & X & X & X \end{bmatrix}$$

(The pixels in the source image which are no longer significant have been shown as crosses).

2. *Applications of discrete convolution: smoothing, accentuating and detecting contours*

a) Smoothing

We now come back to example 2 above. The source image exhibits a sudden transition between a left-hand part with values of 0 and a right-hand part with values of 10. After convolution the transition has been softened, since values range from 0 on the left to 160 on the right, passing through intermediate values 40 and 120 in between. Thus the image has been *smoothed*, corresponding to an attenuation of the higher spatial frequencies.

This operation is often used to attenuate noise and irregularities in the image which are of a higher frequency than the details needing to be retained. It can be carried out several times, creating a soft-focus effect. In practice it is necessary to reach a compromise between noise reduction and the retention of significant details and contours.

It is also a fact that the edge effect becomes wider each time convolution is repeated, so caution is required.

Note: a side-effect of the matrix used in example 2 above, in the form of a pyramid, is to change the mean level in the image. To eliminate this effect it is usual to normalise the impulse response matrix by dividing it by the sum of its coefficients. Thus we shall use:

$$\frac{1}{16} \begin{bmatrix} 1 & 2 & 1 \\ 2 & 4 & 2 \\ 1 & 2 & 1 \end{bmatrix}$$

Figure IX.11 shows a digital smoothing of the test-pattern in figure IX.7.a. It is first digitized as 256 x 256 pixels of side 50μ, then convoluted with the 3 x 3 matrix above. The resulting image is very close to that derived from analogue smoothing with a 140μ aperture. Another example of digital smoothing is shown in figure IX.12, where two smoothing operations in succession have been carried out on the image shown in figure V.3.a using the 3 x 3 matrix described above.

Non-linear smoothing

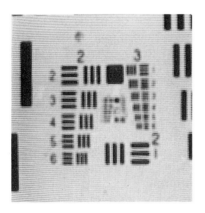

Fig.IX.11 - The image from figure IX.7.a was digitized as 256 x 256 pixels. It can be smoothed by convoluting it with the 3 x 3 window consisting of the matrix:

$$\frac{1}{16} \begin{bmatrix} 1 & 2 & 1 \\ 2 & 4 & 2 \\ 1 & 2 & 1 \end{bmatrix}.$$

Fig.IX.12 - The object in figure V.3.a after digital smoothing. Two smoothing operations have been carried out in succession using the 3 x 3 matrix:

$$\frac{1}{16} \begin{bmatrix} 1 & 2 & 1 \\ 2 & 4 & 2 \\ 1 & 2 & 1 \end{bmatrix}$$

The disadvantage of linear smoothing is that it treats useful signals, superimposed noise and interference alike. It is sometimes helpful to make use of non-linear algorithms. These will eliminate preferentially or attenuate any values which seem to differ abnormally from the values of neighbouring pixels. Here are two examples [3].

1) "Out-of-range" algorithm

If $\left| e_{\ell\ell'} - \frac{1}{8}[e_{\ell-1,\ell'-1} + \dots e_{\ell+1,\ell'+1}] \right| < \epsilon$ where the value of ϵ is arbitrary, the following matrix is used:

$$\frac{1}{8} \begin{bmatrix} 1 & 1 & 1 \\ 1 & 0 & 1 \\ 1 & 1 & 1 \end{bmatrix}$$

In all other cases the pixel remains unaltered.

2) Median filter

When there is an odd number of pixels in the window, the central pixel is assigned the median value of the set of pixels within the window. We know that the classic statistical definition of the median value of a sequence of N numbers from a_1 to a_N (where N is an odd number) is the number a_M in the series such that $\frac{N-1}{2}$ of the other numbers have a value $\leq a_M$ and $\frac{N-1}{2}$ have a value $\geq a_M$. For example in the sequence 50, 60, 155, 82, 75 the median value is $a_M = 75$.

This method eliminates isolated values related to noise spikes whilst giving rise to lower resolution loss than with linear filtering.

b) Detecting and accentuating contours

To some extent these operations are the opposite of smoothing in the sense that they amplify the higher spatial frequencies, so emphasising sudden transitions. They can be carried out in various ways:

1. By taking the *difference between the source image and the smoothed image*, both being weighted as necessary.

Consider a one-dimensional signal composed of seven unit samples from a rectangle (fig.IX.13.a). Convolution with the matrix I = [0 4 0] has the effect of multiplying the signal by 4. Convolution with L = [1 2 1] is a smoothing operation.

The operation I-L = [-1 2 -1] is an edge detection operator. The left-hand edge gives two samples equal to -1 and +1, the right-hand edge gives two samples +1 and -1 (fig.IX.13.b).

Since I-L has made the rectangle itself disappear it can be superimposed by adding I, that is by using the operator 2I-L = [-1 6 -1]. The result of convolution with this operator is shown in figure IX.13.c. The edges of the source image (multiplied by 4) have in fact been accentuated (they are also said to have been "raised").

In two-dimensions the following 3 x 3 accentuation windows are commonly used:

$$\begin{bmatrix} 0 & -1 & 0 \\ -1 & 5 & -1 \\ 0 & -1 & 0 \end{bmatrix} \quad \begin{bmatrix} -1 & -1 & -1 \\ -1 & 9 & -1 \\ -1 & -1 & -1 \end{bmatrix} \quad \begin{bmatrix} 1 & -2 & 1 \\ -2 & 5 & -2 \\ 1 & -2 & 1 \end{bmatrix}$$

By using derivative operators

We shall first consider a continuous one-dimensional signal $f(x)$. Its

derivative is $f'(x) = \dfrac{df}{dx} = \lim\limits_{h \to 0} \left(\dfrac{f(x) - f(x-h)}{h} \right)$. For a sampled

signal, and assuming the sampling period to be unity, we can say that the closest values of x correspond to $h = 1$. These are $f(x)$ and $f(x-1)$. An approximate derivative of the signal can therefore be obtained by taking the difference $f(x) - f(x-1)$, which amounts to convoluting with the matrix $[-1\ 1\ 0]$. The result of this operation for the object shown in figure IX.13.a may be seen in figure IX.13.d.

It may be seen that this process is the same as taking the difference between the object and the same object shifted towards the right by one sample (see fig.VII.3). This has the disadvantage of shifting the descending transition to the right by one sample.

It is possible to avoid such a shift by using Taylor's equation to obtain another approximation of the derivative. In fact this equation makes it possible to write:

$$f(x+1) = f(x-1) + 2f'(x_0) \qquad x-1 < x_0 < x+1$$

therefore $\qquad f(x+1) \simeq f(x-1) + 2f'(x)$

giving $f'(x) \simeq 2\,(f(x+1) - f(x-1))$.

To the nearest factor of $\dfrac{1}{2}$ this operation can be performed by convolution with the matrix $[-1\ 0\ 1]$. The result can be seen in figure IX.13.e. It shows that the transitions are symmetrical but twice as wide as in the previous case.

In two dimensions, the previous results make it possible to derive directly the 3 x 3 matrix producing the partial derivative $\dfrac{\partial f}{\partial x}$ known as the horizontal derivation:

We can use

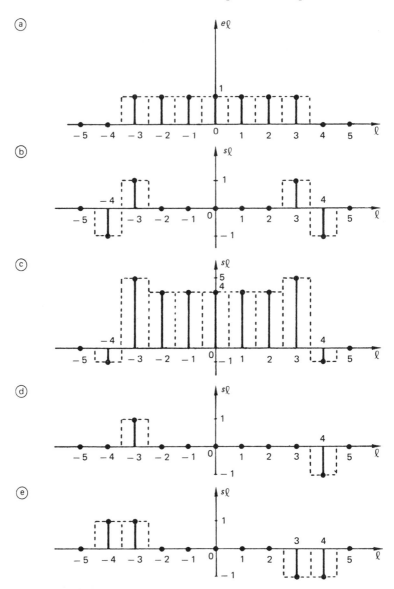

Fig.IX.13 - One-dimensional examples of edge accentuation and detection using discrete convolution; a) input signal e_ℓ consisting of seven unit samples, b) the result of convolution with [-1 2 -1]: edge detection, c) the result of convolution with [-1 6 -1]: accentuation or "raising" of the edges, d) the result of convolution with [-1 1 0]: derivation (the same as the difference between the object and the same object shifted by one sample), e) the result of convolution with [-1 0 -1]: derivation.

$$\begin{bmatrix} 0 & 0 & 0 \\ -1 & 1 & 0 \\ 0 & 0 & 0 \end{bmatrix} \quad \text{or} \quad \begin{bmatrix} 0 & 0 & 0 \\ -1 & 0 & 1 \\ 0 & 0 & 0 \end{bmatrix}.$$

Similarly the vertical derivative $\frac{\partial f}{\partial y}$ will have corresponding matrices of the following type:

$$\begin{bmatrix} 0 & 0 & 0 \\ 0 & 1 & 0 \\ 0 & -1 & 0 \end{bmatrix} \quad \text{or} \quad \begin{bmatrix} 0 & 1 & 0 \\ 0 & 0 & 0 \\ 0 & -1 & 0 \end{bmatrix}.$$

It is possible to calculate by way of exercise the convolutions for the image in example 2 of section 1 with the four matrices above, ignoring the edge effect. We find:

$$\begin{bmatrix} 0 & 0 & 0 & 10 & 10 & 10 & 10 \\ 0 & 0 & 0 & 10 & 10 & 10 & 10 \\ 0 & 0 & 0 & 10 & 10 & 10 & 10 \\ 0 & 0 & 0 & 10 & 10 & 10 & 10 \\ 0 & 0 & 0 & 10 & 10 & 10 & 10 \\ 0 & 0 & 0 & 10 & 10 & 10 & 10 \\ 0 & 0 & 0 & 10 & 10 & 10 & 10 \end{bmatrix} * \begin{bmatrix} 0 & 0 & 0 \\ -1 & 1 & 0 \\ 0 & 0 & 0 \end{bmatrix}$$

$$= \begin{bmatrix} X & X & X & X & X & X & X \\ X & 0 & 0 & 10 & 0 & 0 & X \\ X & 0 & 0 & 10 & 0 & 0 & X \\ X & 0 & 0 & 10 & 0 & 0 & X \\ X & 0 & 0 & 10 & 0 & 0 & X \\ X & 0 & 0 & 10 & 0 & 0 & X \\ X & X & X & X & X & X & X \end{bmatrix}$$

Similarly, if we write E for the matrix representing the unprocessed image, we have:

$$
E * \begin{bmatrix} 0 & 0 & 0 \\ 0 & 1 & 0 \\ 0 & -1 & 0 \end{bmatrix} = \begin{bmatrix} X & X & X & X & X & X & X \\ X & 0 & 0 & 0 & 0 & 0 & X \\ X & 0 & 0 & 0 & 0 & 0 & X \\ X & 0 & 0 & 0 & 0 & 0 & X \\ X & 0 & 0 & 0 & 0 & 0 & X \\ X & 0 & 0 & 0 & 0 & 0 & X \\ X & X & X & X & X & X & X \end{bmatrix}
$$

$$
= E * \begin{bmatrix} 0 & 1 & 0 \\ 0 & 0 & 0 \\ 0 & -1 & 0 \end{bmatrix}
$$

(In this case the vertical derivation gives a null result).

It should be remembered that a good non-directional contour detector is the length of the vector *gradient* (chap. VII, section B.1)

written as $\sqrt{\left(\dfrac{\partial f}{\partial x}\right)^2 + \left(\dfrac{\partial f}{\partial y}\right)^2}$ which is often calculated as an approxi-

mation by $\left|\dfrac{\partial f}{\partial x}\right| + \left|\dfrac{\partial f}{\partial y}\right|$ or by sup $\left(\left|\dfrac{\partial f}{\partial x}\right|, \left|\dfrac{\partial f}{\partial y}\right|\right)$.

- *The secondary partials derivative:*

By taking Taylor's equation to the second order, it is possible to derive an approximation for $\dfrac{\partial^2 f}{\partial x^2}$:

$$
f(x+1) = f(x) + 1.f'(x) + \tfrac{1}{2}f''(x_0) \quad x < x_0 < x+1
$$

giving
$$
f(x+1) \simeq f(x) + f'(x) + \tfrac{1}{2}f''(x)
$$

Replacing $f'(x)$ by the approximation $f(x) - f(x-1)$ we find:

$$
f(x+1) \simeq 2f(x) - f(x-1) + \tfrac{1}{2}f''(x)
$$

giving
$$
f''(x) \simeq 2f(x+1) - 4f(x) + 2f(x-1).
$$

To the nearest factor of 2, this expression gives us the matrix:

$$\begin{bmatrix} 0 & 0 & 0 \\ 1 & -2 & 1 \\ 0 & 0 & 0 \end{bmatrix}$$

Similarly for $\dfrac{\partial^2 f}{\partial y^2}$ we find:

$$\begin{bmatrix} 0 & 1 & 0 \\ 0 & -2 & 0 \\ 0 & 1 & 0 \end{bmatrix}$$

Thus for image E (example 2, section 1) we derive:

$$\begin{bmatrix} 0 & 0 & 0 \\ 1 & -2 & 1 \\ 0 & 0 & 0 \end{bmatrix} * = \begin{bmatrix} X & X & X & X & X & X & X \\ X & 0 & 10 & -10 & 0 & 0 & X \\ X & 0 & 10 & -10 & 0 & 0 & X \\ X & 0 & 10 & -10 & 0 & 0 & X \\ X & 0 & 10 & -10 & 0 & 0 & X \\ X & 0 & 10 & -10 & 0 & 0 & X \\ X & X & X & X & X & X & X \end{bmatrix}$$

$$E * \begin{bmatrix} 0 & 1 & 0 \\ 0 & -2 & 0 \\ 0 & 1 & 0 \end{bmatrix} = \begin{bmatrix} X & X & X & X & X & X & X \\ X & 0 & 0 & 0 & 0 & 0 & X \\ X & 0 & 0 & 0 & 0 & 0 & X \\ X & 0 & 0 & 0 & 0 & 0 & X \\ X & 0 & 0 & 0 & 0 & 0 & X \\ X & 0 & 0 & 0 & 0 & 0 & X \\ X & X & X & X & X & X & X \end{bmatrix}$$

Laplacian operator: this is written as $\dfrac{\partial^2 f}{\partial x^2} + \dfrac{\partial^2 f}{\partial y^2}$ giving the matrix

$$\begin{bmatrix} 0 & 1 & 0 \\ 1 & -4 & 1 \\ 0 & 1 & 0 \end{bmatrix} \text{ or even, changing signs, } \begin{bmatrix} 0 & -1 & 0 \\ -1 & 4 & -1 \\ 0 & -1 & 0 \end{bmatrix}.$$

Other matrices are also used as an approximation for the Laplacian operator. It is a good contour detector and isotropic, that is non-directional in nature, though it does have the disadvantage of emphasising noise:

$$\begin{bmatrix} 1 & -2 & 1 \\ -2 & 4 & -2 \\ 1 & -2 & 1 \end{bmatrix} \quad \begin{bmatrix} -1 & 0 & -1 \\ 0 & 4 & 0 \\ -1 & 0 & -1 \end{bmatrix} \quad \begin{bmatrix} -1 & -1 & -1 \\ -1 & 8 & -1 \\ -1 & -1 & -1 \end{bmatrix}$$

For example:

$$E * \begin{bmatrix} -1 & -1 & -1 \\ -1 & 8 & -1 \\ -1 & -1 & -1 \end{bmatrix} = \begin{bmatrix} X & X & X & X & X & X & X \\ X & 0 & -30 & 30 & 0 & 0 & X \\ X & 0 & -30 & 30 & 0 & 0 & X \\ X & 0 & -30 & 30 & 0 & 0 & X \\ X & 0 & -30 & 30 & 0 & 0 & X \\ X & 0 & -30 & 30 & 0 & 0 & X \\ X & X & X & X & X & X & X \end{bmatrix}$$

- *Note*: a fault with derivation operators is that they show up negative values, as could be seen in the foregoing examples. Since this is an unwanted feature, a positive constant is added in order to shift the values of the derived image.

- *Directional derivation operators*

There is often a need to emphasise the transitions in a particular direction. Thus the operator $\frac{\partial f}{\partial x}$ shows up vertical contours whilst tending to conceal horizontal outlines.

Sobel operators are often used. These operators are for derivation with respect to one of the eight possible directions: North → South, South → North, West → East, East → West, North-East → South-West, South-West → North-East, North-West → South-East and South-East → North-West. For example the N-E → S-W derivative accentuates contours oriented N-W → S-E, casting shadows over the image as if illuminated horizontally from the North-East.

The corresponding matrices are as follows:

$$
\begin{bmatrix} -2 & -1 & 0 \\ -1 & 0 & 1 \\ 0 & 1 & 2 \end{bmatrix}
\begin{bmatrix} -1 & -2 & -1 \\ 0 & 0 & 0 \\ 1 & 2 & 1 \end{bmatrix}
\begin{bmatrix} 0 & -1 & -2 \\ 1 & 0 & -1 \\ 2 & 1 & 0 \end{bmatrix}
$$

$$
\begin{bmatrix} -1 & 0 & 1 \\ -2 & 0 & 2 \\ -1 & 0 & 1 \end{bmatrix}
\qquad
\begin{bmatrix} 1 & 0 & -1 \\ 2 & 0 & -2 \\ 1 & 0 & -1 \end{bmatrix}
$$

$$
\begin{bmatrix} 0 & 1 & 1 \\ -1 & 0 & 1 \\ -2 & -1 & 0 \end{bmatrix}
\begin{bmatrix} 1 & 2 & 1 \\ 0 & 0 & 0 \\ -1 & -2 & -1 \end{bmatrix}
\begin{bmatrix} 2 & 1 & 0 \\ 1 & 0 & -1 \\ 0 & -1 & -2 \end{bmatrix}
$$

- *Miscellaneous examples*: Figures IX.14 to IX.18 show some examples of image processing operations such as accentuation, Laplacian operator and directional filtering.

C. Fourier transform and discrete fourier transform of digital signals [1, 3, 6]

1. In one dimension

Basing our reasoning on a continuous, finite one-dimensional signal $s(x)$ (fig.IX.19.a) we can show that its F.T. $S(f)$ is semi-infinite. In practice there is a relatively high cut-off frequency. Figure IX.19.b gives two examples, one shown as a solid line, the other broken.

1) Let $s(x)$ be sampled at an interval of T (fig.IX.19.c). We then obtain m samples during a signal interval of mT (some samples possibly being zero). These samples form a signal $c(x)$ which has a F.T. of $C(f)$ derived by multiplying $S(f)$ by $\frac{1}{T}$ and repeating the component with a period of $\frac{1}{T}$ (fig.IX.19.d). $C(f)$ is a periodic function giving rise to aliasing. For any given value of T, the degree of aliasing increases with the frequencies in $S(f)$.

(a)   (b)

Fig.IX.14 - a) The image in figure V.3.a, here accentuated by subtracting the smoothed image from the source image, b) smoothing image a) "softens" the overall effect.

Fig.IX.15 - Detecting the contours in the image from figure V.3.a. A close approximation to the Laplacian operator is obtained from convolution with the 3 x 3 matrix

$$\begin{bmatrix} -1 & 0 & -1 \\ 0 & 4 & 0 \\ -1 & 0 & -1 \end{bmatrix}.$$

Fig.IX.16 - West-East directional filtering of the image in figure V.3.a using a Sobel operator. The discrete 3 x 3 matrix used is:

$$\begin{bmatrix} 1 & 0 & -1 \\ 2 & 0 & -2 \\ 1 & 0 & -1 \end{bmatrix}.$$

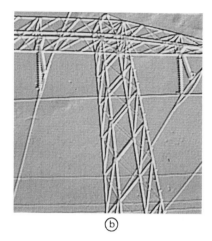

(a)   (b)

Fig.IX.17 - North-East South-West directional filtering using a Sobel operator. The 3 x 3 matrix used is as follows: $\begin{bmatrix} 2 & 1 & 0 \\ 1 & 0 & -1 \\ 0 & -1 & -2 \end{bmatrix}$; a) the unprocessed image, b) the processed image.

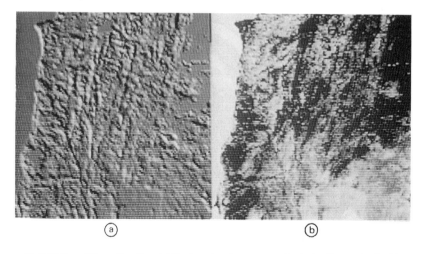

(a)   (b)

Fig.IX.18 - Using directional filtering to show up geological alignments in the South Lebanon region; a) the processed image showing North-West South-East and East-West alignments, b) the original satellite image from Landsat after contrast enhancement (from P.Masson, P.Chavel, S.Equilbey and A.Marion). [16]

For the moment let us repeat signal $c(x)$ with a period of mT (fig. IX.19.e). Signal $b(x)$ is obtained, with a F.T. of $B(f)$ which can be derived from $C(f)$ by multiplying by $\dfrac{1}{mT}$ and sampling at an interval of $\dfrac{1}{mT}$ (fig.IX.19.f).

$B(f)$ is a sampled periodic function. In order to calculate samples B_k appearing in the expression:

$$B(f) = \sum_{k=-\infty}^{+\infty} B_k\, \delta(f-mT),$$

we first calculate $C(f)$ from $c(x)$:

$$c(x) = \sum_{n} s(nT)\, \delta(x-nT)$$

Since $\mathscr{F}\,(\delta(x-nT)) = e^{-2\pi jnTf}$ we can derive:

$$C(f) = \sum_{n} s(nT)\, e^{-2\pi jnTf}$$

representing the F.T. of the digital signal $c(x)$.

Thus when we multiply by $\dfrac{1}{mT}$ and sample at a period of $\dfrac{1}{mT}$ we derive samples of B_k.

$$\boxed{\; B_k = \frac{1}{mT} \sum_{n} s(nT)\, e^{-2\pi jk\frac{n}{m}} \;} \tag{4}$$

The above summation covers the m samples of the signal.

Since $B(f)$ is periodic, we in fact need calculate only the samples for the central component of width $\dfrac{1}{T}$. We therefore have m samples of B_k.

This expression connects values of the m signal samples $s_n = s(nT)$ to the m samples of B_k. It is the discrete Fourier transform (abbreviated to D.F.T.) of the digital signal.

It must be stressed that when we start out with m signal samples at a separation of T (thus with width mT) we derive m samples of B_k at

a separation of $\dfrac{1}{mT}$ $\left(\text{thus with width } \dfrac{1}{T}\right)$.

2) We should arrive at the same result if we considered that the signal $b(x)$ is obtained by first repeating $s(x)$ with a period of mT, giving a signal $a(x)$ (fig.IX.19.g). Its F.T. is $A(f)$, which is a sampled function (fig.IX.19.h).

Let A_k be the samples. Then we can write:

$$A(f) = \sum_{k=-\infty}^{+\infty} A_k \, \delta\left(f - \frac{1}{mT}\right)$$

We then sample $a(x)$ at a period of T, which gives $b(x)$ (fig.IX.19.i) of spectrum $B(f)$ (fig.IX.19.j). $B(f)$ is derived from $A(f)$ by multiplying by $\dfrac{1}{T}$ and repeating the component with a period of

$\dfrac{1}{T}$. This inevitably causes overlap (aliasing) so that the B_k and A_k features are not equal, as is obvious from comparing figures h) and j). We can show the relation:

$$B_k = \sum_{n=-\infty}^{+\infty} A_{k-nm}$$

Consequently the D.F.T. takes account of aliasing errors arising from sampling the analogue signal. Nevertheless it is possible to work back without error from the B_k coefficients, not to $s(x)$ but to the samples $s(nT)$. In fact let us consider $b(x)$ and $B(f)$. The samples $s(nT)$ may be considered as the coefficients of the Fourier series development of the periodic signal $B(f)$. We can therefore write:

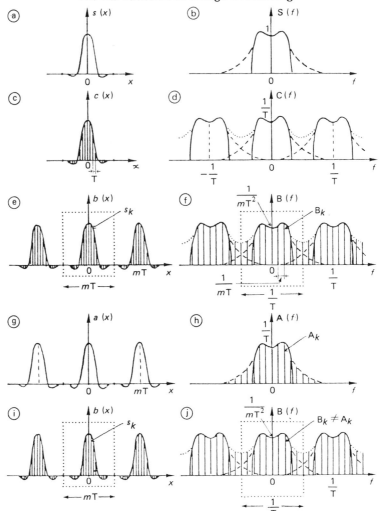

Fig.IX.19 - Fourier transform and discrete Fourier transform of a one-dimensional
signal; a) finite analogue signal s(x), b) its Fourier transform S(f), theoretically
semi-infinite but in practice with a very high cut-off frequency (broken or
unbroken lines), c) c(x) derived from sampling s(x) at an interval of T giving
m samples with separation of T, d) the spectrum C(f) of c(x) derived by multiplying S(f) by $\frac{1}{T}$ and repeating the component at intervals of $\frac{1}{T}$. The solid
curve is derived where there is no aliasing. The broken line gives the shaded
spectrum where there is aliasing, e) f(x) being c(x) repeated at intervals of
mT,

f) the spectrum B(f) of b(x) derived from C(f) by multiplying by $\frac{1}{mT}$ and sam-

pling at intervals of $\frac{1}{mT}$. Features B_k are the samples belonging to the cen-

tral component of width $\frac{1}{T}$: they are the D.F.T. (discrete Fourier transform)

of the digital signal composed of samples s_k also derived from the central component of length mT from b(x), g) a(x) being s(x) repeated at intervals of mT, h) the spectrum A(f) of a(x), composed of samples A_k, i) if a(x) is sampled at intervals of T, function b(x) from figure e) is derived, j) the spectrum

B(f) of b(x) is derived from A(f) by multiplying by $\frac{1}{T}$ and repeating the com-

ponent at intervals of $\frac{1}{T}$. In general B_k features differ from A_k features

because of aliasing. Features s_k and B_k are each other's D.F.T.

$$s(nT) = T \int_{-1/2T}^{1/2T} B(f)\, e^{2\pi jnTf}\, df$$

but $B(f) = \sum_{k=-\infty}^{+\infty} B_k \delta\left(f - \frac{k}{mT}\right)$ giving:

$$s(nT) = T \int_{-1/2T}^{1/2T} \sum_{k=-\infty}^{+\infty} B_k \delta\left(f - \frac{k}{mT}\right) e^{2\pi jnTf}\, df$$

$$= T \sum_{k(\text{period } 1/T)} B_k \int_{-\infty}^{+\infty} \delta\left(f - \frac{k}{mT}\right) e^{2\pi jnTf}\, df$$

Since $\delta\left(f - \frac{k}{mT}\right) e^{2\pi jnTf} = \delta\left(f - \frac{k}{mT}\right) e^{2\pi jk \frac{n}{m}}$ we have:

$$s(nT) = T \underbrace{\sum_{k(\text{period } 1/T)}} B_k \, e^{2\pi jk \frac{n}{m}} \underbrace{\int_{-\infty}^{+\infty} \delta\left(f - \frac{k}{mT}\right) df}_{= 1}$$

$$\boxed{s(nT) = T \sum_{k(\text{period } 1/T)} B_k \, e^{2\pi jk \frac{n}{m}}} \qquad (5)$$

This expression, which is perfectly symmetrical with (4), expresses the fact that the s_k and B_k features are each other's D.F.T. They are samples of the central components of $b(x)$ and $B(f)$ (fig.e and f).

It takes m multiplications and m additions of each sample to calculate a D.F.T., giving m^2 multiplications and m^2 additions in total. In order to reduce calculation time and overheads, algorithms have been developed which use fewer operations. The best known of these is the Fast Fourier Transform (F.F.T.) developed by Cooley and Tukey, which uses $m\log_2 m$ multiplications and additions. The saving increases with m.

Figure IX.10 provides an illustration of the D.F.T. concept. Here we see the D.F.T. of a gate function defined by three samples. Figures a) and b) represent the gate $s(x)$ of width τ and its spectrum $S(f) = \text{sinc } \pi\tau f$. Figures c) and d) represent $c(x)$ derived from sampling $s(x)$ at intervals of $T = \frac{\tau}{3}$, together with its spectrum

$$C(f) = \frac{1}{\tau}\left[1 + 2 \cos 2\pi \frac{3f}{\tau}\right].$$

Function $b(x)$ is $c(x)$ repeated at intervals of $3\tau = 9T$. Over this period there are nine samples s_k (s_{-4} to s_4). Only s_{-1}, s_0 and s_1 are non-zero (fig.e). Figure f) shows the function $B(f)$, being the F.T. of $b(x)$. In the width $\frac{1}{T} = \frac{3}{\tau}$ of the central component there are nine coefficients B_k (B_{-4} to B_4) forming the D.F.T. of the s_k features in figure e). It can easily be shown that if we consider the function $a(x)$, being $s(x)$ repeated at intervals of 3τ (fig.g), its F.T. $A(f)$ is composed of samples A_k which are plainly different from features B_k (fig.h) because of aliasing.

2. Extension to images

The above concepts can easily be extended to include images, considered as two-dimensional signals.

Naturally the number of operations is squared, so that the usefulness of the fast Fourier transform is even more evident in such cases.

This is because the F.T. is a global operation involving every pixel in the image.

Figure IX.21 shows eight images and their discrete Fourier transforms.

D. Comparison of digital processing by convolution and by fourier transform

First we should recapitulate the errors introduced by digitization and reconstruction. They are the same in both cases:

- *sampling errors* creating an effect of overlapping spectra (aliasing). This error is always present for finite signals. It can be reduced by oversampling, but this increases the amount of information to be handled, and with it the required memory capacity, calculation time and, therefore, the overheads.

- the *aperture effect* of the digitizer. It attenuates the higher frequencies thereby reducing image detail, but also reduces aliasing and high frequency noise.

- *reconstruction error* due to interpolation by a filter which differs from the ideal filter (cardinal filter). A one-order blocking filter is in general better than a zero-order blocking filter, except for certain "square" signals such as test patterns.

- *quantization error* due to the number of levels in the digitizer. The error can be reduced by using digitizers which give higher resolution and by carrying out calculations with greater precision.

When filtering has to be carried out, the method using convolution is faster and more efficient if one of the signals is narrow in extent (such as using a 3 x 3 or 5 x 5 matrix on a 256 x 256 or 512 x 512 image).

When two digitized signals are convoluted digitization errors are summed.

If filtering is done via the spectrum and the D.F.T., that is by operating in the frequency domain, it is necessary to calculate one or two discrete Fourier transforms, multiply in the spectral domain and then return to the spatial domain by reversed F.T. In general this is longer and more costly. This method is therefore to be avoided unless sophisticated filtering is being carried out which does not correspond to simple convolution windows of limited size.

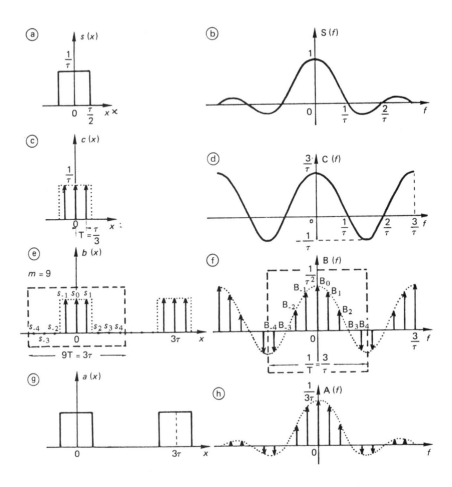

Fig.IX.20 - Example D.F.T.: a) $s(x)$, being a gate of width τ, b) $S(f) = \text{sinc } \pi\tau f$, being the spectrum of $s(x)$, c) $c(x)$ being $s(x)$ sampled at intervals of $T = \frac{\tau}{3}$, d) the spectrum $C(f)$ of $c(x)$ is a cosine of period $\frac{3}{\tau}$, e) $b(x)$ being $c(x)$ repeated at intervals of 3τ. Over the period $9T = 3\tau$ there are nine samples s_k (s_{-4} to s_4), f) the spectrum $B(f)$ of $b(x)$; in the width $\frac{1}{T} = \frac{1}{\tau}$ there are nine coefficients B_k (B_{-4} to B_4) forming the D.F.T. of the s_k features in figure e, g) $a(x)$ being $s(x)$ repeated at intervals of 3τ, h) the spectrum $A(f)$ of $a(x)$ with coefficients $A_k \neq B_{*k}$.

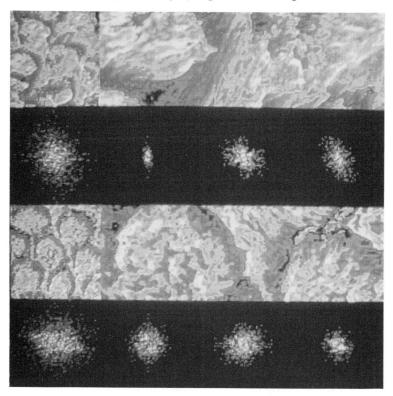

Fig.IX.21 - Eight images and their discrete Fourier transforms.

We should observe that if we wish merely to reconstruct a digitized signal without carrying out any processing, the D.F.T. does not introduce any additional errors. On the other hand, if we filter by multiplying the D.F.T.'s of two signals, we introduce an additional error which may be considered an aliasing error in the spatial domain. In fact, if $B(f)$ (fig.IX.19.f) is multiplied by a filtering function $F(f)$, then the periodic function $b(x)$ is convoluted with the impulse response $R(x)$ which corresponds to $F(f)$. But this function is also a periodic function and tends to make adjacent cycles of $b(x)$ overlap with the primary component, particularly in regions close to $x = \pm \dfrac{mT}{2}$.

If the component of $R(x)$ is narrow and $b(x)$ is gradually variable in these regions, the effect is minimal. If on the other hand there are rapid variations, especially if $b(x)$ does not equal $\pm \dfrac{mT}{2}$ (i.e. the two extremes of the aperture), the resulting function will be heavily marked by artefacts. This effect can be kept to a minimum, either by choosing a window of sufficient width for $b(x)$ to be weak at each of the extremes, or by artificially removing the discontinuities.

These solutions all require more processing time, make the calculations more complicated and add overheads.

E. Restoration of images [1,2,3,4,6,12,14]

So far this book has shown that the various processes involved in image formation introduce errors and disturbances which degrade the image of the scanned object. These problems arise when the image of the object is being formed optically, when it is being recorded on photographic medium, during digitization, and during the calculations needed to process and reconstruct the image for display purposes. Sensors introduce non-linear features, noise and various other errors. The same is also true of matters such as transmission systems and atmospheric disturbances.

There is often a need to use the degraded image in order to produce a "closest possible" resemblance to the original undisturbed image, that is to *restore* the original image. To achieve this the degradation or degradations must be modelled as accurately as possible, and the term "closest possible" must be defined precisely.

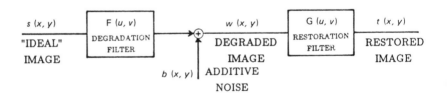

Fig.IX.22 - Model of the degradation and restoration of an image.

A commonly used model is shown in figure IX.22. Here the degradation is produced by a linear filter of transfer function $F(u, v)$ and all sources of noise have been simplified to an additive noise $b(x, y)$. The ideal image $s(x, y)$ is therefore giving a degraded image $w(x, y)$. Restoration will be carried out also using a linear filter with a transfer function of $G(u, v)$ to produce a restored image $t(x, y)$ which must be as close as possible to $s(x, y)$.

1. Inverse filtering

First, let the noise be negligible, that is let $b(x, y) = 0$.

It is natural to think of using a restoration filter having a transfer function of

$$\boxed{G(u, v) = \frac{1}{F(u, v)}} \tag{6}$$

This is known as an *inverse filter*, and performs deconvolution in the *spatial domain*.

The restored image will have a F.T. of

$$T(u, v) = \frac{W(u, v)}{F(u, v)} = \frac{F(u, v)S(u, v)}{F(u, v)} = S(u, v)$$

and must then be equal to the ideal, non-degraded image. This is theoretical, however, because in practice problems arise:

- $F(u, v)$ may be cancelled out at certain frequencies. $T(u, v)$ then becomes semi-infinite and unattainable.
- $F(u, v)$ and $W(u, v)$ may cancel one another at certain frequencies: $T(u, v)$ is then an indeterminate function.
- noise $b(x, y)$ is never strictly zero. When $F(u, v)$ is very small, that is towards the higher frequencies of the spectrum, noise is usually the dominant factor. A common situation is represented in figure IX.23, where the F.T. of the ideal signal $S(u, v)$ has been shown schematically along with the power spectrum (or Wiener's spectrum) of the noise $P_B(u, v)$, the transfer function of the degradation $F(u, v)$ and the transfer function of the inverse filter $G(u, v) = \frac{1}{F(u, v)}$. Since it is disadvantageous to amplify the noise alone beyond the maximum useful frequency u_0 in the signal, $G(u, v)$ may be limited to a constant value beyond u_0 (fig.IX.23.e).

2. Wiener's method

This method ascribes a meaning to the expression "a restored image resembling the ideal image as closely as possible". It is in fact a method of estimation by least squares, in which it is considered that the images are occurrences of a stationary and ergodic random process. The aim is then to make the mean of the squares of the differences between the original image and the restored image as small as possible.

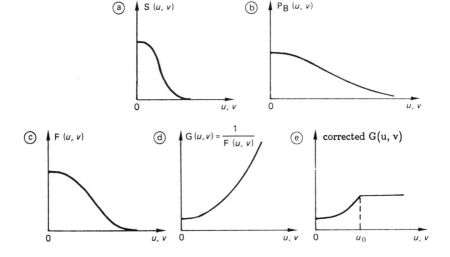

Fig.IX.23 - Restoration by inverse filtering: a) the spectrum S(u, v) of the "ideal" image, b) Wiener's spectrum P_B (u, v) of the noise, c) the transfer function F(u, v) of the model degradation filter, d) the transfer function G(u, v) = $\dfrac{1}{F(u, v)}$ of the inverse filter, e) corrected G(u, v), the transfer function of the restoration filter.

Let us clarify this concept by first assuming that $F(u, v) = 1$, meaning that the degradation is due entirely to noise.

a) **Wiener's estimator**

The model is shown in figure IX.24, where $F(u, v)$ is non-existent. The functions for the ideal image $s(x, y)$ and the noise $b(x, y)$ are random, ergodic and stationary. So too are the functions for the degraded image $w(x, y)$ and the restored image $t(x, y)$. It is assumed that their power spectra are known or measured in advance, and the aim is to make the mean quadratic error $\langle e^2(x, y)\rangle$ as small as possible.

$$\langle e^2(x, y)\rangle = \overline{e^2(x, y)} = \frac{1}{S} \iint_S e^2(x, y)\, dx\, dy$$

with $e(x, y) = s(x, y) - t(x, y)$ and S the surface area of the images.

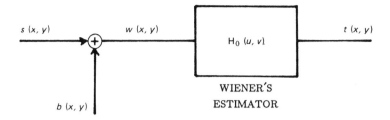

Fig.IX.24 - Wiener's estimator: a model.

It can be shown that the impulse response $h_0(x, y)$ of the filter giving this result, known as *Wiener's estimator*, is such that:

$$C_{ws} = h_0 * C_w \tag{7}$$

where $C_w(x, y)$ is the *autocorrelation function* of the image $w(x, y)$ and $C_{ws}(x, y)$ is the *cross-correlation function* of the images $w(x, y)$ and $s(x, y)$, defined in the same way.

Taking the Fourier transforms of both sides of equation (7) it is possible to derive the transfer function of Wiener's estimator:

$$H_0(u, v) = \frac{P_{ws}(u, v)}{P_w(u, v)} \tag{8}$$

$P_w(u, v)$ is the power spectrum of the degraded image $w(x, y)$. Similarly $P_{ws}(u, v)$, being the F.T. of $C_{ws}(x, y)$, is called the interaction power spectrum of $w(x, y)$ and $s(x, y)$.

A case of special importance is one in which *the signal and the noise are not correlated*. It can then be shown that:

$$P_w = P_s + P_b \quad \text{and} \quad P_{ws} = P_s$$

where $P_b(u, v)$ is the power spectrum of the noise $b(x, y)$ and $P_s(u, v)$ is the power spectrum of the non-degraded image $s(x, y)$.

Equation (8) becomes:
$$H_0(u, v) = \frac{P_s(u, v)}{P_s(u, v) + P_B(u, v)} \tag{9}$$

b) **Wiener's filter**

Deconvolution by Wiener's filter is shown schematically in figure IX.25.a, where $F(u, v) \neq 1$. By using the inverse filter $\dfrac{1}{F(u, v)}$ it is easy to arrive at an equivalent of the diagram shown in figure IX.25.b. This corresponds to restoration using Wiener's estimator with the power spectrum of the noise $b_1(x, y)$ at $P_{b_1} = \dfrac{P_b}{|F(u, v)|^2}$ (see section IV.F.3).

In the case where there is no correlation between the signal and the noise, equation (9) gives us the estimator transfer function:

$$H_0(u, v) = \frac{P_S(u, v)}{P_S(u, v) + P_{b_1}(u, v)}$$

giving

$$H_0(u, v) = \frac{P_S(u, v)}{P_S(u, v) + \dfrac{P_b(u, v)}{|F(u, v)^2|}} = \frac{P_S(u, v)\,|F(u, v)|^2}{P_S(u, v)\,|F(u, v)|^2 + P_b(u, v)} \, .$$

Upon re-examining diagram IX.25.a it is possible to derive the transfer function of Wiener's filter. This turns out to be the filter resulting from cascading the inverse filter with the previous estimator:

$$G(u, v) = \frac{H_0(u, v)}{F(u, v)}$$

giving

$$G(u, v) = \frac{F^*(u, v)\,P_S(u, v)}{|F(u, v)|^2\,P_S(u, v) + P_b(u, v)} \tag{10}$$

where $F^*(u, v)$ represents the conjugate complex of $F(u, v)$.

It should be observed that where there is no noise, that is if $P_b(u, v) = 0$, Wiener's filter resumes the function of an inverse filter.

The examples in figure IX.26 enable a comparison to be made between the effects of inverse filtering and Wiener's filtering on degraded images in the presence of increasing noise. The superior performance of Wiener's filter becomes all the more marked as the noise increases.

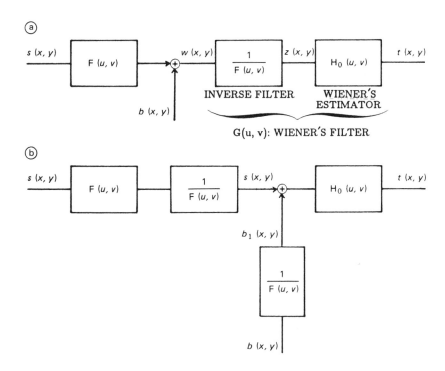

Fig.IX.25 - Deconvolution by Wiener's filter; a) the method in principle, b) an
equivalent of the diagram shown in figure a).

3. Adaptive filter (or)

The technique of adaptive filtering (or matched detection) is of long
standing, since it was originally developed for detecting radar and
sonar signals. The technique is not concerned with restoration in the
strictest sense, since here the aim of the filter is not to restore the
"best possible" shape of a signal degraded by noise and various other
forms of contamination, but simply to detect the actual presence of a
signal of known shape which is submerged by noise. It is therefore a
detection or location problem. In the context of images it amounts to
an example of pattern recognition.

The model used is shown in figure IX.27, where it is assumed that
the noise $b(x, y)$ is superimposed additively on the signal $s(x, y)$. It is
assumed that signal $s(x, y)$ is known and as such is a deterministic
function. The noise $b(x, y)$ is a stationary random function with a

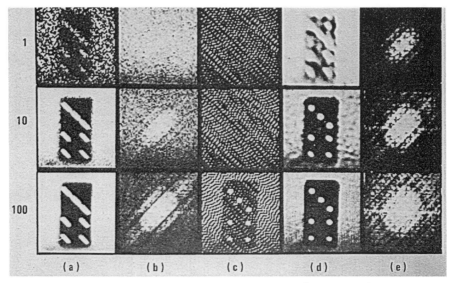

Fig.IX.26 - Examples of inverse filtering and Wiener's filtering; a) degraded images, b) their Fourier spectra, c) the images restored by inverse filtering, d) the images restored by Wiener's filtering, e) Fourier spectra of the images in d) (from R.C.Gonzalez and P.Wintz).[1] (Source: J.L.Harris, NASA Publication, 1968).

power spectrum $P_b(u, v)$ which is assumed to be known.

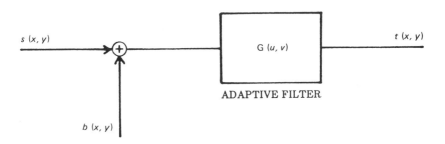

Fig.IX.27 - Adaptive filtering: a model.

The selected detection criterion involves making the signal-to-noise ratio which leaves the filter as large as possible. This ratio is defined as follows:

$$\text{SNR} = \frac{\text{output signal power at } (x_0, y_0)}{\text{mean noise power}}$$

But the signal power is equal to the square of the modulus, that is $|t(x_0, y_0)|^2$. The noise power is obtained by integrating $P_b(u, v)$ over all possible frequencies. This gives:

$$\text{SNR} = \frac{|t(x_0, y_0)|^2}{\iint P_b(u, v)\, du\, dv}$$

By using Schwartz's mathematical inequality it can be shown that the transfer function of the filter which fulfils this condition is of the form:

$$G(u, v) = C\, \frac{S^*(u, v)}{P_b(u, v)}\, e^{-2\pi j(ux_0 + vy_0)} \tag{11}$$

where C is an arbitrary constant and $S^*(u, v)$ is the conjugate complex of the F.T. of the useful signal $s(x, y)$.

In the particularly important case of *white noise* with spectral power density of P_0 it is possible to deduce:

$$G(u, v) = \frac{C}{P_0} S^*(u, v)\, e^{-2\pi j(ux_0 + vy_0)} \tag{12}$$

This corresponds to an impulse response of:

$$\boxed{g(x, y) = \frac{C}{P_0}\, s(x_0 - x, y_0 - y)} \tag{13}$$

In other words it is necessary to use a filter having an impulse response which is, to the nearest coefficient $\dfrac{C}{P_0}$, the signal itself reversed and shifted about the scanning point (x_0, y_0). It is therefore called an adaptive filter or matched detector because it is adapted or matched to the signal.

The output signal from the matched detector is then derived as:

$$t(x, y) = \frac{C}{P_0} C_S(x-x_0, y-y_0) \qquad (14)$$

that is, to the nearest coefficient $\frac{C}{P_0}$, an expression of the autocorrelation function for signal $s(x, y)$ shifted about point (x_0, y_0). A crest or signal maximum is therefore observed at this point, since an autocorrelation function is always at a maximum at the origin. It should be noted that the shape of the signal is not restored since we are retrieving the autocorrelation function rather than the signal itself.

4. Other filters. Interactive restoration

The literature contains numerous examples of filters which various authors have developed.

Here are some examples among others:
- filter for restoring the power spectrum of the non-degraded image [3,4].

Its transfer function (fig.IX.22) is:

$$G(u, v) = \left[\frac{P_S(u, v)}{|F(u, v)|^2 P_S(u, v) + P_b(u, v)} \right]^{1/2}$$

As with Wiener's filter, it will be observed that it returns to an inverse filter in the absence of noise.

But in general it gives better results since its transfer function is not zero when $F(u, v)$ is zero, unlike Wiener's filter.
- Geometric mean filters [3,4] in the form:

$$G(u, v) = \left[\frac{F^*(u, v)}{|F(u, v)|^2} \right]^{\alpha} \left[\frac{F^*(u, v)}{|F(u, v)|^2 + \beta \frac{P_b(u, v)}{P_S(u, v)}} \right]^{1-\alpha}$$

where parameters α and β are positive.

For α = 1 or β = 0 we have the reverse filter again.

For α = 0 and β = 1 we have Wiener's filter again. Where α = 0, β ≠ 1 we have the filter known as Wiener's parametric filter.

Finally for α = $\frac{1}{2}$, β = 1 we have the filter for restoring the power spectrum of the image.

We should note that in the last of these cases the transfer function is the geometric mean of the F.T.'s of the inverse filter and of Wiener's filter, which is why these filters are given this name.

- restoration filters using the "method of least squares under constraint" [3,4].

- homomorphic filters, being non-linear systems broadly applying linear filters [6].

- filters used in *interactive restoration* [1]. This method is especially useful for removing noise or periodic raster lines from an image, that is for removing an undesirable interference pattern.

For this purpose it is possible to make interactive use of manually adjusted band-elimination filters to obtain the best noise rejection characteristics. Figure IX.28 shows an example of results obtained using this method.

It is also possible to try to subtract the interference pattern itself from the noise-affected image. This pattern is found interactively by trial and error, using low-pass filters which isolate it but always admit unwanted frequencies. In general, rather than subtracting the figure so derived, it is preferable to subtract a suitably weighted version of it. An example of this technique used for removing raster frame lines from an image of the planet Mars is shown in figure IX.29.

F. Examples of application

Finally we give some examples of simple processing used in archaeology.

Figure IX.30 shows various processing operations used to reveal the outlines of a deserted mediaeval village. These outlines made it possible to draw up the most likely schematic plan for the layout of the village.

Figure IX.31 shows two superimposed drawings of animals on a wall in the Lascaux caves. Since these drawings were represented in markedly different levels of grey it was easy to separate them clearly using functions with variable threshold and slope.

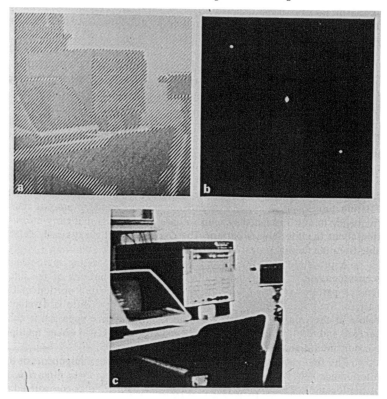

Fig.IX.28 - An example of interactive restoration: removing a periodic raster line;
a) the original lined image, b) D.F.T. of the raster, c) the restored image (from
R.C.Gonzalez and P.Wintz) [1].

Figure IX.32 shows the use of true colour digitization. Photograph
a) shows a cave wall bearing the imprint of a hand which is not
directly visible on the photograph, but exists in the form of traces of
ochre. True colour analysis using linear combinations of the three
components has made it possible to isolate the wall. This has then been
subtracted from the original image, bringing out the hand-print alone.
This print is shown in figure b) following contrast enhancement. The
shape of the hand stands out clearly thanks to a contour detection
operator (fig.c).

Finally figure IX.33 involves an image exhibiting two zones of
quite different mean grey levels which could not be processed at the
same time. By masking, each zone was processed independently to
enhance their contrast whilst bringing them to the same mean level,
then the two halves were "glued back together". Image c) obtained in

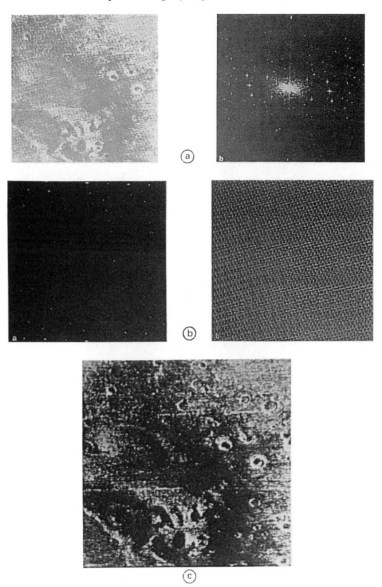

Fig.IX.29 - Interactive restoration: removing raster lines from an image of the planet Mars; a) the original image and its Fourier transform, b) D.F.T. of the raster lines and the raster itself, c) the restored image (from R.C.Gonzalez and P.Wintz) [1]. (Source: NASA Jet Propulsion Laboratory)

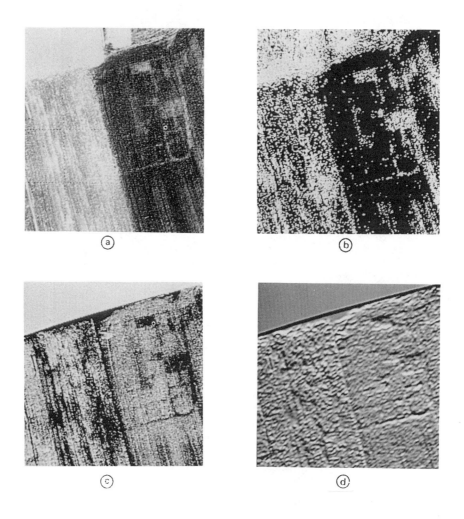

Fig.IX.30 - Archaeological application: example 4; a) aerial view of the village of Venafro (Italy) showing the contours of a fortified town, b) the image with contrast enhanced overall, c) the image enhanced by processing each zone independently, d) after applying directional filtering to image c) (from G.Chouquer and A.Marion) [17].

this way was then processed with directional operators to reveal the contours of the fortified town.

Index